Drawings by Cetra Hearne.
Photographs by Peter Baker, Roy Westlake and Tony Kersting.
Text filmset in Times Roman by Keyspools Ltd., Golborne, Lancashire

Plans based upon the Ordnance Survey map with the sanction
of the Controller of Her Majesty's Stationery Office.

Printed and bound by Editorial Fher S.A., Bilbao, Spain.

RED GUIDE

The Highlands of Scotland

Following road, rail
and steamer routes with
tours from each centre

Edited by Reginald J. W. Hammond F.R.G.S.

WARD LOCK LIMITED

116 Baker Street, London W1M 2BB

Maps and Plans

Contents

CONTENTS

Illustrations

THE RED GUIDES

Edited by Reginald J. W. Hammond

Barmouth and District

Bournemouth, New Forest

Channel Islands

Cornwall : North

Cornwall : South

Cornwall : West

Cotswolds

Dorset Coast

Isle of Man

Isle of Wight

Lake District

Llandudno, Colwyn Bay

London

Norfolk and the Broads

Peak District

St. Ives and W. Cornwall

Tenby and South Wales

Wales N. (Northn. Section)

Wales N. (Southn. Section)

Yorkshire Dales

Northern Ireland

SCOTLAND

Aberdeen, Deeside, etc.

Edinburgh and District

Highlands

Northern Scotland

Western Scotland

RED TOURIST GUIDES

Complete England

Complete Scotland

Complete Ireland

Complete Wales

Lake District (Baddeley)

Complete Devon

Complete West Country

Complete South-East Coast

Complete Yorkshire

Complete Scottish Lowlands

Britain

Portugal (Sarah Bradford)

Japan (William Duncan)

WARD LOCK LIMITED

Introductory

The Highlands may be roughly defined as being that portion of Scotland which lies north and west of a line drawn from Greenock to Stonehaven. This definition has in the main determined the southern boundary of the region described in this volume, although the line includes certain districts – e.g. the coastal belt from Dundee to Elgin; Caithness, and the Orkney and Shetland Islands–which are not really parts of the Highlands. Over the whole of the interesting area thus comprised we have traced the principal routes by road, rail and steamer, pointing out the chief objects of interest and indicating the most attractive tours that can be made from each centre.

A comprehensive road tour is outlined on later pages of this chapter; detailed descriptions of the more important roads, and the scenery passed, will be readily found by consulting either the Contents Pages or the Index to this Guide.

It is not, of course, merely altitude that distinguishes the Highlands from the Lowlands – which are indeed mountainous to no small extent. Apart from the races and Celtic survivals and traditions, there is also a difference in the rocks of the two regions, and that is the cause of other distinctive features. In the Lowlands the rocks consist chiefly of sandstones and conglomerates; in the Highlands slaty rocks, greywacke, mica schist and various igneous rocks, of which granite is the best known, are common.

More detailed descriptions of the respective areas than are possible in a general volume such as this will be found in our *Guides* to *Aberdeen, Inverness and Northern Scotland*; to *Oban and Western Scotland*; and to *The Scottish Lowlands*. *The Complete Scotland* is the most up-to-date handbook including the entire country north of the Border. Those breaking journey in Edinburgh should see our *Guide to Edinburgh*.

ROUTES TO THE HIGHLANDS*

From England there is a choice of three **Railway Routes** to the northern side of the Border. The *London Midland Region of British Railways* operates the West Coast and Midland Routes; while the *Eastern* and *North-Eastern*

Regions operate the East Coast Route. (The *Waverley Route* through the Scott Country from Carlisle—part of the Midland Route to Edinburgh—is over North-Eastern Region lines.) Car-sleeper services are run between London (King's Cross)–Perth, York–Inverness, Newcastle–Inverness, Sutton Coldfield–Stirling, Newhaven–Stirling, Newton-le-Willows–Stirling, Newton Abbot–Edinburgh, Bristol–Edinburgh, on certain nights in summer.

Through carriages and first- and second-class corridor carriages are run on the principal expresses. Restaurant cars are attached to most through trains, and refreshments may be obtained from most of the leading stations *en route*. Sleeping cars are attached to the chief night expresses, the charge for a berth being supplementary to the respective first- and second-class fares.

Coach Routes. By various routes the journey to Scotland from many parts of England and Wales may be made by motor-coach. Details of current services are contained in the *ABC Coach Guide* for Great Britain, or enquiries may be made from *Scottish Omnibuses, Ltd.*, 45 Princes Street, Edinburgh; 298 Regent Street, London, etc. There are a number of other companies.

To Scotland by Air. Those pressed for time may effect a considerable saving by using the air services of B.E.A. The flying time from London to Glasgow or Edinburgh direct is under 2 hours. A much greater saving results when the Hebrides (Tiree, Barra, Benbecula, Lewis) or Orkney and Shetland are the destination, Stornoway being brought within $2\frac{1}{2}$ hours flying time from Glasgow, 1 hour from Inverness; Orkney within 1 hour from Aberdeen, Shetland 2 hours. There are also services from Glasgow to Islay and to Campbeltown, and from Inverness and Wick to Orkney.

Transport Services in Scotland*

Railway facilities in Scotland are under the control of the Scottish Region of British Railways. The particular lines opening out the Highlands are the *West Highland Line* linking Glasgow with Fort William, Banavie and Mallaig; the *Highland Line* which connects Perth with Inverness, Kyle of Lochalsh, and Caithness; and the *Great North of Scotland* section serving Aberdeen and stations in the north-eastern area and Elgin. The services are supplemented by the steamers belonging to the *David Mac-Brayne Company*, Glasgow, which call at a great number of the harbours on the west coast and at many of the adjacent islands; and the boats of the *North of Scotland and Orkney and Shetland Company*, Aberdeen, which serve the Orkney and Shetland Islands and the north coast of Great Britain; and various others.

Coaches and buses, besides linking up all the principal towns, run along many of the roads which wind through the passes and glens, and afford

*Throughout this Guide references to travel facilities require verification by current time-tables or announcements.

easy access to places that, until quite recent years, were almost inaccessible except on foot or by bicycle.

Reference has already been made to the time-saving advantages of the air services when available (*see* above).

Time-Tables. Time-tables issued by British Rail, the steamer companies and the chief bus and coach concerns will be found invaluable when planning extended excursions.

Scenic Attractions

It has been well said that the Highlands of Scotland present the geographical characteristics of all the holiday grounds of the world. Travellers go to Switzerland in search of the mountain scenery which is offered on a smaller scale by the Cuillins, the Grampians and the Cairngorms. They go to Northern Italy for lakes whose scenic beauty is rivalled by that of Loch Earn, Loch Lomond, Loch Ness, Loch Maree or Loch Duich. They go to the Continent for river scenery whilst ignorant of the witching Tay, Spey and Findhorn; to Norway for rushing waters and bounding cataracts that are challenged in impetuousness by the Highland falls; to the Giant's Causeway for rock wonders which for grandeur have their counterpart in Staffa.

Sport

Besides romantic scenery there is sport, and plenty of it; sport by land and water. Those who desire more detailed information respecting the facilities for fishing than can be given in a book for the general holiday-maker are recommended to procure *Scotland for Fishing*, a Scottish Tourist Board publication. The trout-fishing season in Scotland is from March 15 to October 6 (both dates inclusive). Salmon fishing (rod) generally is open February 11 to October 31, but begins and closes earlier or later on several of the rivers and lochs.

Lonely moor and mountain-side provide a home for grouse, partridge, pheasant, deer and other game – and a happy hunting ground for the sportsman. With the approach of "The Twelfth" all roads lead to the Highlands.

Shinty (Gaelic, *Camanachd*), to which reference is made in the most ancient of Highland tales, is still popular; hockey is derived from it. Putting the stone and tossing the caber are also Highland sports seen to advantage at annual gatherings held in late summer at centres such as Braemar, Crieff, Oban and Inverness; and there is probably no town without a green for the old Scottish game of bowls. In winter, curling, the "roaring game," is indulged in whenever the weather conditions are suitable. Ski-ing is increasing in popularity, especially in the Cairngorms and Glencoe. Even Loch Lomond sometimes lends itself for skating purposes; and as a playground for Winter Sport generally, increased attention is being paid to the Highlands. In the large cities there are indoor skating rinks.

But the Scottish pastime which appeals most strongly to English and Americans is the royal and ancient game of golf. For the convenience and information of golfers who visit the Highlands we indicate the numerous courses. The Clyde is one of the chief centres of yachting, which has votaries also at Oban and other stations on the north-west coast. The Highlands afford one of the most arduous and fascinating fields for the walker.

The Highland Gatherings

A unique feature of the Scottish season is the series of "Gatherings" or "Games," many of which have a world-wide celebrity. At these gatherings one sees the Scot in all the pride of kilt and tartan; the pipes are heard from morning to evening and the national dances take a prominent part in the programme. The sporting events include tossing the caber – the stem of a fir tree – putting the weight and other feats requiring not only strength but skill for their proper performance. Sheep-dog trials are also an interesting feature of the Scottish season.

The "Games" season extends from June to September, during which are held the Braemar Gathering – usually attended by Royalty – and the Aboyne Games. Skye Week is observed in June, Mull Games take place in July at Tobermory, the Lochaber Gathering is at Fort William in August, in which month also are held the Ballater Games.

Mountaineering

For walking over the mountains boots should be nailed – rubber soles are apt to be treacherous on wet rock or on grass. Carry a reliable compass and in reading the map do not attend only to details of route but study the conformation of the ground over which you pass – such information may be invaluable in helping you to "feel" your way down in case of mist. Also in case of mist or other causes of delay, it is always wise to carry an emergency ration – such as chocolate – and to *reserve it* at least until one is definitely on a beaten track.

Midges, clegs and other winged pests can prove a trial, and it is well to carry a midge repellent.

For many reasons, June is the best month for walking in Scotland. Later in the year routes are apt to be restricted by deer-stalking, grouse-shooting and similar sports. Against certain unjust restrictions the Rights-of-Way Society have fought with much success, and their sign-post is an increasingly familiar and welcome feature, but strangers should note that the right on such routes is confined to the actual paths and does not assume leave to wander at will.

Most of the mountain walks are described in our *Complete Scotland*. For climbs and the least frequented routes the *Journals* and other publications of the Scottish Mountaineering Club (obtainable from Messrs. Douglas and Foulis, 9 Castle Street, Edinburgh) and of the Cairngorm Club (Aberdeen) will be found invaluable.

Sunday in Scotland

It should be noted that both local and main line services are restricted on Sundays. Times are changing, however, and current announcements should be consulted. Buses are generally available on Sunday near the larger centres of population.

Hiking and Hostelling

In many of the wildest and grandest parts of the Highlands, hotels are few and far between, and in the season are liable to be full up. Hence the growing number of Youth Hostels in these northern and western regions: they supply the needs of those who look askance at hotel comforts and hotel charges. Hardy hikers, cyclists and mountaineers – from all over Britain and also from overseas – flock annually to the hostels of the Scottish Youth Hostels Association, whose headquarters are at 7 Bruntsfield Crescent, Edinburgh, 10. In the area covered in this volume there is now a choice of over seventy such hostels – ranging from modest huts to palatial mansions. Their locality is indicated in the following pages. They are intended primarily for "those who travel by their own efforts."

For those who like to holiday under canvas, the Camping Club of Great Britain (11 Lower Grosvenor Place, London, S.W.1) issues, as do British Railways, a helpful list of camping sites.

Car Touring

Well-equipped garages will be found in all the principal towns and the more important isolated hotels supply oil and petrol, while some hold small stocks of spares, such as tyres, but it is a wise rule to keep petrol and oil topped up, as in outlying districts filling stations are often few and far between.

The following tour includes most of the better-known places of interest in the Highlands. In order to allow comfortable time for sightseeing and breaks of journey the average daily mileage has been kept down to about 60; those for whom such progress is too leisurely can easily make the tour in fewer stages. Detailed descriptions of each Highland section of this tour will be readily found by means of the Index at the end of this Guide. Those whose tour includes also the Lowlands should see our *Complete Scotland*.

Edinburgh to Callander (51½ miles), *viâ* Linlithgow (17), Falkirk (24½), Bannockburn (33), Stirling (35½), Bridge of Allan (38½), Callander (51½). Objects of interest – Edinburgh: Palace of Holyroodhouse Castle, etc.; Linlithgow: Palace; Bannockburn: Field of Battle; Stirling: Castle, Wallace Monument (all described in our *Guide to Edinburgh and District*); Callander: Falls of Bracklinn.

Callander to the Trossachs. The Trossachs may be included in a fine circular run from Callander of about 30 miles. There is no road along Loch Katrine, but from Aberfoyle there is a road to Stronachlachar, near the far end of the Loch, and down Glen Arklet to Inversnaid on Loch Lomond (23½); returning same way from Inversnaid. The scenery throughout is very fine.

Callander to Crieff (70 miles), *viâ* Strathyre (8½), Balquhidder (13: for Rob Roy's Grave), Lochearnhead (17), Killin Junction (20½), Killin Village (24½), Kenmore (41), Aberfeldy (47), Amulree (58), Crieff (70). Again fine scenery. Long steep climb up Glen Ogle to Killin Junction, but level surface along north bank of Loch Tay to Kenmore.

Crieff to Dundee (39½ miles), *viâ* Methven (11), Perth (17½), Inchture (30½), Dundee (39½).

Dundee to Aberdeen (67 miles), *viâ* Arbroath (17), Montrose (29), Bervie (42), Stonehaven (52), Aberdeen (67). Objects of interest – Arbroath Abbey; Dunnottar Castle near Stonehaven.

Aberdeen to Braemar (58½ miles), *viâ* Banchory (17), Kincardine O'Neil (25), Aboyne (30), Ballater (41), Crathie (49), Braemar (58½). Scenery very fine up Deeside from Banchory onwards. Objects of interest – Balmoral Castle, Crathie Church, Mar Castle and Invercauld House at Braemar, and numerous waterfalls near Braemar.

Braemar to Dunkeld (47 miles), *viâ* Spital of Glenshee (15), Persie Inn (26), Bridge of Cally (29), Blairgowrie (35), Dunkeld (47). The highest through road in Scotland (2,199 feet), with several dangerous hills, but good surface and the scenery well repays the labour or care involved.

Dunkeld to Kingussie (58 miles), *viâ* Pitlochry (12), Blair Atholl (19½), Struan (24), Dalwhinnie (43½), Kingussie (58). Note that there is neither inn nor hotel between Struan and Dalwhinnie (nearly twenty miles of climb and descent: summit 1,506 feet). Objects of interest – Dunkeld Cathedral; Birnam Hill and Wood; Pass of Killiecrankie, Blair Castle, Falls of Bruar.

Kingussie to Inverness (44 miles), *viâ* Aviemore (12), Carrbridge (19½), Inverness (44). Fine scenery.

From Inverness a good road runs north to **John o' Groats** by way of Beauly, Dingwall, Tain, Bonar Bridge, Dornoch and Wick (141 miles). The return to Inverness might be made *viâ* Thurso, Tongue and Lairg (161 miles), or by Laxford Bridge and Lairg (217 miles). (*See* pp. 118–158 and our *Guide to Northern Scotland*.)

Inverness to Fort William (67 miles), *viâ* Drumnadrochit Hotel (14), Invermoriston Hotel (27), Fort Augustus (34), Invergarry Hotel (41½), Fort William (67). This splendid road skirts Loch Ness and the Caledonian Canal most of the way, and the views are very fine. Objects of interest – Inverness Castle, Tomnahurich, Urquhart Castle, Fort Augustus Monastery. From Fort William, Ben Nevis (the highest mountain in Great Britain) can be climbed, but a whole day must be allowed for it. The view is glorious on a clear day.

Fort William to Oban (95 miles), *viâ* Onich (10), Kinlochleven (rounding Loch Leven), up Glencoe and over the modern road by Bridge of Orchy to Tyndrum; thence by Dalmally to Oban. A splendid run. The ferry boats at Ballachulish are large and carry both motor and cycle, saving the 20-mile detour by Kinlochleven.

Oban to Arrochar or Tarbet (85 miles), *viâ* Lochgilphead (38), Inveraray (63), Cairndow and "Rest and Be Thankful." From Lochgilphead to Cairndow the road skirts Loch Fyne, and at Arrochar or Tarbet one is in touch both with Loch Long and Loch Lomond. (Loch Awe may be included by taking the Dalmally route from Oban to join the Lochgilphead route at Kilmartin; or from Dalmally it is a good route by Glen Aray to Inveraray.)

Arrochar or Tarbet to Edinburgh. The first part of the route is down the western side of Loch Lomond by Luss to Balloch and Dumbarton, whence the way to Glasgow is mainly suburban. Those with time should, from Arrochar, make direct for Garelochhead (fine view from Whistlefield), and from Helensburgh take the road on the left to Loch Lomond, where again turn left and follow the loch all the way to Ardlui. Hence to Edinburgh by Crianlarich, Killin and Stirling.

Ferries

As might be expected, with such an indented coastline, ferries play an important part in certain of the road communications. Those, however, who propose to use the outlying ferries on the wild west coast should bear in mind that their operations are subject to tidal conditions and that occasionally a fairly long wait is necessary before one can make the crossing: this is the case, for instance, at Kyle of Lochalsh.

The well-known ferry crossing the Firth of Forth at Queensferry gave way in 1964 to the magnificent new Forth Road Bridge; while that from Newport to Dundee across the Firth of Tay was likewise superseded by a new road bridge in 1966.

Cycling

Much depends upon the standard set, but if good riding over good roads through beautiful scenery is required, then Scotland is a cyclist's Paradise. Except on the wild north-west coast (where one learns anew the meaning of "off the beaten track") the hills are for the most part long and well graded and capable of being ridden by any good cyclist unhampered by a head wind. The cyclist, too, can use many of the ferries which are not big enough to carry cars, and in various other ways he has a greater freedom. He can penetrate into many parts of Western Scotland that are inaccessible to the motorist, and can explore quite a number of islands on which no car has yet been landed. Although the tour on foregoing pages has been compiled for motorists, it is to be recommended to cyclists wishing for a lengthy tour taking in all that is best worth seeing in the Highlands; but later pages in this Guide will suggest many attractive alternatives.

The Cyclists' Touring Club supply, on application, a list of cottages and boarding houses in the Highlands which cater for members.

Ward Lock's
Red Guides

Edited by Reginald J. W. Hammond

Complete England

Complete Scotland

Complete Wales

Complete Ireland

Lake District (*Baddeley*)

Complete West Country

Complete Devon

Complete South-East Coast

Complete Yorkshire

Complete Scottish Lowlands

WARD LOCK LIMITED

Perth to Inverness via Aviemore

PERTH

Access from the South. – *Road:* Buses run from Edinburgh (change at Stirling) and Glasgow.
Rail: From Glasgow *viâ* Larbert, Stirling and Gleneagles. From Edinburgh (Waverley Station) *viâ* the Forth Bridge, in continuation of the East Coast and Midland Routes from England. From Carlisle and the South by Stirling.

Angling. – The Tay is famous for its salmon. Fishing on the river is permissible within the burgh boundaries. Permits may be obtained from the City Chamberlain. Elsewhere the river is strictly preserved but information as to beats and angling conditions may be had from Perth Anglers' Club, 1, Scoonieburn, Perth.

Distances by Road. – Aberdeen, 82 miles; Braemar, 50; Dundee, 21; Edinburgh, 42 (*viâ* Forth Road Bridge), 70 (*viâ* Stirling); Glasgow, 61; Inverness, 116; Oban, 95; Stirling, 34.

Early Closing. – Wednesday.

Golf. – Three courses adjacent to the town. *King James VI Course* is on the Moncreiffe Island, half a mile from the town. *Craigie Hill Course.* The third is a *Public Course* on the North Inch. (Public *Putting Courses* have been laid out on both Inches.) For *Gleneagles*, 15¼ miles south from Perth, *see* p. 19.

Hotels. – *Station, Royal George, Salutation, Isle of Skye, Huntingtower, Waverley, Victoria, County, Atholl* (unl.), *Queen's,* etc.

Population. – 42,000.

Post Office. – Near centre of High Street.

Youth Hostel (open all the year round and much frequented) in Glasgow Road.

Perth, onetime capital of Scotland and of considerable antiquity, has little to show in old buildings and historical relics. This is in great part due to the destruction of the religious houses by the populace in 1559, after listening to the fiery harangues of John Knox, and to the removal of other visible evidences of the city's historic glories by the civic authorities in the early years of the nineteenth century. The buildings destroyed at the Reformation included the Blackfriars Monastery where James I was killed; the Carthusian Monastery which he founded, and where he and Joan Beaufort, his Queen, and Margaret, the Queen of James IV, were buried; the Greyfriars Monastery, which stood on the present churchyard of that name, and the Carmelites or Whitefriars House, situated a little west of the city. The nineteenth-century demolition included the removal of Earl Gowrie's Palace (*see* below) to make room for the County Buildings; the destruction of the Mercat Cross (erected in 1668 in place of one taken down by Cromwell; a copy has been erected in memory of King Edward VII); and the clearing away, in 1818, of the Parliament House, where the ancient Diets of Scotland were held. Until the seventeenth century Perth was also known as *St. Johnstoun*, in honour of the patron saint of the city.

Most of the show-places of Perth are within a few yards of the river. Towards the southern end is the **South Inch,** a large recreation ground,

Perth Bridge over the Tay

with the **Railway Station** on one side and at the other **Tay Street,** which runs alongside the river to the **North Inch** at the opposite end of the city. In midstream is Moncreiffe Island, on which is one of the golf courses. Following Tay Street northward one reaches the **County Buildings.**

St. John Street, a turning on the right out of South Street, near the County Buildings, leads to the principal church and the oldest building in Perth, **St. John's Church;** here John Knox preached his famous sermon against "idolatry" (1559). Its records go back to the twelfth century; it has a nave and transept dating from the thirteenth century and a choir of fifteenth-century design. For many years the church sheltered three separate congregations, but as part of a War Memorial scheme the partitions were removed and one now sees the fine cruciform building as a whole. From the other end of St. John Street a return can be made to Tay Street, which leads north to the **Perth Bridge** of nine arches, built by Smeaton in 1771. Near it is the **Art Gallery** and **Museum,** and here the North Inch begins.

From the Bridge, Charlotte Street may be followed to North Port (on the left), which quickly brings one to Pullar's Dye Works and North Port, where, marked by a tablet, stands **Simon Glover's House,** the supposed home (now Corporation property) of the "Fair Maid of Perth." Readers of her story, as told by Sir Walter Scott, will regard the **North Inch** with special interest as the scene of the memorable combat (1396) between the

Clan Chattan and the Clan Quhele (Kay). The spacious greensward is now a public golf course and recreation ground. From its south-western corner Atholl Street leads to **St. Ninian's Cathedral,** which is an Episcopal Cathedral. Methven Street leads the visitor south and westward to the Railway Station, near which are large cattle-markets.

The best view of Perth is obtained from **Kinnoull Hill** (729 feet), a great part of which was presented to the town by Lord Dewar in 1924. It is about three-quarters of an hour's walk eastward from the station across the river (buses run in summer). From its summit a spacious view is obtained of Strathearn, the Ochils and the Grampians, and the Firth of Tay, widening between the fertile shores of the Carse of Gowrie and of Fife.

Branklyn Gardens, property of the National Trust for Scotland, look southward over the Tay. In this two-acre garden there is a fine collection of plants, particularly alpines, assembled by the late John Renton and his wife.

Short Excursions from Perth

1. To **Moncreiffe Hill** (725 feet), about 3 miles south-east. The route lies across the South Inch, along the Edinburgh high-road for a couple of miles and then along a cart-road to the left. **Bridge of Earn,** a pretty holiday resort, is 4 miles from Perth: **Abernethy** (ancient Pictish capital: round tower) is 8 miles, on the Newburgh road.

2. To the ruins of **Elcho Castle** (sixteenth century), about 4 miles (road) south-east of the city.

3. To **Huntingtower Castle,** 2¼ miles out on the Crieff road. As Ruthven Castle, it was the scene of the *Raid of Ruthven*, in 1582, when the Earl of Gowrie seized his boy-guest, James VI. It is a mysterious affair, in which many, at the time and since, have discovered a plot on James's part to ruin the House of the Ruthvens, Earls of Gowrie (open weekdays, 10–4 or 7; Sundays, 2–4 or 7; *admission fee*).

4. To **Scone Palace,** 2½ miles to the north-east, a modern castellated mansion belonging to Lord Mansfield. It adjoins the site of the old Abbey of Scone (destroyed 1559), which held the Coronation Stone of the Scottish Kings, now kept with the Coronation Chair in Westminster Abbey. At Scone (pronounced *Skoon*)–Pictish capital from the eighth century– Scottish monarchs were crowned in the twelfth to fifteenth centuries. (*Palace, grounds, pinetum, daily except Fridays, fee*).

5. To **King's Seat, Dunsinane,** the scene of a portion of Shakespeare's *Macbeth*. It is 8 or 9 miles to the north-east among the Sidlaws.

6. To **Gleneagles,** 15 or 16 miles south-west by road or rail. Buses from the station to the famous golf courses ("King's" and "Queen's," 18 holes each; "Wee," 9 holes. Sunday play). A round trip of under 50 miles can be made by Gleneagles, Glen Devon, Rumbling Bridge, Kinross (Loch Leven) and Glenfarg.

7. To **Methven** (6½ miles west), where Bruce was defeated by Pembroke in 1306, and **Glenalmond** (10¼ miles). W. E. Gladstone had a hand in founding (1847) Trinity College, Glenalmond. Logiealmond, across the river, is the "Drumtochty" of Ian Maclaren's novels. Through the Sma' Glen and Amulree, Aberfeldy (32 miles) can be reached.

8. To **Crieff** and **Strathearn** by road.

PERTH TO LOCHEARNHEAD

Before we proceed northward from Perth to Inverness by Aviemore (*see* p. 23), a few pages must be devoted to the country westward, along the route to Lochhearnhead, *viâ–*

Crieff

Early Closing.–Wednesday.
Golf. A splendid 18-hole course. Sunday play. *Gleneagles* (see above) is within 9 miles.
Hotels.–*Star, Drummond Arms, Crown, George, Murray Park, Victoria, The Birches.* Unlicensed: *Ancaster, Strathearn Hydro,* etc.
Population.–5,600.

Post Office.–In High Street. Open 9 a.m. to 1 p.m. and 2 p.m. to 5.30 p.m.
Recreation.–Golf, bowls, tennis, cricket. Boating and fishing (salmon and trout) in the Earn and other waters. There is also a library, and the Strathearn Institute has billiard and reading rooms.

Crieff, which lies 17 miles west of Perth (A85), claims to be the most picturesquely situated hill-town of Scotland, and is a very popular health resort. Built close to the river *Earn* on the southern face of a wooded hill called the Knock, near the foot of the Grampians, it is sheltered from cold winds, has a gravelly sub-soil, and is the centre of a district full of historical and general interest, and of great scenic beauty.

At the door of the Town Hall, in High Street, are the ancient stocks, and near them is the Cross of the Burgh of the Regality of Drummond, an antiquarian relic associated with exploits of Rob Roy. The **Cross of Crieff** is believed to be a ninth-century preaching cross.

The **Knock of Crieff** (911 feet: view indicator), to the north of the town, commands a view of nearly the whole of Upper and Lower Strathearn.

Short Excursions from Crieff

Buses run to the **Sma' Glen** (a rugged, deep and narrow valley, small only in name, where Ossian is said to sleep) and **Amulree** (visitors at the hotel can fish Loch Freuchie and the Bran); **Mill o' Fortune,** and **Muthill,** a pretty village containing an ancient tower and the ruins of a fifteenth-century church; **Braco** (near the famous Ardoch Roman camp). They also run past **Drummond Castle,** the seat of the Earl of Ancaster. The mansion contains a fine collection of portraits. The old castle, built in the fifteenth century and restored in the nineteenth, stands apart from the modern house. The gardens are very attractive. (*Closed to the public when the house is occupied.*)

Other objects of interest in the neighbourhood are **Ochtertyre Grounds** (2 miles), the **Falls of Turret** (4 miles), **Loch Turret** (6 miles), and the **Falls of Barvick** ($2\frac{1}{2}$ miles).

Other places easily reached from Crieff include Loch Earn, Balquhidder, Loch Tay, Loch Awe, and other centres on the Oban line. There are buses to Perth, Callander, Edinburgh, Glasgow, and in summer to Aberfeldy.

From Crieff to Comrie, the road (7 miles) runs along the north bank of the river *Earn*, and 2 miles from Crieff passes close under the hill of **Tomachastle,** the obelisk on which commemorates General Sir David Baird, who overthrew Tippoo Sahib at Seringapatam in 1799, and died at Ferntower, Crieff, in 1829.

Comrie

Hotels. – *Ancaster Arms, Royal, Comrie, St.* K.... **Recreation.** – 9-hole golf course, and pleasant angling
Population. – 1,836.   in *Earn* and other waters.

Comrie is in the Earn valley. On the south the nearer hills are low and are covered with trees or grass; on the north and west they are bold and rugged and rise to a height of 3,000 feet. While the climate is genial in winter and spring, it is bracing during the warmer months through breezes from the uplands. The town has a reputation for cleanliness and neatness; also for harmless earthquakes. The best views are obtained from **Dunmore** and the so-called **Druidical Stones.** The former is a hill (837 feet) to the north, crowned by a monument of the first Lord Melville.

Short Excursions from Comrie

1. The **Devil's Cauldron,** a deep wood-clad ravine into which the *Lednock* dives, is 1½ miles north by the direct road. It may also be reached from the Melville monument on Dunmore by a zigzag path.
2. **Glen Lednock,** a beautiful wooded valley. At the upper end, 5 miles from Comrie, is **Spout Rollo,** where the stream throws itself over a huge rock. A path leads on to Ardeonaig (12 miles) on Loch Tay.
3. **Strowan** (4 miles), where may be seen the ivy-clad ruins of the ancient **Church of St. Rowan,** the cross of which marks the site of the old market-place.
4. **Roman Camp** and **Glen Artney.** A supposed Roman Camp on the way to Glen Artney has by some been identified as *Mons Graupius,* the scene of a memorable fight (A.D. 86) narrated by Tacitus (*see also* p. 61). Glen Artney was the starting-point of the stag in the adventurous hunting described in Scott's *Lady of the Lake.* About 8 miles from Comrie is **Glenartney Lodge,** a seat of the Earl of Ancaster. A path leads over to Callander (15 miles).

From Comrie to St. Fillans is 6 miles by road. Near St. Fillans, but on the south side of the river, is the green hill of **Dunfillan** (600 feet), on which St. Fillan, the patron saint of Robert Bruce, is said to have prayed so assiduously as to leave the marks of his knees in the rocks. At the foot of Dunfillan, a few feet from the Dundurn burn, is **St. Fillan's Well,** formerly believed to possess miraculous healing powers.

Comrie is connected with St. Fillans and Lochearnhead by bus.

St. Fillans

Distances by road. – Oban, 65 miles; Perth, 29½;   **Recreation.** – Angling (in the Earn and Loch Earn);
  Stirling, 37; Gleneagles, 20; Comrie, 6; Crieff, 12.   sailing and boating on Loch Earn.
Golf. – Excellent 9-hole course available to visitors.
  Daily rates.

This pretty village of cottages and villas lies along the eastern end of Loch Earn and the outlet of the river. The houses extend in a long line on the narrow strip between the mountains and the water. The scenery of the vicinity is remarkably fine.

In an enclosure opposite the *Drummond Arms Hotel* are twin oak trees called the **Goose Oaks,** because they were planted in 1818 over the grave of a goose that was said to have lived for 106 years and to have warned the

Neishes, the clan then occupying the site of St. Fillans, of the approach of hostile M'Nabs.

Saint Fillan, to whom the village owes its name, lived in the eighth century, and was the son of an Irish princess. After being abbot of a monastery on the Holy Loch he wandered about the West Highlands and built churches at Killin and Dundurn. He died at Dundurn, on the other side of the Earn from St. Fillans, and his original chapel remained there until about 1500, when the building now in ruins took its place.

Loch Earn is about 7 miles long and averages a mile in breadth. On both sides are hills and mountains that are in great part clothed with rich woods. The loch can be fished by visitors at the *Drummond Arms Hotel* and it is also a popular boating centre. Near the St. Fillans end is the little wooded **Neish's Isle,** with a ruined stronghold of the Neishes.

There is a road on each side of the loch; that on the south commands the better view, but the other has the advantage of being more level. About 2 miles along the northern road is **Glen Tarken,** a couple of miles up which is a huge boulder of mushroom shape.

Towards the western end of the loch is the scant ruin of **Ardveich Castle,** and on the southern side of the water is **Ardvorlich House,** the "Darnlinvarach" of the *Legend of Montrose*. Behind the house rises **Ben Vorlich** (3,224 feet). Nearer Lochearnhead are **Edinample Castle** and **Falls,** close to the mouth of **Glen Ample.**

Lochearnhead

Distances by road.–St. Fillans, $7\frac{1}{8}$ miles; Comrie, $12\frac{1}{8}$; Crieff, $19\frac{1}{8}$; Perth, $36\frac{5}{8}$; Killin, $7\frac{5}{8}$; Crianlarich, $16\frac{7}{8}$; Balquhidder Station, $2\frac{1}{8}$; Callander, $13\frac{3}{4}$.

Lochearnhead is an attractive hamlet that makes an admirable centre for excursions. There is trout fishing and boating on Loch Earn. The *Lochearnhead Hotel* is prettily situated half a mile from the loch.

Besides the castles just named in connection with Loch Earn, other places of interest in the immediate vicinity of Lochearnhead are:

Glen Ogle, 3 to 4 miles long, through which the road runs north-westward for Killin and Crianlarich, at either end of Glen Dochart.

About 2 miles west of Kingshouse Hotel is the **Kirk of Balquhidder,** with its very old font and the stone of St. Angus, Celtic saint and preacher. To the east of the ruined church of 1631 and within the walls of a still older building are the graves of **Rob Roy MacGregor,** his wife and two of his sons. Two of the stones within the railing obviously belong to a much earlier period. Robert Kirk, student of fairy lore (fl. 1680), and the Clan MacLaurin are also associated with the district. The road follows Lochs Voil and Doine for some 6 miles after which sheep tracks link up the charred ruins of homes burned out in 1746. *Stronvar House* on the south shore of Loch Voil is a Youth Hostel.

For the route northward from Lochearnhead by road, and then westward, passing Loch Awe, to **Oban,** *see* pp. 90–94; for the road southward by Strathyre and Loch Lubnaig to **Callander** *see* p. 90.

Wade Bridge, Aberfeldy

PERTH TO PITLOCHRY AND AVIEMORE

Road and railway run side by side practically all the way, the most notable separation occurring a few miles north of Perth, when, after passing in view of Scone Palace across the river (p. 19) and through **Luncarty** (scene of a memorable defeat of the Danes, *c.* 990) the road continues through Bankfoot to Birnam, leaving the railway to swing eastward to Stanley Junction (7¼ miles), where the Highland line for Pitlochry, Blair Atholl, Kingussie, Inverness, etc., begins.

The river *Tay* at this spot and for some miles above is renowned for its trout and salmon fishing.

A quarter of a mile from Stanley is **Campsie Linn,** the scene of one of the closing incidents in *The Fair Maid of Perth*.

The route now closely follows the beautiful valley of the Tay. We pass below **Birnam Hill** with the ruins of "Duncan's Castle" (*see Macbeth*) to—

Dunkeld and Birnam

Golf (9-hole course) at Birnam.
Hotels.—Dunkeld: *Royal, Atholl Arms, Perth Arms, Taybank, Dunkeld House*. Birnam: *Birnam, Merlewood* (unl.).
Population.—About 1,000.
Public Library and Reading Room.—High Street.
Recreation.—Tennis, bowls, angling, golf (*see* above).

(Visitors at the *Birnam Hotel* can fish 1½ miles of the Tay for salmon and its tributary, the Braan, for trout. There are also waters open to visitors at the *Atholl Arms Hotel*.)
Youth Hostel (open summer) at south end of Birnam.

Dunkeld and Birnam are charmingly situated on opposite banks of the *Tay*, and are the centre of many delightful walks and drives. Dunkeld (i.e. Fort of the Culdees; according to others, Hill of the Caledonians), an early seat of Scottish sovereignty and of Celtic Christianity, is a quiet town,

23

its most interesting object being the **Cathedral,** the earliest portion of which dates from the thirteenth century. It was wrecked by the Reformers in 1560, and lay in ruins until 1600, when Stewart of Ladywell repaired and re-roofed the choir. In 1691 the Cathedral was repaired by the Atholl family, and fitted as the Parish Church. In 1908 the choir was restored after the original design through the munificence of Sir Donald Currie. The building was, in 1927, handed over to the nation by the Duke of Atholl (open daily: *standard hours*). The roofless nave is now a burial-ground: here is the effigy in armour of "the Wolf of Badenoch." One of the bishops of Dunkeld was the Scottish poet, Gawain Douglas (*c.* 1474–1522), son of Archibald Bell-the-Cat.

The Cathedral is charmingly situated among shaded lawns beside the river. Adjoining the Cathedral are the grounds of *Dunkeld House*, formerly a seat of the Duke of Atholl but now an hotel. Within the grounds, at a spot quite near the churchyard, is a remarkably fine larch tree, one of two that grew side by side and were known as "the mother larches," as they were said to be the first of the kind grown in Britain. They were brought from Tyrol in 1738.

About 1¼ miles from the Cathedral, by the Aberfeldy road (on the south or Birnam side of the river), are the grounds of the **Hermitage,** or "Ossian's Hall" (*open to the public*), near which are the **Lower Falls of Braan,** hard by a little bridge.

Excursions from Dunkeld and Birnam

1. **Birnam Hill** (1,324 feet), ascended by way of a path which starts from a lane at the north end of the railway station. The summit seen from Birnam affords the best near view, but is not the actual top.

2. **Craigie-Barns,** a rocky height clothed with woods through which are beautiful walks. The entrance is at Cally Lodge on the Blairgowrie road.

3. **The Hermitage Bridge.** Follow the Aberfeldy road and take the road to the left just before reaching Inver bridge. After crossing the railway go through a gate on the right and take a rough cart-track across the fields. Where this dips down to the fields keep straight on by a faint path which soon gets better and, keeping close to the stream, affords fine views of the **Hermitage Bridge.** This is a delightful spot. On the far bank of the river is the large summer-house known as *Ossian's Hall,* and beyond it the path on the left bank of the stream is joined.

4. **Rumbling Bridge and the Falls of Braan.**

(*a*) By path from Inver. Take the Aberfeldy road to Inver and about a quarter of a mile beyond the last house take a path which strikes off to the left. With the stream on its left, this path passes close to the Hermitage Bridge, latterly becomes a grassy track and joins a road at a point about a quarter of a mile from Rumbling Bridge.

(*b*) By road. Follow the main Amulree road for 2½ miles and take a branch road to the right which leads down to the bridge. The return to Dunkeld may be made by either of the paths mentioned above.

5. **Aberfeldy,** 18 miles by a good road. The usual road route is that near the right bank of the Tay, passing Inver, **Dalguise, Balnaguard** and **Grandtully,** the last-named village adjoining, say some, the original of "Tullyveolan," the Castle of Baron Bradwardine in Scott's *Waverley*. The return may be made by crossing the Tay by General Wade's Bridge and proceeding along the north bank to Logierait, crossing the *Tummel* by the bridge, and thence following the Great North Road through **Guay** and the **King's Pass;** or by way of Loch na Craige, Glen Cochill, and Scotston to Kinloch Lodge, and thence down **Strathbraan** by way of Trochie, the Rumbling Bridge and Inver.

6. **Kenmore, Loch Tay** and **Killin.** By road to Aberfeldy (17 miles) as in (4). Thence continuing (6½ miles: bus service) to Kenmore, skirting the grounds of *Taymouth Castle*, the former seat of the Marquis of Breadalbane, sheltering under the wooded heights of **Drummond**

Hill. The green of the model village of **Kenmore,** at the park gates, saw the execution of a chief of the MacGregors and other "limmers" (*see also* p. 92). *Breadalbane Hotel* has a good golf course. South of the Aberfeldy road is a stone circle. Kenmore has bus connection with **Killin** (16 or 17 miles) at the south-west of Loch Tay. From Kenmore a rough road climbs abruptly to 1,750 feet, plunges into Glen Quaich, passes Loch Freuchie, and joins the main road in Strath Braan at Amulree (11 miles from Kenmore; 9 miles from Dunkeld).

7. To **Blairgowrie** (p. 53), a romantic and interesting route (12 miles, regular bus service), following the course of the *Lunan*, and passing, among other lochs, **Loch Clunie,** on an island in which are the remains of a castle, the seat of the Bishops of Dunkeld, and an early home of the "Admirable Crichton" (1560–82).

About 10 miles south-west of Dunkeld is the village of **Logiealmond,** of which realistic glimpses are given by the Rev. D. M. Forrester in *At the Edge of the Heather.*

From Dunkeld the road (A9) from Perth to Aviemore and Inverness follows the *left* bank of the Tay. The railway continues on the right bank and, immediately on leaving Dunkeld station, passes to the domains of the Duke of Atholl.

Ballinluig is important as the meeting-point of the Tay and the Tummel and of the roads which accompany those rivers over this part of their courses. It stands at the junction of the Great North Road with the very fine road to the west coast at Oban by Kenmore and alongside Loch Tay to Killin, and on by Crianlarich to Dalmally, Loch Awe and the Pass of Brander as described on other pages.

Main Route to Aviemore resumed on p. 26.

Ballinluig to Aberfeldy. From Ballinluig a good road runs westward through picturesque scenery alongside the Tay to Aberfeldy. **Logierait,** a mile west of Ballinluig on the Aberfeldy road, was the seat of a Court of Regality in which the Lords of Atholl administered feudal justice. The ancient prison once held that famous outlaw Rob Roy. In the hotel garden a hollow oak tree, estimated at a thousand years old, is used as a tea-room.

The road keeps to the north side of the river for four miles and then crosses Grandtully Bridge and thence follows the south side past Grandtully Castle.

Aberfeldy

Angling. The local Angling Club issues permits for its waters for day or season, for trout fishing.

Caravan site. Municipal site alongside Grandtully road.

Distances by road. Perth, 32 miles; Crieff, 23; Dunkeld, 17; Killin, 22; Tummel Bridge, 13.

Early Closing. Wednesday.

Golf. A 9-hole course along the banks of the river.

The 18-hole course at *Taymouth Castle* is also open to the public.

Hotels. *Breadalbane Arms, Cruachan, Crown, Moness House, Palace, Station.* Various guest houses.

Park, with tennis and bowling clubs open to visitors on payment of a small subscription.

Population. 1,558.

Aberfeldy, pleasantly situated amidst grand scenery, is one of the best health resorts in the country. Robert Burns was here in 1787, having come over the hills from Crieff by Amulree and Glen Quaich. Of the lovely scenery in the neighbourhood he sang in his *Birks of Aberfeldy*. The song is to the air of an older lyric, "The Birks of Abergeldy." The birches at the latter place, on Deeside, are famous, but curiously there are very few at the Falls of Moness.

The bridge (1723–33) was one of the works of General Wade: note the inscription relating to its erection. The Monument to the Black Watch marks the place where that gallant regiment was originally enrolled.

The three **Falls of Moness,** which inspired Burns's song, are a short distance south of the town. The entrance to the path leading to them is opposite the *Breadalbane Arms.* About two hours are required in making the circuit of the falls. The lowest fall is a mile from the entrance, and is inferior to the others. The next is a quarter of a mile farther, and the third half a mile beyond that. A rustic bridge, a little above the last fall, leads back by a gentle descent. A Nature Trail has been sign posted. *Admission free.*

Short Walks from Aberfeldy

1. To **Weem.** An avenue of poplars leads from the farther end of Aberfeldy Bridge to the village of **Weem** (1 mile). The **Rock of Weem** (800 feet) rises behind the *Weem Hotel* and commands beautiful views. Castle Menzies, a fine old baronial mansion which bears the date 1571, is situated at the foot of the Rock. Nearly half-way up is **St. David's Well,** the original stonework of which, a memorial of the Menzies family, is now in the mausoleum of Sir Robert Menzies.

2. To the summit of **Farragon** (2,559 feet), to the north of the Rock of Weem. The ascent will occupy about 2 hours.

3. To **Dull,** a village 4 miles west, on the north side of the Tay. The Rock of Dull commands a wide prospect.

4. To the **Torr,** a small tract of moorland above Aberfeldy. The highest point affords a fine view of the town.

Drives from Aberfeldy

1. To **Kenmore** (*see* pp. 24 and 92), at the eastern end of **Loch Tay.** Hence one can continue by A827 to **Killin** (16 miles farther), at the western end of the loch (*see* p. 91).

2. To **Acharn, Fearnan** and **Lawers.** Another Loch Tay excursion. Buses run regularly from Aberfeldy *viâ* Kenmore to Acharn (8 miles), on the south side of Loch Tay, and to Fearnan (10 miles) and Lawers (14 miles) on the north side.

3. To **Fortingall** and **Glen Lyon.** From Aberfeldy to Fortingall (8 miles) and up Glen Lyon (Bridge of Balgie, 20 miles). Bus from Aberfeldy. There is an hotel at Fortingall and a Youth Hostel one mile to the east. The Lawers hydro-electric scheme includes two dams in Glen Lyon.

Fortingall has a famous yew tree, reputed to be 3,000 years old, the oldest specimen of vegetation in Europe, and the remains of a supposed Roman camp. A bell of the early Celtic Church is preserved in the little church rebuilt by Sir Donald Currie. The "longest Glen in Scotland," **Glen Lyon,** runs east and west for 30 miles in the very heart of Scotland, between Schiehallion (3,547 feet) and Ben Lawers (3,984 feet). **Bridge of Balgie** is connected with Killin (9 miles) by a hill road that runs southwards to Loch Tay; and a delightful but testing footpath leads northward (9 miles) to Loch Rannoch at Dall. The road up Glen Lyon passes **Meggernie Castle** and peters out at the Hydro-Electric Board's dam at Lubreoch (29 miles from Aberfeldy: 1,000 feet above sea level), whence a bridle path finds its way along the side of Loch Lyon, and past Beinn Dorain over to the road between Bridge of Orchy (*see* p. 96) and Tyndrum (44 miles).

The works of the North of Scotland Hydro-Electric Board have transformed this grand glen by tunnels, generating stations and dams, Loch Lyon being greatly enlarged.

Main Route resumed (from p. 25).

From Ballinluig rail and road follow the east bank of the *Tummel,* which except after heavy rain occupies but a small part of its wide and stony bed. On the lower spur of a hill on the left is a monumental Celtic cross to the sixth Duke of Atholl. *Moulinearn Farm,* 1¾ miles from Ballinluig, was an

The Tummel and Fish Pass, Pitlochry

important inn in pre-railway days. Here, in the rebellion of 1745, Prince Charles breakfasted when northward bound, and almost a century later (1844) Queen Victoria partook of "Atholl brose" (a mixture of oatmeal, honey and whisky) while on her way to Blair Castle.

Pitlochry

Angling. – Good fishing for trout and salmon in Loch and River.

Distances by road. – Inverness, 88½ miles; Kingussie, 44½; Perth, 27¼; Blair Atholl, 7; Dunkeld, 13; Aberfeldy, 15.

Early Closing. – Thursday.

Golf. – 18-hole course on high ground with good turf. There are private 9-hole courses at the *Atholl Palace Hotel* and *Pitlochry Hydro Hotel*.

Highland Games. – Early in September.

Hotels. – *Atholl Palace, Pitlochry Hydro, Fisher's, Airdaniar, Dundarach, McKays', Castlebeigh, Green Park, Scotland's.* Unlicensed hotels include: *Pine Trees, Tighnacloich,* etc.

Population. – 2,400.

Post Office. – Main Street 9 a.m. to 5.30 p.m. (Sats: 4.30).

Recreation. – Tennis, bowls, golf (*see* above), putting, boating on Loch Faskally, recreation ground, cinemas, Festival Theatre.

Pitlochry, raised to Burgh status in 1947, stands on the sunny slopes of the Grampians, on the north bank of the River Tummel, and is one of the most attractive and convenient summer resorts in the Highlands. The vicinity is exceedingly lovely, the valleys of the Tummel and the Garry affording beautiful glen scenery.

The main street forms part of the road made by General Wade to the Northern Highlands across the Grampians (now A9). The railway station in on the main Perth Inverness line.

Pitlochry is a fine centre; there are walking and motor excursions in all directions, and good bus services radiate from it. In the Festival Theatre plays are presented from April–September, and there are concerts and Art exhibitions. The advent of the Pitlochry hydro-electric schemes has provided still further attraction. The loch formed by the damming of the River Tummel is very beautiful, and a unique fish-pass, enabling salmon to get to the upper reaches of the river is of continual interest.

Short Excursions from Pitlochry

1. To **Moulin,** a charming village (*Moulin Hotel*), about three-quarters of a mile to the north-east, at the foot of Ben Vrackie. The Parish Church, reconstructed in 1874, stands on what has been a sacred site from time immemorial. In the churchyard are several curious tombstones and an ash tree to which culprits were chained while waiting sentence by the Council of Lairds, the old-time administrators of justice. Kinnaird Cottage, 1 mile east of Moulin, was the residence of Robert Louis Stevenson in 1881, when he wrote *The Merry Men* and *Thrawn Janet*.

2. To the summit of **Ben Vrackie** (2,757 feet), north of Pitlochry (3½ to 4 hours up and back). The descent can be made to Killiecrankie.

3. The **Black Spout** (1½ miles). A picturesque waterfall in a densely wooded ravine. Proceed by Knockfarrie Road (at east side of *Atholl Palace Hotel* entrance), south-east until just before the second burn is reached; there turn to the left.

4. **Queen's View and Loch Tummel** (*see* p. 29).

5. To **Linn of Tummel.** These falls (some 4 miles from Pitlochry, above the junction of the Tummel and the Garry) were formerly among the finest cascades in Scotland. While the flow has been reduced as a result of the Tummel–Garry hydro-electric scheme, it is fortunate that the beauty of the river has not been impaired. The Falls can be reached by crossing the aluminium footbridge which replaces the old Clunie Bridge, and thence along the road to Foss. Beyond the falls another footbridge across the Tummel allows return to be made to Pitlochry by a walk alongside the Garry to Garry Bridge.

Motorists proceeding from Pitlochry may do so by Aldour Bridge, south of the town, which leads across the Tummel to Foss Road. The construction of Loch Faskally necessitated a new road being made at a higher level and one may now proceed along the southern side of Loch Tummel to Tummel Bridge. On the way to the Falls is passed the *Memorial Arch* in memory of men who lost their lives in driving the tunnel which carries the waters of Loch Tummel to Clunie power station. The Linn of Tummel and the neighbouring Pass of Killiecrankie are National Trust properties.

6. The **Pass of Killiecrankie.** Three miles north of Pitlochry the Great North Road begins to run high above the famed Pass of Killiecrankie, and from openings among the trees on the left one can look down to where the river rushes along its rocky bed. The railway viaduct is prominent at the end of the vista, and beyond rises the pointed peak of Beinn a'Ghlo.

The walk along the pass is best entered by the gate beyond the car-parking place.

Through this dark defile, General Mackay led the royalist force which encountered the rebellious Highlanders under Claverhouse (Viscount Dundee) on the plain about half a mile north of Killiecrankie Station, July 27, 1689. It will be remembered that while King William's soldiers were routed, Dundee fell mortally wounded, and his death was the ruin for the time of the Jacobite cause.

At the top of the Pass is the **Soldier's Leap.** A fugitive royalist, pursued by one of Dundee's Highlanders, is said to have cleared the river here at a bound–a feat successfully emulated by an English visitor in 1912.

7. **Falls of Bruar,** 10 miles from Pitlochry by the Great North Road. *Motel* beside falls.

8. To **Kirkmichael** (12½ miles). A bus runs to and from this pretty village on the left bank of the *Ardle*, 800 feet above sea-level. Kirkmichael is about 7 miles from Bridge of Cally, and 13 miles from Blairgowrie, with which it is linked by bus (*see* p. 53). (Hotels: *Aldchlappie, Kirkmichael*.)

9. **Dunkeld** (train or road: 13 miles) and **Rumbling Bridge,** near the falls of Braan (*see* p. 24).

10. **Tummel Bridge** (14 miles) and **Kinloch Rannoch** (21 miles) (*see* p. 29).

11. **Aberfeldy** (by road: 14 miles) *via* Ballinluig (*see* p. 25).

Pitlochry to Kinloch Rannoch

As an alternative to the southern route (p. 29) one can cross the Garry, turn westward and follow the north bank of the *Tummel*, passing the mansion of Bonskeid (used as a Y.M.C.A. holiday home). Beyond the mouth of the **Glen of Fincastle,** at the foot of Loch Tummel, is a lofty projecting rock, reached through a wicket, that affords a magnificent prospect known as the **Queen's View.** Strathtummel Youth Hostel is half a mile to the east.

Loch Tummel is about 7 miles long by half a mile broad, and contains pike and large trout.

From the Queen's View the road runs parallel with the loch, and $10\frac{1}{2}$ miles from Pitlochry reaches *Loch Tummel Hotel*, a favourite resort of anglers. Three and a half miles beyond the hotel is **Tummel Bridge,** from the southern end of which a road strikes off to Fortingall, Aberfeldy and Kenmore (on a clear day the view northward from the highest point of this road is extraordinarily fine).

The high-road to Kinloch Rannoch does not cross the Bridge, but continues along the northern bank of the river. A short mile from the Bridge is the junction of the Trinafour road (*see* p. 31). *Dunalastair House* stands on a lovely stretch of the Tummel, opposite to the base of **Schiehallion,** and near by it is the Hydro-Electric Board's Dunalastair Reservoir.

Kinloch Rannoch (*Dunalastair, Bunrannoch, Loch Rannoch*) is a flourishing little village situated – despite its name – at the lower end of **Loch Rannoch.** [Buses daily to and from Pitlochry; and also to and from Rannoch Station (18 miles) on the Crianlarich–Fort William line.] Loch Rannoch is a fine sheet of water, a mile wide and $9\frac{1}{2}$ miles long. It is bordered by gently sloping hills in regular and unbroken outline, on the north; on its southern side the hills are higher and steeper. The main road runs along the north side of the loch, but a secondary road skirts the southern shore, passing the **Black Wood of Rannoch,** famed for its grand Scots pines.

The water is famous for brown trout of large size. The hotel guests have the privilege of fishing the loch and also part of the Tummel which flows from it. Near its western extremity (the better end for trout) is the mouth of the *Ericht*, which comes from the loch of the same name. A tunnel connects Loch Ericht with a power station in Loch Rannoch, near CamaserICht. Into the head of Loch Rannoch flows the *Gaur*, which has its origin in Loch Laidon or Lydoch, in the Moor of Rannoch; it is one of the best trouting lochs in the country.

Excursions from Kinloch Rannoch

1. To **Struan** (*see* p. 31), 13 miles.
2. The ascent of the sharply pyramidal peak of **Schiehallion** (3,547 feet): from two to three hours. Variety may be had by ascending from Tummel Bridge (on the bus route) and descending to Kinloch Rannoch, or *vice versa*. The ascent from the Bridge takes about an hour longer.
3. **The circuit of Loch Rannoch** (22 miles). The road is almost level and is shaded by trees, part of the old Caledonian Forest, for a good way.
4. To **Rannoch Station** on the Crianlarich–Fort William line (18 miles: bus service). The road along the north side of the lake affords fine views of Schiehallion. A mile short of the

western end of the lake, beyond the power-house referred to above, it crosses the Ericht at **Camasericht,** so called from its situation at a "bend of the Ericht." At the head of the loch *Rannoch Lodge* is passed, and a mile westward, on the Gaur River, *Dunan Lodge.* Beyond is bare moorland to **Rannoch Station** (*hotel*).

5. To **Pitlochry** (as on p. 29).

6. To **Glen Lyon** (Innerwick, 15 miles), by **Dall,** on the south side of the Loch, and thence afoot by a glorious hill path. There is no inn at Innerwick or Bridge of Balgie, but a bus runs from there to Fortingall and Aberfeldy (*see* p. 26).

7. To **Aberfeldy** *viâ* White Bridge and Strath Appin (*Coshieville Hotel*), 18 miles.

Main route resumed (from p. 27).

From Pitlochry, high-road and railway run up the **Pass of Killiecrankie,** though, owing to a tunnel, train passengers obtain only a glimpse of the Pass (from the *left* side of the carriage). The hills on both sides are clothed with woods, and the foliage is so profuse as often to hide the river tumultuously forcing its way over the rocks and eddying through the pools. At the northern end of the Pass is pretty **Killiecrankie** (*Killiecrankie House Hotel*), 32½ miles from Perth, and 3¾ from Pitlochry.

Another 3 miles bring us to–

Blair Atholl

Angling.–On the River Garry, a tributary of the Tummel (permit necessary from local angling club).
Caravan site.–In castle grounds.

Golf.–9-hole course at Invertilt, ¼ mile from station.
Hotels.–*Atholl Arms, Tilt.*

This pleasant village stands at an elevation of 450 feet above the sea, and has a climate even more bracing than that of Pitlochry.

Blair Castle is the principal residence of the Duke of Atholl. It is old and has many historic associations. In 1644 it was garrisoned by Montrose; stormed by Cromwell in 1653; occupied by Claverhouse in 1689; besieged by the Jacobites in 1746. It was afterwards dismantled and deprived of its battlements and upper storeys. In 1869 it was restored. Queen Victoria was more than once a guest within its walls. The castle is open to the public (fee) at stated times.

Excursions from Blair Atholl

1. The **Hill of Tulloch,** or **Tulach,** "The Knoll" (1,541 feet), about a mile south-west of Blair Atholl.

2. The **Falls of Bruar,** nearly 4 miles westward. (Northbound bus services pass the entrance to the glen (*see* below.) *Motel* beside the falls.) Nearby is the Clan Donnachaidh museum.

3. To **Braemar by Glen Tilt.** There is a fairly good road as far as the *Forest Lodge* (8 miles), and a rough bridle-path thence to the upper waters of the Dee at *Bynack Lodge* (18 miles from Blair), from which there is a road (impracticable for motors until Linn of Dee) to Braemar (30 miles). Cyclists occasionally take this route, but between the Forest Lodge and Bynack the cycle and its rider must often change places. It should be clearly understood that this is a long and arduous tramp. Indifferent walkers should not attempt it – especially unaccompanied. Small Youth Hostel at Inverey, 5 miles from Braemar.

Glen Tilt is entered at Blair Atholl from the high-road near the Tilt Hotel, and the route lies by the side of the stream to the Old Bridge of Tilt, a distance of half a mile; walkers, stopping short of the Old Bridge, ascend to the Fender Bridge, from which they will descend, in full sight of the peaks of **Beinn a'Ghlo** (3,505 and 3,671 feet), to the road, regaining it about a mile from the Fender. Near the bridge are the pretty **Falls of Fender.** The Glen Tilt road is private, and before using it permission must be obtained from the Estates Office, Blair Atholl.

Three miles beyond Blair Atholl a wide parking-place in a bend of the Great North Road marks the proximity of the **Falls of the Bruar** (*see* above). A little way up the stream are the lower bridge and one of the falls, and from this spot there is a good path on each side of the burn to the upper bridge, which is about a mile from the main road, and just beyond the highest and best of the three falls, which consists of three cascades, having a combined height of 200 feet. It is sad to say that the falls are likely to dry up in summer due to hydro-electric development.

The banks of the Bruar are clothed with fir plantations, thanks to the "Humble Petition of Bruar Water to the noble Duke of Athole," penned by Burns.

A mile westward of the Bruar Water is **Calvine,** a small hamlet at the foot of Glen Garry. To the left is **Struan** (hotel), whence a minor road goes off by **Glen Errochty** to Kinloch Rannoch (p. 29), climbing to over 1,000 feet near Trinafour, above which the Errochty Water has been dammed to create a large reservoir. The road offers grand views in the descent to the Tummel Valley.

For the next 20 miles the main route is concerned in crossing the Grampians. It is through scenery that so increases in its impressiveness as the summit is approached that even the electric cables on their striding pylons are dwarfed into insignificance. Between Struan and Dalwhinnie – some 20 miles – is neither hotel or garage, hardly, indeed, any permanent habitation. The first 12 miles are through **Glen Garry,** railway, road and river travelling side by side.

From **Dalnacardoch Lodge** (6 miles beyond Struan) a rough road runs 6 miles over the hills to the south to Trinafour and so to Kinloch Rannoch (*see* above); while, on the north, a private road follows the Edendon Water, and is continued, as a footpath, along a chain of lochs, to the secluded **Gaick Forest,** noted for its deer, at the head of the *Tromie,* whence there is access to the valley of the Spey at Kingussie (20 miles from Dalnacardoch).

Loch Garry, a splendid trouting water (strictly preserved), is passed on the left. A delightful footpath runs from Dalnaspidal, *viâ* Loch Garry, over to Loch Rannoch, about a dozen miles to the south. Just beyond **Dalnaspidal** (51 miles from Perth), the summit level of the railway is reached. This is 1,484 feet above the sea, the highest level attained by any ordinary type of railway in the British Isles. The point coincides with the boundary between the counties of Perth and Inverness. Dal-na-spidal means "the field of the spital or hospice," and the name is thought to indicate that the spot was once the site of a hospice – a feature which many weary travellers have wished to revive, for now the place is very quiet, bleak – the reverse of hospitable. Snow lingers late on the neighbouring mountains, and the stoutly-built fences which protect the railway and road from snow-drifts in winter, add further to the wildness of the scene.

Beyond Dalnaspidal, road and rail run in close company through the

Loch Garry

Pass of Druimuachdar (Drumochter: "the upper ridge"), a narrow gap in the long range of hills. On the west are two mountains, the Atholl Sow and the Badenoch Boar (2,422 feet). Running down to Dalwhinnie the views open out and there is a grand panorama of the Monadhliath mountains. Just before reaching the hamlet of **Dalwhinnie** (58 miles from Perth, and 1,169 feet above sea-level) the War Memorial is conspicuous on the right, and a little short of it is a concrete dam (with salmon ladder) in connection with the hydro-electric schemes. Dalwhinnie has two hotels (*Loch Ericht, Grampian*), a guest-house, tea-room, filling-stations and a distillery.

There is a track across the hills from Dalwhinnie into **Strath Mashie** (7 miles), entering the Fort William road 4 miles beyond Drumgask and 3 east of Loch Laggan (*see* p. 34).

Loch Ericht, 16 miles long, is situated partly in Perth and partly in Inverness. It is one of the wildest and most solitary lakes of Scotland. In many places it is extremely deep. Its water, though very cold even in the hottest days of summer, seldom freezes. Loch Ericht is now being used in connection with the Grampians Electricity Scheme. **Cluny's Cage,** where Prince Charlie sheltered in 1746, is on the west side, towards the foot of the Loch, where it is overshadowed by **Ben Alder** (3,757 feet). Loch Ericht is the home *par excellence* of brown trout, and therefore a great attraction to anglers. It may be fished by visitors at the *Loch Ericht Hotel* (about a mile from Dalwhinnie station), which has boats.

From Dalwhinnie we descend **Glen Truim** for 7 or 8 miles, and, entering the valley of the *Spey*, find ourselves in the heart of the district of **Badenoch.** (A hill-road, A889, runs due north from Dalwhinnie to Drumgask and Laggan Bridge, *see* p. 33.)

Newtonmore

has rapidly developed as a summer resort. It has commodious private residences, boarding houses and hotels (*Balavil Arms, Glen, Main's Badenoch* (unl.), *Craig Mhor, Lodge*). There is an 18-hole golf course, bowling green, tennis courts and good trout fishing in the Spey and smaller streams. Pony trekking, which is growing in popularity, originated here. Situated not far below the junction of the *Truim* with the Spey – the scene of a famous clan battle between Camerons and Mackintoshes in 1386 – it has nearer access than Kingussie to the scenery of the Upper Spey, described in the excursions mentioned below. The Clan Macpherson Museum contains interesting clan relics (*open Easter to end of September*).

Three miles farther north is–

Kingussie

Angling.–Permit fishing for salmon and trout in the Spey. Good fishing in Loch Laggan.
Bowls and Tennis.–Clubs open to visitors.
Caravan Site.–By golf course.
Distances by road. Inverness. 44 miles; Pitlochry, 44½; Perth, 71.
Early Closing Day.–Wednesday.
Golf. An 18-hole course. Sunday play. The course at Newtonmore is also available.
Highland Folk Museum.–Am Fasgadh.
Hotels.–*Royal, Duke of Gordon, Silverfjord, Hyeres, Columba Guest House.*
Population.–1,050.
Post Office.–Spey Street.
Youth Hostel.–East Terrace.

The name (pronounced *king-yew-sie*) is derived from the Gaelic equivalent of "the end of the pine-wood."

The town is the centre of a wide district of great beauty. It is situated, at a height of 764 feet above sea-level, midway, and where Scotland is widest, between the Atlantic Ocean and the North Sea, and is a capital point from which to explore some of the most magnificent Highland scenery. The Grampians keep back biting blasts from the east, while the Monadhliath (*monaleé-ah*) mountains largely intercept the rain-clouds from the Atlantic. Pine-woods abound. Near the station is a unique Highland Folk Museum, open May to September 10–1, 2–5. Admission charge.

In the vicinity of Kingussie there are many splendid walks, unhampered by restrictions. Near the town are **Gynack Glen** and **Loch,** both highly popular resorts. The *Gynack* is a tributary of the Spey. The loch lies between Creag Mhor and Creag Bheag, a good mile from the principal street. Creag Bheag is a pine-clad height whose summit (1,593 feet), but a mile and a half from the town, commands a fine view of the Grampians, the Monadhliath hills and the lower Valley of Badenoch.

Excursions from Kingussie

1. To **Loch Laggan** (18 miles). The route is part of that followed in the next excursion. (Bus service.)

2. To **Tulloch** (31 miles), for **Fort William** (49 miles). Bus service to Tulloch station, on West Highland Line for Fort William, etc.

From Kingussie the road (A86) takes a south-westerly direction, along the course of the Spey. Running through **Newtonmore**, it continues along the north side of the river, having, on the right, **Creag Dhubh** (2,550 feet), the "black crag," whose name was the gathering cry of the Macphersons, and passing **Cluny Castle** (9 miles), the seat of Cluny Macpherson.

Two miles beyond the Castle is **Laggan Bridge.**

LOCH LAGGAN

Laggan Dam

This hamlet is connected with Dalwhinnie station, on the Highland line – Perth, Kingussie, Inverness – by a hilly but well-surfaced road, about 8 miles long. It is also connected with Fort Augustus, 24 miles distant, by "Wade's Road" (followed by Prince Charlie in the '45), of which about 10 miles only are drivable, and on which there is no inn. It leads over the Corrieyairack Pass, rising to 2,507 feet. This is a very popular route for walkers, but it is emphatically one for strong walkers only.

At Laggan Bridge the road crosses the Spey and follows the *Mashie*, one of its tributaries. In the angle formed by the Spey and the Mashie is the British fort of **Dundalair,** having thick walls of slate, and said to be one of the most perfect British strongholds in Scotland. Soon after the Mashie is left the road reaches its highest point and then descends to **Loch Laggan,** a beautiful sheet of water 820 feet above sea-level, and about two-thirds of a mile wide. Originally 7 miles in length it has been lengthened by 4½ miles artificially as part of the Lochaber Water Power Scheme, the waters being impounded by the great **Laggan Dam** – of concrete and 700 feet long with a height of 130 feet – and led by a 3¾ mile tunnel into Loch Treig. Loch Laggan contains an abundance of small trout. Boats may be obtained from the *Loch Laggan Inn* (18 miles from Kingussie) at its eastern end. Around the lake are lofty mountains, well wooded on the south side, and on its surface are two small islets, named respectively *King's Isle* and *Dog's Isle*, from the tradition that Fergus, "the first of the Scottish kings," lived on one and kept his dogs on the other.

From Loch Laggan Inn a track runs in a north-easterly direction to the Corrieyairack Pass to Fort Augustus (21 miles, *see* above), which it strikes at the end of 3 miles; and running in a south-easterly direction there is a wild track to Dalwhinnie.

For some 6 or 7 miles beyond Loch Laggan the road passes through a pastoral district and then through a more diversified tract to **Tulloch,** where the West Highland Line is joined. The way thence is through Glen Spean, passing the Braes of Lochaber and the dashing Monessie Falls, by Roy Bridge (noted for its parallel roads) and Spean Bridge to Fort William (*see* pp. 115, 97).

3. To **Insh** and **Tromie Bridge.** Out and return, 15½ miles. Follow the high-road, which runs parallel to the railway, to **Kincraig** (6 miles); cross the railway and Spey to Insh Church (6½ miles); thence skirt the north end of **Loch Insh,** and return up the right bank of the Spey, at a distance of three-quarters of a mile or so from the river, to **Tromie Bridge** (12½ miles),

and then past the ruins of **Ruthven Barracks** to the bridge leading to Kingussie station. The Ruthven Barracks supplanted the residence of the Comyns, lords of Badenoch. They were erected in 1718 to overawe the Highlanders. In February, 1746, they were captured by Jacobites. "Ossian" Macpherson was born at Ruthven.

4. To **Glen Feshie** (16 miles *viâ* the Manse of Insh, 10 miles *viâ* Tromie Bridge). Those who elect to make the circular tour should go *viâ* the Manse Road, as it gives the better view in approaching the Glen. The routes are identical to Tromie Bridge (3 miles). The Manse Road lies through the village of **Insh,** and beyond that is the *Manse of Insh,* near the loch, where the rather rough driving road up **Glen Feshie** branches off from the turnpike.

By the alternative route, turn to the left after crossing Tromie Bridge. Two or three hundred yards beyond it, the road to Glen Feshie strikes off to the right up a steep brae. Two or three miles from the summit of the hill is **Baileguish,** where vehicles must go through a tributary of the *Feshie.* The spot is 1,000 feet above sea-level and commands a magnificent view of the Glen. Having crossed the stream, keep straight on for a mile, where our road joins that coming from the Manse of Insh and then leads up Glen Feshie to the lodge, where it ends. A proposal has been made to build a high-road up Glen Feshie and over to Deeside by Geldie Lodge.

5. To **Loch an Eilean.** A favourite excursion with those bound upon a picnic. The loch can be reached by taking train to Aviemore station, thence by road (3 miles). By road from Kingussie the distance is 14 miles *viâ* Aviemore. The Loch, which can also be approached *viâ* Tromie Bridge and Feshie Bridge, is described on p. 36.

On leaving Kingussie there are good views on the right of the Glen Feshie mountains, which, as we proceed, give place to a view of the Cairngorm group.

Road and railway closely follow the Spey, which winds through a succession of rich meadows, along which are pools abounding in water-fowl and covered with tall reeds and water-lilies. To protect the railway from inundations extensive and costly embankments are necessary for several miles.

Rather more than 2 miles from Kingussie, in a small larch plantation on the left, is a *Monument to James Macpherson* (1736–96), the translator or compiler of the ancient Gaelic poems ascribed to Ossian.

Close by is **Balavil House,** occupying the site of the old Castle of Raits, originally a stronghold of the Comyns, and for a time in the possession of "Ossian Macpherson," and afterwards of his son-in-law, Sir David Brewster.

About a couple of miles farther, we pass on the right **Loch Insh,** a beautiful sheet of water – an enlargement of the Spey – roughly a mile long by three-quarters of a mile wide. Permission must be obtained for fishing the loch. Just beyond the loch is **Kincraig,** 72 miles from Perth. The village has a 9-hole golf course opposite the *Suie Hotel.*

Beyond Kincraig, pretty **Loch Alvie** appears on the left, and opposite is **Tor Alvie,** or the Hill of **Kinrara** (1,175 feet). Upon it are two monuments – a lofty pillar in memory of the last of the old Dukes of Gordon, and a cairn in memory of Highland soldiers who fell at Waterloo. The summit of the hill commands a magnificent view of Strathspey. Tor Alvie is within the private policies of Kinrara Lodge.

So past the clachan of **Lynwilg,** in which is a comfortable hotel that may serve as headquarters for walkers wishing to explore the Monadhliaths. On the left is the Rock of **Craigellachie** (pronounced *craig-ell′-achy*), the trysting-place of the Grant clan, whose slogan or war-cry was "Stand fast, Craigellachie."

Some 78 miles from Perth is—

Aviemore

Aviemore (Hotels—*Cairngorm, Altnacraig, High Range, Badenoch, Post House, Strathspey, Red MacGregor. Dell* at Rothiemurchas, and *Lynwilg* at Loch Alvie) is an excellent centre for tourists. It is a good starting-place for the summits of the Cairngorms. It also has attractions of its own, including a Stone Circle and other archaeological remains, and the fine Aviemore Centre comprising ice rink, swimming pool, dry Ski slope, bars, cinema/theatre, kart track, ballroom and children's amusements. There is plenty of accommodation and good fishing is available. There are excellent facilities for nearby ski-ing in the Cairngorms with ski-tows, chairlifts and licensed restaurants.

For continuation of Main Route to Inverness by Carrbridge, see p. 38; by Forres, see p. 39.

Excursions from Aviemore

1. To **Loch an Eilean** and **Loch Gamhna** *viâ* Inverdruie and the Croft, returning *viâ* Polchar and Inverdruie.
Loch an Eilean, "the Lake of the Island," is about 3 miles south of Aviemore. On a small island are the ruins of a stronghold originally constructed by Lachlan Macintosh, Chief of Clan Chattan, in the mid-fifteenth century and over the following two hundred years was added to until it covered the whole island. The ruin is the home of a fine echo. **Loch Gamhna,** a small loch at the upper end of Loch an Eilean, is adorned with water-lilies. **Polchar** was for many years the summer and autumn residence of Dr. Martineau, the eminent Unitarian Divine, in memory of whom a roadside column was erected in 1913.

2. To **Lynwilg, Kinrara House,** and **Tor Alvie.** Lynwilg and Tor Alvie have been briefly noticed on p. 35. **Kinrara House,** at the foot of the Tor, was the favourite residence of the mother of the fifth and (before the re-creation of the title in favour of the Duke of Richmond) the last Duke of Gordon. She was the beautiful Jean Maxwell, the friend and hostess of Robert Burns. Her grave is marked by a granite monument on the site of St. Eada's Chapel. On the opposite side of the Spey is **South Kinrara House.** Purchased by Adam Black, the publisher, it was enlarged and improved.

3. **A Circular Tour by Kincraig.** The outward route passes through Lynwilg and by Loch Alvie and Loch Tor. **Kincraig** is a tiny place of about 400 people and Highland line trains now pass right through its former station. Nearby is **Insh Church,** which has a bronze bell believed to date from the Culdee period. After skirting the north end of **Loch Insh** (*see* p. 35) the road turns sharp left and in about a mile reaches the picturesque **Feshie Bridge.** Crossing it, the road follows the right bank of the Spey to Inverdruie and the bridge over the Spey to Aviemore.

4. **Round by Boat of Garten.** The route follows the main road northward, passing Loch Vaa, for about 4 miles, and then branches right to **Boat of Garten,** after a former ferry, a growing summer resort. The return is made by crossing the Spey and turning south by the road which leads past **Kincardine Church,** an old building with a "squint" or leper window, and a rude stone font, and Loch Pityoulish, to **Coylum Bridge,** 2 miles distant from Aviemore. (Total distance 15 miles.) From near Kincardine the **Slugan Pass** runs up the Milton Burn and through the Queen's Forest to Loch Morlich.

5. To **Loch Einich.** The route is *viâ* Inverdruie, and, if on foot, the return journey may be made *viâ* Loch an Eilean. **Loch Einich** is a long, narrow sheet of water about 9 miles from Aviemore. It is 1,650 feet above sea-level. Above it tower the rocky ridge of **Sgoran Dubh** (3,658 feet) and the lower slopes of **Braeriach** (4,248 feet). The Loch contains char and trout.

Glen Einich is the best starting-point for the ascent of **Braeriach, Cairn Toul** (4,241 feet) and Sgoran Dubh.

Loch an Eilean

6. The **Ascent of Cairn Gorm** (14 miles to the summit, 4,084 feet). Vehicles can proceed to a car park at a height of some 2,000 feet, passing the shores of Loch Morlich. Glenmore is the heart of a superb National Forest Park (24 sq. miles) which extends to the very top of Cairn Gorm. At Loch Morlich are camping grounds, huts for youth organizations, bathing and boating, and courses in mountain craft. The **Cairngorms National Nature Reserve** (39,689 acres), between Rothiemurchus and Braemar, is the largest in Britain. The Cairngorm chairlift operates winter and summer.

7. **Across the Cairngorm Mountains by the Larig Ghru Pass to Braemar** (30 miles). The route lies along the course of the Druie to the hamlet of **Coylum Bridge** (2 miles), where is the last permanently-occupied habitation that will be passed until Derry Lodge is reached, 10 miles short of Braemar. Beyond the summit (2,733 feet) of the pass are ice-cold pools, called the **Pools of Dee,** 12 miles from Aviemore. Thence the path crosses the stream and leads down the east side of the valley, with **Ben Macdhui** (4,296 feet) on the left, and on the right the entrance to the wild Garrachory between **Braeriach** (4,248 feet) and Cairn Toul (4,241 feet). High up the Garrachory the infant *Dee* may be seen, a delicate streak of white falling over the face of the cliffs from its source, the **Wells of Dee** (4,000 feet). Four miles beyond the Pools of Dee, and opposite the Devil's Point (3,303 feet), the path turns left and just rounding the south side of Carn a'Mhaim enters Glen Lui Beg, reaching *Derry Lodge* at the junction of the Derry Burn and the Lui Water. From here there is a private road down Glen Lui which is closed to vehicles unless permission has been obtained. Vehicles may be ordered to meet one at the Linn of Dee, 6 miles from Braemar. The wild scenery of this excursion well repays the exertion involved, but the Larig Ghru should not be lightly undertaken if the weather conditions are not favourable, and the danger of mist must be borne in mind.

8. Over to **Nethy Bridge** (17 miles) *viâ* **Glenmore Lodge,** and afoot (or by cycle) through the extensive pine-woods of Glenmore and Abernethy, by the fairy-haunted Green Loch and the **Revoan Pass.**

9. Westward, on foot, over the hills by the "Burma Road" to the Dulnain and down the valley to Carrbridge (14 miles).

The Aviemore Centre

AVIEMORE TO INVERNESS VIA CARRBRIDGE

The Great North Road takes this direct route from Aviemore to Inverness (33 miles), running now on one side of the railway, now on the other, and making straight for Inverness across Drummossie Moor from Daviot without any detour such as the railway is obliged to make.

From **Carrbridge** (7 miles, *see* p. 42), we begin to ascend the southern slope of the Monadhliath mountains. At the deep **Pass of Slochd Mor** there is a remarkable echo. Emerging from the Pass we reach an open, trackless expanse of furze and heather. In excavating the enormous railway cutting on this portion of the route, there were discovered at a depth of 25 feet below the surface three successive crops of pine-trees, showing that in pre-historic times the region was tree-clad, although now there is not a twig to be seen. A viaduct, a quarter of a mile in length, carries the line across the *Findhorn*, a river that has always been famed for its salmon and trout fishing. On 2 miles of the stream, visitors at the *Freeburn Hotel* at **Tomatin,** the very heart of the Mackintosh country, have the privilege of fishing both for salmon and trout. Three miles farther will be seen on the right **Loch Moy,** with the magnificent residence of The Mackintosh of Mackintosh in the vicinity. On approaching **Daviot** a glorious panorama of mountain scenery comes into view. Beyond Daviot, the Great Glen of Scotland opens on the left, and far away in the north-west rises the huge mass of **Ben Wyvis** (3,429 feet). Soon there may be seen towards the north, across the River Nairn, a ridge that is a site of great historic interest, for it is the battlefield of **Culloden** (*see* p. 50). From Daviot the railway swings northward in a wide detour, giving glorious views. The road makes more directly for **Inverness** (*see* pp. 49–50).

AVIEMORE TO INVERNESS VIA FORRES

On leaving Aviemore, the **Kinveachy Woods** will be seen on the left, covering the slopes of the hills, and sheltering Loch Vaa and other pretty lakes.

Five miles from Aviemore and a little eastward of the main road, is **Boat of Garten,** a favourite holiday resort. Hotels include *The Boat* and *Craigard,* with several guest-houses. The road comes in from the left a mile or so north of Boat of Garten, and then passes the farm of *Tulloch-gorum,* a name familiar to Scots as that of a celebrated reel and of the Rev. John Skinner's verses, which Burns declared to be "the best Scotch song that Scotland ever heard." So to –

Grantown-on-Spey

Angling. – The Strathspey Angling Improvement Association has 13 miles of fishings on the Spey, Dulnain and Loch Garten. Salmon and trouting tickets are issued by the Secretary (High Street, Grantown). There is free trout fishing in certain tributaries of the Spey, and there are many streams and lochs in the vicinity.

Camping and Caravanning. – Modern up-to-date site.

Distances *By road.* Aviemore, 15; Carrbridge, 10; Craigellachie, 24; Elgin, 37; Forres, 22; Inver- ness, 33; Nairn, 23; Tomintoul, 13.

Early Closing. – Thursday.

Golf. – A sporting 18-hole course.

Hotels. – *Grant Arms, Palace, Strathspey, Craig-lynne, Ben Mhor* and many others.

Population. – About 1,600.

Post Office. – High Street.

Recreation. – Tennis courts, 8 courts in Heathfield Road, where important tournaments are held in August. Bowling green. Curling. 18-hole golf course.

Grantown, the capital of **Strathspey,** is situated in the midst of varied and pleasant scenery at an altitude exceeding 700 feet above the sea. It possesses a bracing climate, the salubrity of which is increased by extensive pine-woods. The town stands on gravelly soil, and claims to be one of the driest spots in the Scottish Highlands. It is an extremely popular resort and during the summer and again for the ski-ing season, the town is occupied by holiday-makers in good numbers. Within a mile of the town flows the River Spey, through a level and fertile tract, while in the background are lofty heather-clad mountains. Half a mile or so upstream from the picturesque but old **Spey Bridge** – an old Wade Bridge – a new structure of reinforced concrete spans the river with a single arch of 240 feet, and gives access to the road leading down Strathspey to Craigellachie.

The river contains salmon, pike, sea and river trout. Finnocks abound in the early part of the season, and in the upper reaches char may be found.

At the head of an avenue proceeding from the beautiful grassy Square at the northern end of the main street is the **Seafield Memorial Church,** erected in 1886 by Lady Seafield in memory of her husband, the seventh Earl, and her son. The pulpit is most beautifully carved in black Italian oak.

Excursions from Grantown

1. **The Ladies' Walk** (half-mile) is on an eminence overlooking the Spey. It commands some of the most charming views obtainable in the vicinity of Grantown.

2. The **View Point,** a height (1,200 feet) about 1½ miles to the north, is reached by well-marked paths and offers a magnificent panorama of Strathspey.

3. **Inverallan Churchyard** (1¼ miles), on the left bank of the Spey. The churchyard formerly contained the Parish Church. Inside the gateway is **St. Figat's Stone.**

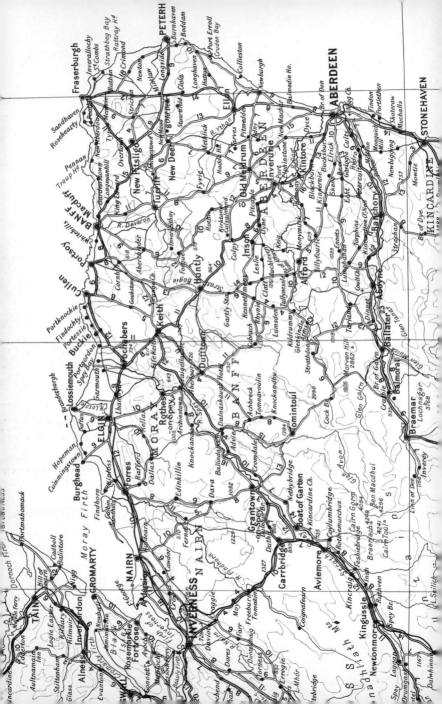

EASTERN HIGHLANDS

WARD, LOCK LIMITED, LONDON

© John Bartholomew & Son Ltd, Edinburgh

0   4   8   12   16   20 Miles

4. **Glen Beg** and **Ben More**. Follow the Dulnain road for about a mile, then turn to the right, and passing under the old railway route proceed up the Glen. **Ben More** (1,545 feet) commands one of the finest views in the district.

5. **Castle Grant,** 2 miles from the centre of the town. (*Not open.*)
Follow the North Road from the Square. The Castle is the family seat of the Earls of Seafield, Chiefs of the Clan Grant (now represented by the Countess of Seafield). There is an imposing entrance gateway and lodge, from which proceeds a beautiful avenue. The view of the **Cromdale Hills**, on the right, is much admired. The Castle is a massive plain building, the oldest part of which is of the Scottish Baronial type, and dates from the fifteenth century. Part has been destroyed by fire.

6. **Lord Huntly's Cave** (3½ miles). Follow the Forces road past the Castle Grant gateway until just beyond the third milestone. There take a footpath on the right guarded by a stile. This path leads to the Glen, at the bottom of which, on the left-hand side, is a cave, the traditional hiding-place of the second Marquis of Huntly, who espoused the cause of Charles I.

7. To **Dulnain Bridge** (3 miles); the ruins of **Muckrach Castle** (4 miles); **Duthil Parish Church** (7 miles); and **Carrbridge** (10 miles): bus service. The road runs from the southern end of the town, and for about a mile and a half lies between the Highland line and the Spey. Then it passes under the line, and after skirting Gaich Wood comes to **Dulnain Bridge**, a charming spot, where the brawling *Dulnain* stream – next to the Avon the largest tributary of the Spey – rushes along its deep rocky bed. The road continues on the north side of the river, and half a mile from the bridge passes *Muckrach House*, and a little farther the ruins of **Muckrach Castle,** built by Patrick Grant in 1598. The lintel stone of its doorway has been built into one of the walls of the Doune mansion in Rothiemurchus.

The road continues to the old church and churchyard of **Duthil.** In ancient times the district was known as Glencharnoch ("Glen of Heroes"), from the number of illustrious dead who were laid to rest under cairns, many of which still remain. The churchyard has been the burial-place of the Grants for three hundred years. The history of the church goes back to the thirteenth century.

A moorland road (B9007) here starts off boldly northwards for Forres (24 miles), but our road crosses the *Duthil Burn* and reaches the attractive village of **Carrbridge**. Some 50 yards from the Bridge, near the hotel, is the arch of the old bridge, built by the Earl of Seafield some 200 years ago. A mile from the hotel is Carrbridge station, on the Highland line. Half a mile from the station is a 9-hole golf course. The return to Grantown may be made by following the old North Road (A9) southwards for 3 miles and then turning left at Kinveachy Lodge into the road down Speyside (A95).

8. To **Castle Roy** (5 miles); **Nethy Bridge** (6 miles); **Abernethy Forest** (8 miles); and **Loch Garten** (10 miles). To the Spey Bridge by the New Road, and having crossed it, turn to the right and follow the road southward.

9. To **Bridge of Broun** (10 miles); and **Tomintoul** (14 miles).
The road from Grantown south-eastward to Tomintoul has been greatly improved; and the scenery, including an extensive prospect of the **Braes of Abernethy**, is very fine. The **Bridge of Broun** is in a most romantic spot. At the point where the stream is spanned, the water flows through a narrow and rocky channel known as the **Linn of Broun.**

Tomintoul is the chief centre of population in the extensive parish of Kirkmichael, in Banffshire. The highest village in the Highlands (1,124 feet), it has bracing air; the district abounds with trout streams, the River Avon has salmon and sea trout, and the place is making a name for itself as one of the holiday resorts of the North. By the *Lecht Road* over to Donside, Tomintoul is in close touch with Deeside. There are hotels (*Gordon Arms, Richmond Arms, White Heather, Glenavon*) and a Youth Hostel, and buses run daily except Tuesday and Wednesday, to and from Dufftown.

For routes between Tomintoul and Deeside, *see* pp. 68 and 71, and for route between Tomintoul and Strathdon, *see* p. 73.

10. **Lochindorb,** the "lake of black water," to the north-west of Grantown, may be reached by tramping across the moor, or by road (10 miles). On an island in its midst is a Castle that has been the scene of many stirring historic events. In 1303 it was captured by Edward I of England. Later, in the fourteenth century, it was a stronghold of the Wolf of Badenoch, who burned Elgin Cathedral (*see* p. 83). Lochindorb is the scene of Maurice Walsh's *Key Above the Door.*

11. To **Advie** (*see* p. 83).

12. **Other mountains and hills near Grantown.**

Creag Liath (1,473 feet). One and a half miles west of the Forres road and 3 miles north of Grantown.

Cromdale Hills. Cross Spey Bridge, turn to the left, and follow the Cromdale road for about 2 miles, and then take the road on right by the edge of a wood, leading to Burnside farm. Hence it is about 2 miles in a south-easterly direction to the summit of **Creagan a'Chaise** (2,250 feet), one of the highest of the Cromdale hills. It commands a magnificent view.

At Grantown those bound for Forres leave the valley of the Spey. Passing the policies and woods of Castle Grant, the way is up a rocky defile in which is Lord Huntly's Cave. We emerge on the bleak and extensive moorland district of **Brae Moray,** crowned by the **Knock** (1,500 feet), and 8½ miles from Grantown reach **Dava.** Some 5 miles farther the railway crosses the *Divie* by a fine viaduct 106 feet high, where a romantic peep is caught of **Edinkillie** church and churchyard; and another mile brings us to **Dunphail,** from which the richly-wooded banks of the *Findhorn* are in sight on the west. Dunphail is a good point from which to approach the most charming part of the Findhorn Glen. Three miles beyond Dunphail the route enters the beautiful **Altyre** estate of the Gordon-Cummings, and later a glimpse may be had, beyond the river on the left, of **Darnaway Castle** (*see* p. 44). From time to time, as we proceed, views are obtained of the Moray Firth and the mountains of Ross and Sutherland, the prospect northward extending in fine weather as far as the Ord of Caithness. Approaching Forres we may sight Rafford Church, the ruins of Blervie Castle, and the large hotel on the slope of **Cluny Hill,** the summit of which is crowned by the Nelson Monument.

Forres

Angling.–Salmon, grilse, sea-trout and finnock fishing in the lowest 5 miles of the Findhorn, between Red Craig and the sea. Apply *Forres Angling Association.*

Boating, bathing and sea-fishing at Findhorn, about 5 miles north of the town.

Bowls.–Public green in Grant Park. Green of Forres Bowling Club is open to visitors.

Buses to Findhorn village. Also to Inverness, Elgin, Dallas and Aberdeen.

Distances by road.–Aberdeen, 78¼ miles; Elgin, 12; Grantown, 22; Inverness, 26¼; Nairn, 10½; Perth, 121.

Early Closing.–Wednesday.

Golf.–A good inland course of 18 holes. Putting green in Grant Park.

Hotels. *Royal Victoria, Cluny Hill, Queens, Carlton, Red Lion, Ramnee, Newbold House.*

Museum (Tolbooth Street).–Open daily, except Sundays, 10 a.m. to 5 p.m. Admission fee. (Saturdays free).

Population.–4,665.

Post Office, at the junction of Castle Bridge with the High Street.

Tennis.–Courts in Orchard Road.

Forres, dating from very ancient times, stands on gently rising ground on the eastern bank of the Findhorn, and is largely visited for its fine salmon and trout fishing, the exquisite scenery and the sweet and balmy climate of the district. The annual rainfall is one of the lowest in Scotland. At the west entrance to the town is a striking War Memorial (a bronze figure of a Highland soldier). The **Market Cross,** erected in 1844, was modelled upon the Scott Monument in Edinburgh. Behind is the **Court House,** nearly opposite the interesting **Falconer Museum.** Two sons of Forres who have been benefactors of the place are Lord Strathcona (1820–1914) and Sir Alexander Grant. Lord Strathcona was born in a thatched house which once stood at the west end of the town, between the

Burn of Mosset and the mound that is the site of "King Duncan's Castle," the foundations of which have been excavated.

At the eastern end of the town, about 1¼ miles from the station, is one of the most remarkable stone obelisks of old-world date in Britain. Known as **Sueno's Stone,** it stands 23 feet above ground and bears carvings of warriors, animals and Celtic knots. In popular belief it records the final defeat of the Danes in 1014.

At the same end of the town is the **Nelson Tower,** crowning the summit of the tree-clad **Cluny Hill.** The view from the top is beautiful and extensive, embracing portions of nine or ten counties. The tower was built in 1806.

The **Grant Park,** at the foot of the hill, is attractively laid out for various forms of recreation.

Excursions from Forres

1. **Darnaway Castle,** the seat of the Earl of Moray, about 4 miles south-west of the town. The Castle was mainly built 1802–12, and is in the Italian style. Randolph's Hall, a portion of the old Castle, erected (*c.* 1450) on the site of a hunting lodge of Randolph, Earl of Moray, the nephew of Robert Bruce. It has a carved oak roof, and contains many relics and portraits. The Castle, embosomed in a forest of oak and pine, is not open to the public.

2. **Culbin Sandhills** (5 miles), on the west side of Findhorn Bay, now a State Forest. Much thatching with brushwood and planting of Corsican pine by the Forestry Commission has transformed a desert waste into productive woodlands.

3. From Forres a road runs along the eastern side of the bay to **Findhorn** village, at the mouth of the Findhorn, which here forms a wide estuary at high water. At Findhorn there is fine sea-bathing, fishing and boating in the sea and estuary; and there are hotels.

4. **Kinloss Abbey,** 3 miles to the north-east of Forres along the B9089 road. The Abbey was founded by David I, 1141. Edward I, in 1303, and Edward III, in 1336, lodged within its walls. At the Reformation it was sold and served as a quarry for all the houses and walls in the neighbourhood, but there are still considerable remains left, both of the Abbey Church and of the Abbot's residence, built by Bishop Robert Reid (1526–40).

5. **Pluscarden Priory** (8 miles). *See* p. 85.

6. **Brodie Castle** (4½ miles to the west). Close to the Forres–Nairn highway. The Castle, the seat of Brodie of Brodie, is of great antiquity. The park (*open to public, castle by appointment*) contains a noteworthy "Pictish Stone," with oghams.

7. **Burgie Tower,** 2½ miles south-east of Kinloss, is six storeys high. Visitors can always obtain admission.

8. **Blervie Tower,** 2½ miles south-east of Forres. (*Always open.*) An ancient tower five storeys high, commanding a charming view.

The Findhorn Glen

The **Findhorn Glen** is one of the finest specimens of rock and wood scenery in Scotland. The river is noted for its rapidity and its violent floods.

The road turns off from the main highway by the War Memorial at the west end of Forres and soon reaches an area of rich heath and woodland— **The Forest of Altyre.** The *Findhorn* runs below on the right, and beyond the valley a glimpse may be caught of *Darnaway Castle.* At the fork about 6 miles from Forres turn down to the right. Here is **Relugas,** one of the points at which admission is gained to the lovely **Findhorn Glen.**

The most charming part is between Sluie and Relugas, though to visit Altyre or Relugas grounds special permission would have to be obtained.

At Dulsie Bridge

Considerable forestry planting in this area, and periodic flooding having washed away the former path along the river, restrict movement in the Glen. A bridge over the Divie at Relugas (1½ miles north of Dunphail) gives on to a wall with steps over. Then follow a path which leads back to the bridge, past **Randolph's Leap,** a narrow, rocky gorge in the grounds of Relugas House, a short distance above the confluence of the Divie with the Findhorn. It takes its name from a supposed feat of Randolph, the first Earl of Moray and the builder of Randolph's Hall at Darnaway Castle.

Even those who do not leave the highway can enjoy the fine scenery of the Glen, beyond which the road climbs to heathery uplands about *Ferness,* 12 miles from Forres and only a mile or two north of **Lochindorb** (*see* p. 42) on the Grantown road.

Another very beautiful part of the Findhorn is at **Dulsie Bridge,** 7 miles upstream from Relugas. It is best approached by driving to Ardclach. The bridge carries General Wade's old military road. It may also be approached from the Forres–Duthil road, crossing the Tomlachlan Burn by a new concrete bridge.

The return to Forres may be made *viâ* Nairn. Turn sharp back northward at the fork at Ferness and after crossing the river by Logie Bridge climb the far side of the valley for the lovely run onward. Just beyond Logie

Bridge a road on the right runs down the west side of the valley to the main road about 3 miles west of Forres, passing through Darnaway Forest and near the Castle. All delightful scenery.

Proceeding westward from Forres, we obtain, in crossing the Findhorn, glimpses of the Culbin Sandhills, away on the right. About 3½ miles on the way is **Brodie Castle** (p. 44). Then, between road and railway, comes a part of **Hardmuir**, the "blasted heath" on which Macbeth is supposed to have met the witches, the traditional spot being a knoll (161 feet) known as **Macbeth's Hill.** About a mile farther westward are the ruins of **Inshoch,** also popularly associated with Macbeth. Ten miles by rail, rather more by road, west of Forres, is –

Nairn

Angling.–Trout and salmon fishing in the *Nairn*. Information from the *Nairn Angling Association*.

Distances.–Forres, 10½ miles; Elgin, 22; Fort George, 8; Inverness, 16.

Early Closing.–Wednesdays.

Golf.–The *Nairn Club* has an 18-hole course, 3½ miles in length, upon the seashore, besides a short 9-hole course (*Newton*).

The *Nairn Dunbar Golf Club* (18 holes) is eastward of the town.

Hotels.–*Ardgour House, Altonburn* (1 mile), *Hermitage, Windsor, Millford, Invernairne House, Washington, Highland, Braeval, Star, Golf View, Newton, Royal,* and many others.

Population.–5,200.

Post Office.–Cawdor Street. Sub-office in Harbour Street.

Sports.–Golf, bowls, cricket, tennis, coach trips and bathing. Highland games, golf and tennis tournaments are held during August. Indoor sea-water swimming pool.

Nairn is a prosperous-looking town situated on the *Nairn* river, where it flows into the Moray Firth. The western end has been very attractively laid out, with a large green, known as the Links, overlooking the shore and used as a cricket and recreation ground in summer. There is splendid bathing, the beach extending eastward for miles. There are two golf courses and facilities for tennis, bowls and other sports, and the residential portion of the town is very pleasant.

Near the town are attractive walks. That by the seaside westward of the Marine Hotel is most popular, but for scenery the walks by the riverside are in great favour.

Excursions from Nairn

1. **The Height of Balblair,** about a mile south-west of the town, was the site of the Duke of Cumberland's last encampment before proceeding to the battlefield of Culloden.

2. **Geddes,** 3 miles *via* the right bank of the river. **Rait Castle,** a ruin, is half a mile south of the ancient churchyard of Geddes.

3. **Auchindoune** (7 miles south-west). The hill half a mile westward has the site of a vitrified fort and commands a magnificent view.

4. **Auldearn,** a village 2½ miles south-east of Nairn, was the scene of Montrose's brilliant victory over the army of the Covenanters in 1645.

5. **Ardclach and Dulsie Bridge.** Follow the main Grantown road for 7½ miles to Redburn, and take the road to the right. After one mile a branch road to the left leads to **Ardclach Church,** which stands on a lovely haugh of the Findhorn, with a belfry on a hill several hundred feet higher. Our road now leads on, with beautiful views of the *Findhorn* near Glenferness, to **Dulsie Bridge** (*see* p. 45).

6. **Cawdor,** 5 miles south-west. **Cawdor Castle** (*grounds only open on occasion*), the seat of the Earl Cawdor, is built on the rocky bank of a mountain burn which flows into the River Nairn. The original castle was built about 1390 and consisted of a very plain square keep

surrounded by a curtain wall, parts of which survive, and outside which was a dry moat. The outer courtyard is approached over a drawbridge, the most perfect specimen, perhaps, of such entrances now in existence. In 1454 the sixth Thane of Cawdor was granted a Royal Charter by James II to complete the fortification of the building, including the battlements and a copehouse on top of the tower. Additions were made between 1660 and 1700 by Sir Hugh Campbell of Calder and his wife, Lady Henrietta Stuart, daughter of the third Earl of Moray.

7. **Kilravock Castle,** 2 miles west of Cawdor and 6 miles from Nairn. The Castle, which is not usually shown, consists of a square tower built in 1460 and other buildings of later date. The modern additions are said to be from designs by Inigo Jones. It has been in the possession of the Rose family since 1290.

Near Kilravock is the **Loch of the Clans,** to which Prince Charlie's army marched on the day before Culloden, intending to give battle to Cumberland's forces. The loch contains curious examples of crannogs or lacustrine dwellings.

8. **Fort George.** On the shore of the Moray Firth, 8 miles by road. Its promontory and that of Chanonry Point in the Black Isle here narrow the Firth to less than a mile. The Fort, covering 15 acres, was constructed shortly after the Battle of Culloden. Now obsolete as a fortress, it serves as a military training depot. The chapel was built in 1767 and contains a three-decker puplpit.

Adjoining Fort George and strung out along the west shore of the promontory is **Ardersier** (for some time known as **Campbeltown**), an old-fashioned village serving as a quiet unconventional holiday headquarters.

The main road to Inverness from Nairn is characterized by some long straight stretches, but on account of the views over the Firth, the slower road across **Culloden Moor** (*see* p. 50) is preferable, apart from its historic interest.

Soon the main road enters the Culloden estate and the scenery becomes more distinctly Highland. The prospect attains its greatest beauty at **Allanfearn,** 12 miles from Nairn and about 3 miles east of Inverness.

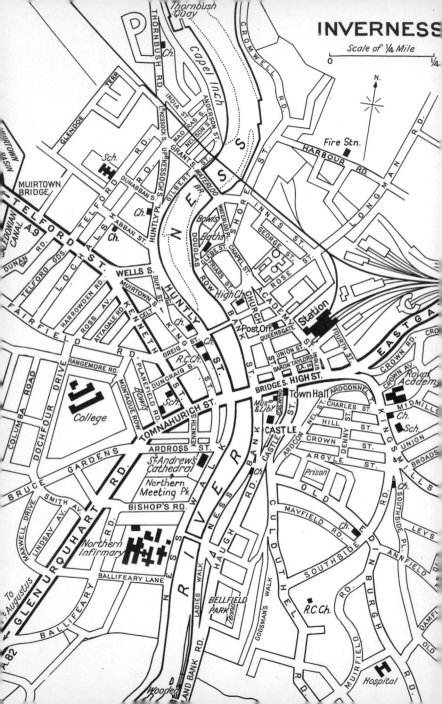

INVERNESS

Airport.—Airport at Dalcross. Services to Glasgow, Wick, Orkney and Stornoway.

Angling.—That portion of the River Ness known as the *Four Cobles Water* is open for fishing from January 15 to October 15. Sea trout and salmon. (Brown trout from March 1.) The *Cobles Water* (or Bught) is owned by the Corporation and leased to the Inverness Angling Club, who issue tickets to visitors. Salmon, sea trout, brown trout, finnock, on stretch of 3 miles. For fishings in the neighbourhood application should be made to any of the fishing-tackle establishments.

Bowling Greens (Municipal).—Waterloo Place, Planefield and MacEwen Drive.

Distances.—Aberdeen, 104 miles; Edinburgh, 160, Fort William, 66; Glasgow, by rail, 207; by water, 213; London, *viâ* Forth Bridge, 541; *viâ* Carlisle, 594; Perth, 116.

Early Closing.—Wednesday.

Enquiry Office.—2 Academy Street.

Golf.—18-hole course at *Culcabock*, three-quarters of a mile south of the town. 18-hole Municipal course at Torvean.

Hotels.—*Station, Caledonian, Palace, Royal, Douglas, Cummings, Albert, Lochness House.* Unlicensed: *Windsor, Crown, MacDougall's,* and many others.

Population.—31,278.

Post Office.—Queensgate.

Swimming Bath.—Corporation Swimming Bath, Albert Place. Sea bathing in the Firth.

Tennis.—Public courts at Bellfield Park. *Inverness Tennis Club* at Bishop's Road.

Youth Hostel in Old Edinburgh Road.

Inverness, the northernmost town of any considerable size in Scotland, occupies a beautiful site at the head of the Inverness Firth and at the north-eastern end of the Great Glen, which contains the Caledonian Canal. Through it flows the River Ness, dividing the town into two unequal portions, the larger part being on the eastern bank.

The best views are from the boulevard along the western bank of the river, from which the dominating features are the Bridge and the County Buildings, of red sandstone. The latter are generally spoken of as **The Castle,** although the Castle that figures in *Macbeth* (as well as the earlier residence of King Brude, according to some) is believed to have stood on the summit of the ridge to the east of the station. The terrace of the Castle, with its statue of Flora Macdonald, is a favourite viewpoint.

Beside the Town Hall, which is above the Bridge, at the foot of Castle Hill, is the **Town Cross.** The upper part is modern; the lower part incorporates a curious blue lozenge-shaped stone, called the *Clach-na-Cudainn,* "the stone of the tubs," and for centuries regarded as the palladium of the burgh. It derives its name from having been the resting-place for the water-pitchers of bygone generations of women as they passed from the river. It is said to have been used by the earlier Lords of the Isles at their coronation, but how it came into the possession of the inhabitants of Inverness is unknown.

On the western bank of the river, nearly opposite Castle Hill, is **St. Andrew's Cathedral** (Episcopalian), the most imposing ecclesiastical structure in the place. Its style is Decorated Gothic, from designs by Alexander Ross, LL.D., himself an Invernessian.

About three-quarters of a mile up the river are the wooded **Islands,** connected with each other and with the roadway on either bank by suspension bridges, and forming a favourite resort in the summer evenings.

Not less worth a visit is the Cemetery on fairy-haunted **Tomnahurich Hill,** a thickly-wooded height rising 223 feet above the level of the sea, and commanding good views. Another good viewpoint is **Craig Phadrig** (550 feet), a wooded height on the farther side of the Canal and about a mile from the Cemetery. On the top is a vitrified fort, identified with the home of the Pictish King Brude, who is said to have been visited here in the sixth century by St. Columba and converted to Christianity.

Five miles east of Inverness is **Culloden Moor** (*see* below), one of the principal excursions. The trip to the Battlefield may be combined with a visit to the **Clava Stone Circles,** or a road runs down to the shores of the Firth by Allanfearn, providing lovely views during the descent.

The most direct route from Inverness to the Black Isle (p. 118) is *viâ* the ferry (cars carried) between **North Kessock** and **South Kessock,** reached by following the road on the western bank of the river down to the rivermouth.

Excursions from Inverness

Inverness has long been renowned as a touring centre; but its full advantages have been emphasized by the increase of motoring and hostelling (Scottish Youth Hostel, 1 Old Edinburgh Road). Roads run east, west, north and south; it is a most convenient centre for rail and motor-coach excursions and for air trips to Orkney.

1. To **Culloden Moor,** some 6 miles by road.

Take the Carrbridge road through the hamlet of **Culcabock** (1½ miles) and almost opposite the entrance to Inshes House (2½ miles) branch off to the left.

Culloden Moor is 500 feet above sea-level. The road passes between the large cairn marking the spot where the contest (April 16, 1746) was fiercest and the graves of the slain, which consist of a number of grass-covered mounds, rising slightly above the adjoining heather. Headstones were erected in 1881 by Duncan Forbes, of Culloden, to indicate the resting-places of the various clans. The Mount whence Prince Charles Edward beheld the battle still stands, a mile to the west. A boulder, known as the **Cumberland Stone,** rests by the roadside a hundred yards or so east of the principal group of graves.

2. **The Stone Circles at Clava** are considered to be "the most splendid series of circles and cairns on the eastern side of the island." From the Cumberland Stone go downhill for about three-quarters of a mile and at the bottom of the hill, after crossing the River Nairn, turn to the right.

3. To **Fortrose** and **Cromarty.** By road *viâ* (*a*) Kessock Ferry; or (*b*) round Beauly Firth by Beauly (38 miles) to Cromarty.

4. To **Beauly,** 12½ miles westward by road. Built around a large square, Beauly has a misleading air of sleepiness: actually it is a brisk little place making good holiday headquarters. The principal sight is the ruin of Beauly Priory (founded 1230), at the northern end of the village. The Priory has been scheduled as an Ancient Monument (open free from 10 to 6 or 7 in summer, till 4 in winter).

5. To **Kirkhill,** in the churchyard of which is the reputed grave of the Lord Lovat of the '45, and **Moniack Burn** and **Castle,** along the Beauly Road.

6. To **Falls of Foyers** on Loch Ness, Fort Augustus, returning by Invermoriston, Drumnadrochit (Glen Urquhart); 68 miles, 4½ hours by motor-coach.

7. To **Strathpeffer** and **Falls of Rogie.**

8. To **Speyside** and **Lossiemouth,** *viâ* Grantown-on-Spey, Craigellachie, Elgin, returning *viâ* Forres, Nairn, Culloden.

9. To **Glen Affric** by Lovat Bridge (near Beauly), Strathglass, Struy, and Cannich; returning by Glen Urquhart and Loch Ness; about 58 miles. This tour (often done in the reverse direction by motor-coaches) leads into the heart of the most spectacular of the Highland hydro-electric undertakings. The hydro-electric scheme has entailed the raising of the levels of Loch Mullardoch and Beneveian by dams built across the respective valleys. The surplus waters of the former are led by tunnel to the latter, thence to the power station at Fasnakyle. Loch Affric itself is therefore not affected.

At Lovat Bridge the Beauly main road turns sharp right, but our road continues ahead for **Kilmorack.** The building of the new hydro-electric schemes have caused the disappearance of the former falls of Kilmorack. Across the river is **Beaufort Castle,** the seat of Lord Lovat, the head of the Clan Fraser. A stretch of the stream just beyond Kilmorack contains craggy wooded islets and is known as the **Druim** (*dreem*). The largest of the islands is called **Eilean Aigas.** It was long the hiding-place of Simon, Lord Lovat.

The River Ness, Inverness

Beyond the Druim the valley soon opens again, and on opposite sides are seen **Aigas House** and **Eskadale,** the latter a hunting-lodge belonging to Lord Lovat. Beyond **Erchless Castle,** of old the seat of The Chisholm, is **Struy** (*hotel*), the point of union of the two valleys– Strathglass and Glen Farrar–and their respective streams (For the fine walk from Struy to Strathcarron, *see* p. 52). The Farrar (issuing from Loch Monar, and flowing through a fine Highland strath) is crossed at Struy and then the road, taking a south-westerly direction through scenery of a pastoral character, the mirror-like surface of the leisurely Glass contrasting strongly with the rapids of the lower river, ascends the left bank of the river to **Invercannich** (*Glen Affric Hotel*). Here the Glass is joined by the Cannich coming in from the west through a fine gorge.

At Cannich a road strikes off to the east, crosses the Glass, and after ascending steeply to a height of 708 feet leads down **Glen Urquhart** to the village of Drumnadrochit (*hotel*).

The main road continues up Strathglass and 2 miles beyond Cannich a road branches off to the left, crosses the Glass by the Fasnakyle Bridge, and, turning right, leads up the right bank of the river to **Tomich** (*hotel*). At the far end of the village are the entrance gates to *Guisachan Estate,* famed for its magnificent forests of Scots pine. In the estate is the very fine **Plodda Fall,** about 3 miles south of Tomich.

The main road to Glen Affric holds to the right and in about 1 mile enters the **Chisholm's Pass,** a defile of great grandeur and beauty. The road, often at a height of 300 feet above the river, winds through a forest of birch. Four miles from Cannich is the best viewpoint. There the road descends close to the water near the small cascade called the **Dog Fall.** The road next reaches **Loch Beneveian** (Beinn a'Mheadhoin), a lovely sheet of water. At the western end of the loch the public road ends, but it is possible to walk a considerable distance westward–to Loch Duich on the west coast, in fact (*see* below).

10. **To the West Coast.** For walkers there are two magnificent walks to the west coast–(*a*) to Loch Duich by Glen Affric and (*b*) to Strathcarron by Glen Farrar.

51

CANNICH TO LOCH DUICH

(a) Cannich to Loch Duich by Glen Affric

This is a long (30 miles) but very fine walk, which has already been described as far as Loch Beneveian. A mile or so farther west is **Loch Affric.** The track skirts the northern shore and 4 miles beyond the west end of the loch passes lonely Alltbeath, with one of Scotland's most secluded Youth Hostels (June to Sept.), in magnificent walking country. Half a mile farther on the path crosses a stream and then runs up **Glen Grivie** for nearly 4 miles to **Loch a'Bhealaich,** from which it ascends steeply to the **Bealach** (or Pass) **of Kintail,** a gorge between **Ben Attow** (3,383 feet) on the left, and A'Ghlas-Bheinn (3,006 feet) on the right. There is a rapid descent to Loch Duich.

Those who wish to visit the **Falls of Glomach** should strike off to the right just before reaching Loch a'Bhealaich and follow a very indistinct path which leads northwards through the glen to the Falls. These are about 370 feet in height and among the highest and wildest in Britain. The tallest falls in Britain are the Eas-Coul-Aulin at Eddrachillis in Sutherland (658 feet). The return to the main route should be made by the path to Dorusduain and Croe Bridge. The Falls of Glomach, like the Kintail Estate, are in the care of the National Trust.

Four miles from the summit of the Pass of Kintail, the rough foot-track joins the high-road to Kyle of Lochalsh at **Morvich:** here, too, comes in an alternative route from Alltbeath, *viâ* the south side of Ben Attow and Glen Lichd. Almost immediately after striking the road, the traveller crosses the bridge over the *Croe Water,* and proceeds along the north shore of **Loch Duich.** Three miles beyond **Croe Bridge** is **Inverinate,** after which the road climbs up to a height of 574 feet above the Loch, and commands a magnificent view of the mountains at its head. The road then descends to **Dornie** (*see* p. 117).

(b) Struy to Strathcarron by Glen Farrar

From **Struy** (p. 51) a gated road goes as far as Loch Monar (15 miles); beyond that the route is for walkers (strong walkers only – the total distance is 35 miles).

The only accommodation to be had on this route is at the keepers' houses in the glen, and naturally this is barred during the shooting season. The birch-woods in the lower part of Glen Farrar are extremely graceful. Above Deannie Lodge the glen becomes barer, but **Loch a'Mhuillinn** is a gem of beauty. Sgurr na Lapaich (3,773 feet), a most prominent and beautiful peak, is well seen above Ardchuilk. A wild and rough gorge (*Garbh-uisge*) leads to the Monar dam where the road ends. The level of water in **Loch Monar** fluctuates widely and there is virtually no defined path as far as the head of Strathmore, but for the next 9 miles there is a faint track.

From Strathmore Lodge the path leads westward through the Bealach an Sgoltaidh (1,847 feet), to Loch an Laoigh, and south to Bendronaig Lodge and then over the hills to the west by the Bealach Alltan Ruairidh to *Strathcarron station (hotel).* The expedition leads through some magnificent scenery, but is only suitable for good and hardy walkers. From Pait Lodge (pronounced *Patt*), west end of Loch Monar, there is a bridle-path to the head of Glen Elchaig, where it joins the road to **Lochalsh** (*see* p. 117) *viâ* Killilan and Ardelve.

Perth to Inverness via Aberdeen

Perth to Aberdeen – Dundee – Aberdeen – Deeside, with Ballater, Balmoral and Braemar – Buchan – Cruden Bay – Peterhead – Fraserburgh – The Don Valley – Banff – Moray Firth Coast Line – Keith to Elgin and Inverness

The usual road route from Perth to Aberdeen (A94; 83 miles) is that which runs by Coupar-Angus and Forfar; but that skirting the coast by Dundee, Montrose and Stonehaven (A85 and A92; about 90 miles) has much to recommend it.

The main road route from Perth to Coupar-Angus passes through **New Scone,** but a more direct route to Blairgowrie is that through Old Scone and by Meikleour. Just beyond Cargill the road crosses the *Isla* after which a right turn leads to Coupar-Angus and a left turn to Meikleour. **Meikleour** is famous for its long lofty beech hedges, nearly 100 feet in height and two hundred years of age. **Coupar-Angus** is reached in 15½ miles. "Angus" is the old name, now officially re-adopted, for the county of Forfar, and is here used to distinguish the town from Cupar in Fife. Coupar-Angus is, however, now wholly in Perthshire. There are still some vestiges of the wealthy Cistercian Abbey founded here by Malcolm IV in 1164.

Five miles north-westward is –

Blairgowrie

Angling in the *Ardle*, the *Blackwater*, of which the upper part is known as the *Shee*, and the *Ericht*, formed by the union of the Ardle and Blackwater. Fishing is free on the *Lunan* and *Loch Stormont. Loch Drummellie* or Marlee, 2 miles from Blairgowrie has good pike.

Early Closing. – Thursday.
Golf. – An 18-hole course and a 9-hole course.
Hotels. – *Queen's Royal, Angus, Station, Glen Ericht, Marlee, Balmoral, Ryefield Gulf, Kinloch House.*
Population. – 5,600.

Blairgowrie is situated on rising ground on the west bank of the *Ericht* at the head of Strathmore. Rattray on the opposite bank forms part of the united burgh. It is a favourite summer resort with beautiful scenery and excellent fishing. There is a most attractive golf course – Rosemount.

A great amount of land is here devoted to growing raspberries, most of the fruit being bought for canning, deep freeze and preserves.

Road tours during summer from Blairgowrie to Braemar, by the **Spittal of Glenshee** and Glen Clunie, 35 miles (*see* p. 71).

Also from Blairgowrie to Glenshee, Glen Ardle and **Kirkmichael** (p. 28), etc. There are also regular bus services to Perth, Dundee and Forfar.

Five miles or so east of Blairgowrie is –

Alyth

Golf. – An 18-hole course. Sunday play.
Hotels. – *Alyth* (formerly *Commercial*), *Lands of Loyal*.

Population. – 1,838.

Alyth (pronounced *ail-lith*) is a featureless but thriving town on the south slope of the Grampians, of interest to tourists chiefly as the centre of some good excursions.

Excursions from Alyth

1. Some 5 miles south of Alyth is **Meigle,** with sculptured stones of much interest to archaeologists and Arthurians, for they are said to mark the grave of Queen Guinevere, who was imprisoned on Barry Hill, a mile or so from Alyth.

2. **Airlie Castle** (5½ miles north-east), an ancient home of the Ogilvys, Earls of Airlie, is prettily situated at the junction of the picturesque Melgam and Isla. It is the subject of the ballad *The Bonnie Hoose o' Airlie*, which house was burned in 1640 by the Earl of Argyll.

3. **The Slug of Auchrannie,** 2 miles from Airlie Castle, a series of falls in a fine sandstone gorge of the Isla.

4. **Reekie Linn** (5 miles north). – Walkers may follow the old road over the **Hill of Alyth** (966 feet); cars turn to left out of road to Airlie Castle. The routes unite about 3 miles from the town; take the right-hand branch at fork, and a mile farther turn up a lane through a farm-gate. At the end of the lane pass through a wicket, from which the linn is but a short distance. The river, in three plunges, falls 60 feet.

5. **Kirkton of Glenisla** (10 miles). – This excursion may be a continuation of that to Reekie Linn. Opposite the lane referred to in No. 4 is a road off the main road. Follow that to its junction with a high-road from Alyth, and then follow the latter for 4 miles. It leads up a hill called the **Druim Dearg** ("Red Ridge"). Near the summit (1,487 feet) a track on the right leads to **Kirkton of Glenisla** (with an hotel and a Youth Hostel). The best road, however, leaves the main road half a mile beyond the Reekie Linn and strikes due north to Dykend, where it joins the road from Kirriemuir to Glenisla. Glenisla is the habitat of many flowers and ferns – among the latter the rare holly fern – and is a good trout-fishing centre.

6. **Mount Blair** (2,441 feet). – From Alyth to the summit is 14 miles. Proceed, as in No. 5, as far as the track near the summit of Druim Dearg. There is then a choice of two routes. For the Kirkton Hotel follow the track; otherwise keep to the main road, as by so doing a mile is saved. Beyond a stone bridge enter a lane leading to the buildings of a farm called Alrich, thence make for the middle of the eastern shoulder of Mount Blair, from which there is an easy climb to the summit. The descent may be made to the Spittal of Glenshee, in a north-westerly direction, or to Blairgowrie, in a south-westerly direction. About a couple of hours' walking will take the tourist to the Spittal of Glenshee Hotel (an anglers' "howff"), while Blairgowrie is about 15 miles from the summit of Mount Blair, and some 12 miles from the point at which the high-road is reached.

Main route resumed on p. 56.

Some 20 miles south-east of Alyth, and connected with it by bus, is Dundee.

Dundee

Access. – *Rail:* Dundee is served by two main lines, the Aberdeen–Glasgow line *viâ* Perth and the Aberdeen–Edinburgh–London (King's Cross) line.
    Road: The Tay and Forth Road Bridges provide road links to all parts. There are regular bus services to all parts.
    Air: All-year-round services.
Early Closing. – Wednesday.

Hotels. – *Queen's, Royal, Angus, Invercarse, Tay Centre.*
Population. – 182,959.
Post Office. – Meadowside (centre of town).
Station. – *Tay Bridge* for Edinburgh, Perth, Arbroath, Montrose and Aberdeen, and local trains for Carnoustie and Arbroath. Perth and Aberdeen.
Youth Hostel. – 77 Constitution Road.

Dundee, the third Scottish town in population, has a finer site than Aberdeen, but has not the same hold on visitors as "the Granite City." Its main industries are jute, flax and linen, engineering, textile machinery and accessories, ship-building – whalers were long a speciality – canning, marmalade, plastics, etc. On the left of the Perth Road as the city centre is approached is **Queen's College,** founded in 1883 and now forming part of Dundee University.

Perth Road becomes Nethergate, where, at the head of Union Street, is the **Old Steeple,** a handsome and massive tower, decorated in style, and more than 150 feet high, surmounting the City Churches (three under the same roof). It dates from the fourteenth century, and was restored at a great cost by Sir Gilbert Scott in 1872.

In the south-west corner of the grounds is a copy of the **Old Town Cross** (1586).

In the City Square is the magnificent **Caird Hall** (1914–23), due to the generosity of Sir James Caird. It has a fine façade of ten Doric columns and includes the City Hall (seating over 3,000) adjoining the municipal chambers.

At the northern end of Reform Street, and fronted by a good statue of Burns, is the **Albert Institute,** one of Sir Gilbert Scott's modern Gothic buildings. It contains a Library, Art Gallery and Museum (*open daily, free*). Around the Institute are congregated the **Howff,** a quaint old burying-ground, given to the city by Mary Queen of Scots, the Post Office, the **Royal Exchange,** the Dundee Savings Bank; the **High School,** with a Greek portico. Panmure Street leads to the **Cowgate** and the **East Port** – the only one remaining—over which a restored inscription records the preaching of George Wishart during the plague of 1544. University College (1882), in Nethergate, was re-named Queen's College of St. Andrews University in 1954 and became Dundee University in 1967.

Riverside Drive, extending from Tay Bridge Station to Ninewells and passing under the Tay Railway Bridge, is a popular promenade affording pleasant views across the Firth.

Dundee Law (572 feet) is a mile north of the Post Office by Constitution Road and Law Road, which goes right to the top of it. On the way one passes near the **Royal Infirmary** and **Dudhope Park,** the latter containing **Dudhope Castle** (sixteenth century), no longer inhabited. From the top of the Law the view extends beyond St. Andrews to the south-east and to the Grampians in the north.

In Caird Park are the ruins of **Mains Castle** and golf courses of 18 and 9 holes. There is another 18-hole course, a zoo and other attractions in Camperdown Park, to the north-west.

The **Tay Bridge,** which carries the railway across the Firth, was the longest of its kind – over 2 miles – when rebuilt in 1883–1887, its predecessor having been destroyed on December 28, 1879, in a disastrous gale.

The **Tay Road Bridge** (*toll for vehicles*) linking Dundee with Newport was opened in 1966. It stretches in 42 spans for a distance of $1\frac{1}{2}$ miles from King William Dock, Dundee, to Craighead of Newport.

East of Dundee is **Broughty Ferry,** a popular resort taking its name from the ferry formerly plying across the Tay to Tayport. Once a Burgh, it was incorporated with Dundee in 1913. The Waterloo Monument between Newport and Tayport is prominent across the river. Broughty Castle dates from the fifteenth century, but has been reconditioned. There is an interesting museum.

Between Monifieth and Carnoustie is a triangular promontory terminating in Buddon Ness and used for artillery camps and ranges. **Carnoustie** (*Bruce, Station, Glencoe, Kinloch Arms*) has come to the fore as one of Scotland's premier golfing resorts, but it has fine sands and other attractions which render it a very popular holiday resort. A dozen miles out at sea may be discerned the lighthouse which has superseded the Bell on the *Inchcape Rock*, with which readers of Southey are familiar.

Arbroath (*Windmill, Cliffburn, Royal, Seaforth*, etc.), 6 miles north-east of Carnoustie, is a busy town, with a small harbour and an interesting Abbey, founded in 1176 by William the Lion, who lies buried here, and dedicated to Thomas à Becket. (*Admission fee.*) The ruin has grand features, but, as a whole, is vast rather than beautiful. It is of red sandstone. The deeply-recessed western doorway, by which we enter after passing through a Gothic arcade, is Norman, but the rest is Early English. The three Pointed windows at the east end help to emphasize the great length of the building. Besides these the south wall of the nave, the south transept and the Chapter House, hard by and still roofed, are nearly all that remain, if we except the Pointed arches and the lower segment of a large rose window over the western doorway. From the transept a stair may be ascended to a passage in the wall that affords a good view over the town. A plain stone in the chancel is said to cover the bones of the founder, William the Lion. The last Abbot was Cardinal Beaton. It was here that the famous Declaration of Scottish Independence was made when Robert the Bruce summoned parliament on 4th April, 1320. The Stone of Destiny, abstracted on Christmas Day 1950 from Westminster Abbey, was deposited on the High Altar in Arbroath Abbey the following April.

Of interest in Arbroath is the large swimming pool with ample accommodation for bathers and spectators. There is a golf course, and the place is noted for its "smokies," smoke-cured haddocks.

Between Arbroath and Montrose the main road runs some way inland, but those interested in caves and rock formations might well turn aside and visit the vicinity of Auchmithie (*Auchmithie Hotel*) and Red Head. At either end of Lunan Bay are collections of fantastic rocks to which various more or less fanciful names have been given.

For **Montrose,** and thence to Aberdeen, *see* pp. 60–63.

Main route resumed (from p. 54).

Those travelling from Perth to Aberdeen by Coupar-Angus will notice on the right soon after passing Alyth Junction, near **Newtyle,** a ruined watch-tower on **Kinpurney Hill** (1,134 feet). Six miles farther is Glamis (pronounced *Glaams*), with **Glamis Castle** (Earl of Strathmore), a magnificent baronial pile, which for seven centuries has looked across the

Glamis Castle

richly-wooded valley of Strathmore to the Grampians. In the village of Glamis is the interesting Angus Folk Museum.

For access to historical parts of Castle and grounds see *local announcements*. It is normally open on Wednesday and Thursday afternoons in summer and additionally on Sunday afternoons from July to September.

The Castle was the headquarters of the Covenanters' army and later of the forces of the Young Pretender. Part of it was rebuilt after a fire in 1800. A beautiful avenue and a wonderful crypt are notable features, and the popular belief is that there is a secret chamber known only to the Earl, his heir-apparent when he comes of age, and his factor. The association of Glamis with Shakespeare's *Macbeth* is well known. The place also awakens memories of a Lady Glamis, falsely accused by a discarded suitor of practising the art of witchcraft against the life of James V, and burned at the stake on Castle Hill, Edinburgh, in 1537. Glamis Castle was forfeited to the Crown, but when Lady Glamis's innocence was proved, it was restored to her son, whose descendant, Patrick Lyon, became Earl of Strathmore in 1677 and to his time dates most of the building seen today. A happier page in the family history was written in 1923, when Lady Elizabeth Bowes-Lyon, daughter of the fourteenth Earl of Strathmore, married the then Duke of York. Here, in 1930, was born their second child, the Princess Margaret Rose, the first royal babe born in Scotland for three hundred years. The proudest page in the history of Glamis, however, was written in 1937 with the Coronation of King George VI and Queen Elizabeth.

Some 5 miles north of Glamis is **Kirriemuir** ("Thrums" – the birthplace of Sir J. M. Barrie, 1860–1937). It is a small town of about 4,000 inhabitants, 6 miles from Forfar, pleasantly situated on the southern slopes of the Braes of Angus. (Hotels, *Airlie Arms, Newton, Thrums*.) It is within easy reach of salmon and trout streams, and has an 18-hole golf course. **Barrie's Birthplace,** a two-storeyed home (in Brechin Road; National Trust), houses a *Museum* of "J.M.B." relics and mementoes and antiquities associated with the district. The Wash-house that was his "first theatre," the "Window," the "Glen" and other scenes in the Barrie novels are in the town or the immediate vicinity.

Northward from Kirriemuir, Glen Clova winds far into the Grampians, **Glen Prosen** coming in from the north-west at Cortachy (5 miles). Bus daily as far as **Clova** (15 miles: *Ogilvy Arms Hotel: Glendoll Youth Hostel*), a hamlet that is the centre of the mountain district known as the *Braes of Angus*.

Clova to Braemar (18 miles). – Follow the road to Braedownie (3 miles), cross the river and take a path which passes to the left of the *Glendol Youth Hostel* and strikes up Glen Doll to "Jock's Road" at the head of that glen. The path then goes north-west, passing high above Loch Esk (on the right) and with **Tolmount** (3,143 feet) on the left, and then drops down into the glen leading to Loch Callater, from the north-west end of which a rough road leads down to join the Cairnwell road, 2 miles short of Braemar.

Clova to Ballater (19 miles). – Proceed as above to Braedownie Bridge. Do not cross it, but follow the cart-track for three-quarters of a mile and there strike up Capel Mount, on the right. The path is indicated by poles and occasional cairns. On either side is a swamp. Descend to the Spittal of Glenmuick, half a mile beyond the end of Loch Muick, from which a road leads down the glen to Ballater. Four miles beyond the Spittal the road passes the Linn of Muick, a fine waterfall, and 5 miles farther reaches Ballater.

Five and a half miles from Glamis or Kirriemuir is –

Forfar

Hotels. – *Royal*, Castle Street; *County*, Castle Street: **Golf.** – 18-hole course.
    Queen's, The Cross. **Population.** – 10.000.
Early Closing. – Thursday.

Forfar, the county town of Angus, with a population of about 10,000, is a Royal Burgh of ancient but unknown origin. It is popularly believed that Malcolm Canmore held his first Parliament here in 1057 and the Inch at Forfar Loch has long been associated with the name of Margaret, his Queen. The loch, which stands to the west of the town, is the traditional scene of the drowning of the murderers of Banquo or Malcolm II. Forfar has figured frequently in Scottish history. Edward I and Robert Bruce both captured its castle, which was destroyed early in the fourteenth century, and the town was sacked by Cromwell's troops in 1651. Charles II, however, confirmed the town's ancient rights in 1665 in recognition of the loyalty of its inhabitants and of Provost Strang's defence of his father, King Charles I. The chief buildings are the Town Hall and the Reid Hall, the latter the gift, along with a public park (above which rises Balmashanner Hill), of a local manufacturer of "rock," a sweetmeat for which Forfar is noted, as it is for its "bridies" or meat pasties. There are also some textile (jute) factories. There is an 18-hole golf course. There are also bowling greens and tennis courts, while several other games are provided for.

About a mile east of Forfar are the remains of **Restenneth Priory** (thirteenth-century chancel. *admission fee*), an offshoot of Jedburgh Abbey. Then, to the left of the road, is **Rescobie Loch.** Farther eastward is **Guthrie Castle,** built in 1468, and much enlarged in modern times. Seven miles beyond Forfar is **Guthrie,** from which one may reach **Arbroath** (*see* p. 56). Between Guthrie and Montrose the principal feature of interest is **Kinnaird Castle,** the seat of the Earl of Southesk, the towers of which may be seen on the left about 5 miles from Guthrie.

Brechin

Angling.—In the Cruick, South Esk, North Esk and West Water by permission.
Distances.—Brechin is 42½ miles from Perth; 41 miles from Aberdeen; 12 miles from Forfar; 26 miles from Dundee.

Early Closing.—Wednesday.
Golf.—An 18-hole course.
Hotels.—*Dalhousie, Jolly's, Star, Northern.*
Population.—6,756.

Brechin, pleasantly situated on the *South Esk,* was formerly a centre of the linen trade. Now its chief manufactures are linen, jute and other artificial fibre cloths, machine tools and light engineering products, children's clothing and whisky. The **Cathedral,** founded in the twelfth century, was restored in 1901, and is used as a parish church. It contains some perfect specimens of Early English architecture, and is of great interest. At the south-western corner is a **Round Tower** (one of two on the mainland of Scotland, the other being at Abernethy, in Strathearn), 103 feet high, similar to the round towers of Ireland. It dates from the tenth or eleventh century. In the centre of the town is a fragment of a thirteenth-century Maisondieu Chapel.

Brechin Castle held out against Edward I. It was then in possession of Sir Thomas Maule, and is still the residence of the representative of the Maule family, the Earl of Dalhousie. It was here that Balliol surrendered the Crown of Scotland to Edward I.

Excursions from Brechin

1. The **Catterthun Hills** (5 miles north-west). On these are concentric rings of loose stones, remains of Iron Age hill forts (*c.* 200 B.C.). The largest collection, known as the *White Catterthun,* is on the left-hand side of the road. Right of the road is the *Brown Catterthun.*
2. **Aldbar Castle** (3 miles south on road to Letham).
3. **Aberlemno** (sculptured stones) and **Melgund** and **Finhaven Castles,** the latter a ruined hold of the "Tiger Earl" of Crawford.
4. The turreted **Kinnaird Castle,** seat of the Earl of Southesk, stands in an extensive park, some 3 miles south-east of Brechin.

Edzell

a small town 6 miles northward from Brechin, in the valley of the *North Esk,* is famed for its beauty. The village has hotels (*Glenesk, Central, Panmure*), and a golf course of 18 holes (Sunday golf), and is but a mile from the *West Water,* a good trout stream. James Inglis, author of *Oor Ain Folk,* born in the manse at Edzell, was the donor of a fine public hall.

Excursions from Edzell

1. **Edzell Castle,** 1¼ miles west. The ornamentation of the garden walls is unique in Scotland and the garden has been laid out by the Ministry of Works in accordance with its character. Open weekdays from 10 a.m.; Sundays, afternoon only. Admission free to garden.
2. **The Burn** (north of Edzell), gifted by Mr. G. H. Russell and later endowed from the funds of the National Thanksgiving Appeal, is a holiday centre for Commonwealth and United States students. A delightful footpath leads up the side of the river *North Esk* through the grounds to **Gannochy Bridge** (1½ miles by road from Edzell).
3. **Edzell to Ballater** (30 miles), *viâ* Tarfside (12 miles), Lochlee Church (16 miles), and thence by path over the west side of Mount Keen (3,077 feet).

The road leads up Glen Esk from beyond Gannochy Bridge and in about 17 miles reaches the ruined Invermark Castle, at the junction of Glen Mark and Glen Lee. The bridle path goes up Glen Mark and in a mile or two reaches the Queen's Well, whence the route (the **Mounth Road**) lies through beautiful and varied scenery. The path, well marked, strikes steeply up the west side of the Ladder Burn and in 2½ miles reaches the watershed (2,504 feet) just to the west of the peak of **Mount Keen,** well worth ascending for the little extra effort required. The path now dips into Glen Tanar and crosses the stream to the remains of a ruined house. From this point a good private road leads down the Glen to Aboyne. The Ballater path strikes northward up the hill-side and when above Etnach turns north-west and passes through the fence on the sky-line by a gate. Thence west, very indistinct, across the head of the Pollagach Burn to cross the next ridge by a dip about half a mile north of Cairn Leuchan. From here a rough road leads down to join the south Deeside road, near the bridge over the Muick, three-quarters of a mile from Ballater.

4. To **Banchory** (22 miles), by road. *Viâ* Gannochy Bridge to the pretty village of **Fettercairn** (4½ miles). Then by the west side of Fenella Hill (1,357 feet) to **Clattering Bridge** (8 miles); **Cairn o' Mounth,** 1,488 feet high and commanding a fine view; **Bridge of Dye** (14 miles); **Bogendreep Bridge** (18 miles); **Strachan** (19 miles); and past the **Bridge of Feugh** into **Banchory.**

Main route resumed.

Montrose

Distances. – Aberdeen, 37 miles; Brechin, 9; Dundee. 29; Stonehaven, 23.
Caravans. – Sites available.
Early Closing. – Wednesday.
Hotels. – *Park, Madeira, Central, Star, Corner House, Links House,* etc.

Population. – 10,252.
Sports. – Bathing, bowls, tennis, cricket, boating, fishing, golf (*see* below), putting.

Montrose, a town of great antiquity, is entered from the south by a bridge over the *South Esk* where it issues from the lagoon-like Montrose Basin, nearly 2 miles square. It is prettily laid out and has many attractions for visitors. A fine medal course, an auxiliary course and several putting courses invite the golfer. There is a fine indoor pool. A magnificent sandy bathing beach extends for 4 miles. William the Lion, Balliol and James VI are among the many historical personages associated with its Castle (now vanished). There is excellent fishing to be had in the South Esk and North Esk rivers.

The more interesting road from Montrose to Stonehaven is by the coast (the other goes inland through Marykirk and through the fertile "Howe of the Mearns" to **Laurencekirk** (*Royal*), a town once famous for the manufacture of snuff-boxes). The coast road needs no description, though motorists who are not in a hurry will find it worth while to turn down some of the side roads for the sake of the unsophisticated villages overlooking the sea and for the fine coast views. The most remunerative halt is at –

Dunnottar Castle

a mile or so short of Stonehaven, and approached from a modern gateway with car park, etc. (*Admission charge.*)

The best view of the Castle is from the edge of the cliff a few hundred yards from the road, and even those unable to explore the interior of this fine old stronghold – one of the most impressive ruins in Britain – should come thus far.

Long the stronghold of the powerful Keiths, Earls Marischal of Scotland, the Castle stands on the summit of a cliff washed on three sides by the sea; on the fourth it is almost separated from the mainland by a deep chasm, from which the ascent is steep and rugged. The ruins cover about three acres and consist of the great square tower, which is almost entire, broken towers and turrets, remains of the palace and the chapel, long ranges of roofless buildings and broken arches, and many dismal halls, vaults and chambers.

The Castle was taken from the English by Wallace in 1297. To the church which then stood on the crags some of the English soldiers fled for sanctuary, but only to find death, for the building was set ablaze.

Forty years later Edward Balliol garrisoned the Castle with English soldiers, but it was again re-taken. In 1645 it was besieged by Montrose. Among those in it were sixteen Covenanting ministers, who urged the Earl Marischal to be firm in its defence, and to come to no terms with Belial, as they styled their foes, assuring him that the smoke of his farmsteads and villages burning on the mainland would be "a sweet-smelling incense in the nostrils of the Lord." Six years later the Castle was besieged by a Parliamentary force, and as starvation threatened to compel surrender, the ancient Scottish Regalia, which had been sent to it for safety, were in danger of being lost. They were smuggled out, through the blockading forces, and until the Restoration the Regalia lay buried under the floor of Kinneff Church.

The last of the cruel memories attached to Dunnottar is of the treatment of imprisoned Covenanters in 1685, when confined in one dungeon in the height of summer were 167 men, women and children. The remains of the prisoners released by death were interred in Dunnottar churchyard, where the **Covenanters' Stone** records their names. It was while clearing the inscription on this stone that Robert Paterson, the original "Old Mortality," was seen by Sir Walter Scott, who was passing the night in the manse.

A mile or so beyond Dunnottar the road swings round a headland to reveal **Stonehaven** spread out below. Originally a fishing port, this place has of recent years taken its place among Scottish seaside resorts, and the quaint old town is now pinned against the Harbour and the protecting cliff by streets of more modern houses. Tennis, boating and golf, bathing and fishing, are the principal amusements. (*Hotels: County, Marine, Crown, Alexandra, Belvedere, Heugh, Mill Inn, Queen's, Eldergrove* (unl.).)

The **"Slug" Road** (A957) to Banchory (16 miles; p. 67) climbs to 757 feet half-way, giving good views of the Cairngorms, and is a handy short cut into Deeside. *Raedykes*, a Roman camp about 5 miles out from Stone-haven, has been identified as the site of the Battle of Mons Graupius (AD 86), in which Agricola decisively defeated the Caledonians under Galgacus (*see also* p. 21).

About 5 miles north of Stonehaven, turnings on the right lead to **Muchalls** (*hotel*), a primitive fishing village perched on the cliff near some of the finest rock scenery in the north-east of Scotland. **Findon** or Finnan, farther north, was once famed for smoked haddocks, which perpetuate its name – "Finnan haddies."

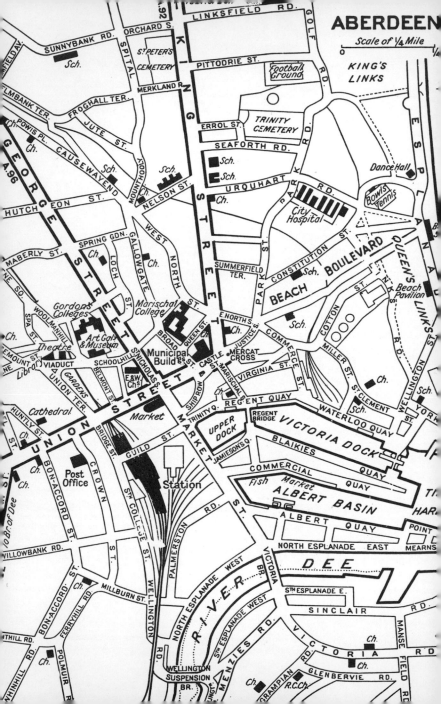

ABERDEEN

Access *by Rail:* The direct route to Aberdeen from Edinburgh and the South (East Coast) is *viâ* the Forth and Tay Bridges, Dundee and Arbroath.

Road: viâ Forth and Tay Road Bridges, Dundee and Arbroath or *viâ* Forth Road Bridge, Perth and Stonehaven; from Blairgowrie *viâ* Ballater and Deeside. Buses run to Aberdeen from Glasgow and Edinburgh.

Steamers to and from North of Scotland ports. Full particulars respecting fares and times of sailing may be obtained from the *North of Scotland and Orkney and Shetland Shipping Company*, Head Office, Matthew's Quay, Aberdeen.

By Air: Aberdeen is within a two-hour journey from London and air services connect the city with Edinburgh, Glasgow, with Orkney and Shetland and Norwich. The airport is at Dyce.

Amusements.—More provision is made for indoor amusement in Aberdeen than, probably, in any other city of like size in the land. Cinemas are numerous; *His Majesty's Theatre* is in Rosemount Viaduct. There are also dance halls, headed by the modern ballroom on the Beach Esplanade, the new Palace Ballroom at Bridge Place and the Palais de Danse in Diamond Street. Ten-pin bowling alley at George Street.

Angling.—Inexpensive angling in the lower part of the *Dee, Don, Ythan* and *Ugie* are within easy reach. Information can be had from the various tackle-makers in the city. Excellent sea-fishing.

Bathing.—Good sea-bathing. Fresh-water baths at municipal bathing establishment overlooking beach. The *Bon Accord Baths,* Justice Mill Lane, house a modern swimming pool, Turkish baths.

Buses.—(good services) connect the most important parts of the city; and there are also numerous buses connecting with places around. For a sightseeing tour the "Circular Route" is useful.

Distances.—Banchory, 18 miles; Banff, 46; Birmingham 429; Braemar 58; Edinburgh 127 (by Forth and Tay Bridges), 152 (*viâ* Stirling); Elgin, 66; Glasgow, 142; Inverness, 104; Liverpool, 361; London, 492; Perth, 81.

Early Closing.—Wednesday and/or Saturday.

Golf.—The principal courses are: *Balgownie Links,* 18 holes, 2 miles from the centre of the city, the magnificent private course of the *Royal Aberdeen Club.* Visitors may be introduced. Adjoining it on the north is the course of the *Murcar Club.* There is also a ladies' course of 9 holes. There are *Municipal Courses*—the old course (18 holes) on the King's links alongside the Beach Esplanade, *Balnagask Golf Course* (18 holes) overlooking the Harbour and the Bay of Nigg, and courses (18 hole and two 9 hole) at Hazlehead, 3 miles west from Castle Street. At Bieldside is the course of the *Deeside Club.*

Guide Book.—See the *Guide to Aberdeen and Northern Scotland in this series.*

Hotels.—*Station,* Guild Street; *Imperial,* Stirling Street; *Douglas,* Market Street; *Gloucester,* Union Street; *Caledonian,* Union Terrace; *Northern,* Great Northern Road; *Earl's Court,* Queen's Road; *Atholl,* King's Gate; *Treetops,* Springfield Road; *Dee Motel,* Garthdee Road. *Prince Regent,* Waverley Place, and many others.

Youth Hostel.—Queen's Road.

Library (Public) in Rosemount Viaduct. Various branch libraries and reading-rooms throughout the city.

Population.—178,441.

Post Office.—The head office is in Crown Street, off south side of Union Street.

Tennis, Bowls, etc. in public parks.

Aberdeen is at once an ancient Cathedral and University city, a very popular seaside resort and a busy seaport with a thriving fishing industry. It lies between the *Don* and the *Dee*, the mouth of the latter river forming also the entrance to the Harbour.

The principal thoroughfare is **Union Street,** running south-west to north-east for three-quarters of a mile. As elsewhere, the buildings are of grey granite, which gives Aberdeen a clean, bright, substantial appearance and its title "the Granite City." Union Bridge carries the street across the hollow in which runs the north-bound railway, with gardens flanking Union Terrace.

At the eastern end of Union Street is Castle Street, on the north side of which are the Town House and Sheriff Court House. Passing along the Beach Boulevard one comes to the **Beach Esplanade,** 2½ miles in length and extending beside the sands from the mouth of the Dee to the mouth of the Don. Here are a fine ballroom, public golf links, tennis courts, a bathing station, and other accessories of Aberdeen's pleasure beach; and turning southward by the Esplanade and then along one of the byways on the right one comes to the busy quays surrounding the Harbour. Such a tour includes most of Aberdeen's sights, notable exceptions being St. Machar's Cathedral. King's College and the Auld Brig o'Balgownie, which lie to the north and are reached by way of King Street, branching off from Castle Street at the beautiful **Mercat Cross,** the finest piece of work of the kind and age in Scotland. The Mercat Cross was erected in 1686 and was designed as a reproduction of an old Edinburgh cross, the destruction of which was lamented by Sir Walter Scott in *Marmion.* The graceful central column is crowned by a unicorn bearing a shield charged with the Scottish lion.

The **Town House,** crowned by a fine tower, is a few yards westward (*daily,* 10–4; *tower is a fine viewpoint*). There are some good pictures by Jamesone, "The Vandyke of Scotland" (1587–1644), William Dyce, R.A., John Phillip, R.A., and Sir George Reid, P.R.S.A., all Aberdonians. The Burgh Records are the most complete collection of civic documents in Scotland. At the east end of the Town House is the old **Tolbooth,** the former Townhouse. The tower dates from 1616; the spire and clock are more modern copies of the originals.

New municipal buildings known as **St. Nicholas House** front on to the west side of Broad Street and house the principal departments of the Corporation other than the Town Clerk's and City Chamberlain's Departments which are to be found in the Town House.

Behind the Town House and fronting on to the east side of Broad Street, is –

Marischal College

Visiting Hours. – Mitchell Tower, Mitchell Hall and Portrait Gallery (admission fee), open throughout the year, but viewing times restricted according to examination requirements. The Anthropology Museum is open daily, free.

This fine pile, 420 feet in breadth and 548 in depth, and with an array of soaring pinnacles, is reputed to be the largest and most imposing granite building in the world. The style of architecture is Gothic, developed from English Perpendicular. The site once held a monastery and gardens belonging to the Order of Grey Friars, who were dispossessed, their property being assigned by James VI to George Keith, fifth Earl Marischal, who, in 1593, converted the monastery into a college. The present buildings were begun in 1840, but were greatly extended between 1890 and 1906.

Entrance from **Broad Street** is by a finely-carved gateway giving on to a courtyard, from the far end of which rises the *Mitchell Tower* (235 feet), which gives entry to the central building. Over the inner door in quaint lettering and still quainter spelling, is the motto of the Keith Marischal family: *Thay haif said, Quhat say thay? Lat thame say.*

The **Mitchell Hall** is very fine, granite and carved oak being well blended, and giving rich effect to the coloured glass in the windows.

The University of Aberdeen was founded in 1494–95 by Bishop Elphinstone, who also founded within it King's College, owing its name to the favour of James IV. Marischal College was founded as a separate university in 1593. After an abortive union in 1640, the two were united in 1860.

King's College, which lies a mile to the north of Marischal College, is prominent for its delightful open lantern in the form of the Imperial crown surmounting its Chapel tower. The Chapel is a good example of Scottish Flamboyant Gothic, begun in 1500, and remarkable for its original timber ceiling and carved stalls and screen, of a design almost unique in Britain. The **Library,** as an institution, dates from the foundation in 1495, and still retains a number of the books given by Bishop Elphinstone and his colleagues.

Up till 1891, when an Amalgamation Act was passed, Aberdeen consisted of two separate burghs, Aberdeen proper and what was known as **Old Aberdeen,** in which are situated St. Machar's Cathedral and King's College. Originally merely the precincts of the Cathedral, Old Aberdeen was in 1498 erected into a Burgh of Barony, and for nearly four centuries it remained a separate burgh with its own municipality. It is today a quaint, old-world, charming northern suburb of the city proper.

A little north of King's College is –

St. Machar's Cathedral

The hours of service on Sundays are 11 a.m. and 6 p.m. The cathedral is open on week-days, free, from 10–8 or dusk.

This now consists of nave and aisles only, built of granite, and used as the parish church of Old Machar. The building occupies the site of a rude church, said to have been erected about 570 by St. Machar, one of Columba's contemporaries. The existing structure was begun about 1378 and completed in 1552. The most striking external features are the twin battlemented towers with short spires, at the west end, and the round-headed portal and the seven-lighted window of the west end. Internally, there is the flat ceiling of panelled oak, "with its eight-and-forty shields, glittering with the heraldries of the Pope (Leo X), the Emperor (Charles V), St. Margaret, the Kings and Princes of Christendom, the Bishops and the Earls of Scotland."

Also in this northern outskirt of the city is **The Auld Brig o'Balgownie,** or old Bridge of Don, a picturesque structure noteworthy as being the oldest first-class bridge in Scotland still in full use. It spans the river with a high, single-pointed Gothic arch, 57 feet wide, and was erected early in the fourteenth century. In 1605 Sir Alexander Hay devised for its maintenance a small property producing a trifling sum each year, but so great became the increase in the value of the legacy that the proceeds sufficed for the erection of the New Bridge.

Westward of the Municipal Buildings, in Union Street, is the building known as the **East and West Churches,** which at the Reformation was the largest parish church in Scotland. It was then divided into separate churches, but each half has been rebuilt since. North of the churches are *Robert Gordon's Colleges,* now a secondary day school and technical college; the **Art Gallery and Regional Museum** (daily, 10–5; Sundays, 2–5), with a large collection of paintings, engravings and sculpture and a series of artists' self-portraits probably unique in this country; and the **Public Library.** In King Street, east of the Municipal Buildings, is **St. Andrew's Episcopal Cathedral,** of interest to American visitors on account of its connection with Samuel Seabury, the first American bishop. Guestrow contains *Provost Skene's House* (seventeenth century) surrounded by new municipal offices. Like *Provost Ross's House* (1596) in Shiprow it is of great antiquarian appeal.

The **Fish Market,** when in "full cry," is by no means the least interesting spot in Aberdeen. The best time to come is at 8 a.m., when often as much as 1,000 tons of fish are auctioned, but during July and August an equally interesting sight is provided throughout the day by the herring industry. Few ports in the world have as large a trade in white fish and herrings: the

Aberdeen trawlers catch about 70 per cent of the white fish landed in Scotland. Aberdeen is also the chief Scottish port for the White Sea and Baltic trades, and the headquarters of the Scottish cattle trade.

Westward of the city and easily reached by public transport is the **Hazlehead** estate, over 400 acres of wood and moorland. Part has been retained in its natural condition; the remainder has been laid out as a public park, with two public golf courses – a very pleasant resort.

Main route to Inverness continued on p. 72.

DEESIDE

Banchory – Aboyne – Ballater – Balmoral – Braemar

Aberdeen is the gateway to Royal Deeside; the lovely valley of the Dee so lavishly endowed with scenic beauty. Beauty in contrast; the pastoral aspect of the lower reaches of the river, to the sublime grandeur of the majestic region of the headwaters. Deeside also means an excursion to Balmoral, now from Aberdeen reached only by road. Throughout the year there is a regular bus service.

Beyond **Cults,** 5 miles from the city, there is an extensive panorama of pleasant scenery, and on the left, almost hidden from view, is **Blairs Roman**

Old Bridge of Dee, near Braemar

Catholic College. Ten miles from Aberdeen, on the right, is **Drum Castle,** seat of the Irvine family (*open Sunday* 2–6, *June-August*). It dates originally from the thirteenth century and has late Jacobean additions. Another 5 miles and there appears on the right **Crathes Castle,** one of the finest of the ancient castellated buildings in the country, and now National Trust property and open to the public during summer in the afternoons (tearoom).

Eighteen miles from Aberdeen (A93) is –

Banchory

nestling in one of the prettiest spots on Deeside. It has good hotels (*Tor-na-Coille, Station, Raemoir, Burnett Arms, Banchory Lodge*), a town hall connected with a reading room and billiard room, a library and facilities for bowls and tennis. One of its leading attractions is a golf course of 18 holes, beautifully situated on the banks of the Dee.

Trout-fishing may be had on the *Feugh*, which enters the Dee at Banchory, and on the *Shiach*.

Among the best excursions from Banchory are –

1. The **Bridge of Feugh,** one of the charms of the neighbourhood, nearly a mile south of the village, across the Dee.
2. The ascent of the **Hill of Fare** (1,545 feet), 5 miles to the north. It commands a view, to the north and east, of Dunecht and Skene, and of the "Granite City" itself.
3. By the left bank of the Feugh to **Whitestone** (6 miles).
4. Through **Strachan, Glen Dye** and over **Cairn o'Mounth** to Fettercairn (19 miles), Edzell (24 miles), and Brechin (30 miles). *See p. 59.*

On leaving Banchory the road (A93) follows more or less the windings of the Dee, passing the village of **Kincardine O'Neil,** formerly a very busy place.

An alternative road A980, but longer, goes north and then northwestward for **Torphins** and **Lumphanan.** Near Lumphanan a cairn is said to mark the *Grave of Macbeth*, who, according to Wyntoun, the chronicler, fled hither after his defeat at Dunsinane, and was killed here, and not at Dunsinane as Shakespeare has taught us to believe. Two miles north-west of Lumphanan the A974 runs off westward for **Tarland** passing on the right Corse Castle (1581). From Tarland the road turns off left for Aboyne passing Coull Castle near the church.

From Kincardine O'Neil, our first road (A93) runs past the Loch of Aboyne to –

Aboyne

(*Huntly Arms, Birse Lodge, Charleston*). Aboyne (properly Charleston of Aboyne) is an attractive Highland village, 31 miles from Aberdeen, fringed by woods and hills. It is about 400 feet above sea-level, and lies chiefly on the north side of the Dee. The climate is bracing, and there is a good 18-hole golf course. There are several miles of good fishing to be had on both banks of the Dee, some salmon fishing in which may be rented through the hotels. A conspicuous feature of the place is the large triangular village green, which affords ample space for outdoor games. Upon it are held, in the first week of September just prior to the *Braemar*, the *Aboyne Highland Games*, the great event of the holiday season. **Aboyne Castle,** long the seat of the Marquises of Huntly, stands in ruins close to the village. Within the policies are the remains of a Druidical circle, a sculptured stone, and what is known to archaeologists as the Aboyne Ogham Stone.

There are many delightful walks in the neighbourhood, particularly one through the glen known as the **Fungle,** skirting the *Ault Dinnie Burn.* From the resting-place at the head a magnificent view is obtained. Another pleasant walk is on the **Hill of Mortlich,** formerly crowned by a monument to the tenth Marquis of Huntly. Other pedestrian excursions recommended are: to **Glen Tanar,** a highly picturesque glen running towards the south-west; to **Mount Keen** (3,077 feet), at the head of the deer forest of Glen Tanar; to the **Forest of Birse,** and to **Lochs Kinord** and **Davan.** Good road connections facilitate a number of motor excursions to be made to several interesting places in the neighbourhood. Further particulars will be found in our *Guide to Aberdeen and Northern Scotland.*

From Aboyne the road runs through woods and across Dinnet Moor to **Dinnet** (*hotel*), a picturesque hamlet, near which is a pretty loch. Flowing into Loch Kinord from Culblean Hill on the west is the *Burn of Vat*, so named from a kind of cave in its course. Westward of Dinnet is **Cambus o' May** (*hotel*), where the pink granite was once quarried. On the other side of the Dee, 3 miles west from Dinnet Bridge, is **Ballaterach,** where Byron spent some of his youthful days, and on this side of the river, but 2 miles farther west, is **Pannanich Wells** (*hotel*), where are chalybeate springs.

Ballater

Angling. Salmon and trout in the *Dee*; fishings rented during the season, so that local enquiry is desirable.
Distances by road.—Aberdeen, 42 miles; Aboyne, 11½; Banchory, 24; Braemar, 16¼.
Early Closing.—Thursday.
Golf.—18-hole course.

Highland Games.—Third Thursday in August.
Hotels.—*Invercauld Arms, Pannanich Wells, Alexandra, Craigard, Loirston, Tullich Lodge, Darroch Learg.*
Population.—1,110.
Youth Hostel in Deebank Road (open April-Sept.).

Ballater is a modern, well-built village, 660 feet above sea-level. It stands like a sentinel at the entrance to the upper and, for many, most characteristic portion of Deeside – the lovely valley between wooded hills which winds past Crathie and Balmoral to Braemar. In addition to golf, fishing, tennis and bowls, etc., indoor entertainments are organized during the season, while the village is an admirable centre for walks and drives. Pony trekking is increasingly popular.

Excursions from Ballater

(For further details, see the Ward Lock Guide to Aberdeen and Northern Scotland.)

1. **Craigendarroch,** 1,250 feet above sea-level, but only 590 feet above Ballater. The summit is thirty to forty-five minutes' walk from the village. There are numerous paths.
2. To **Pannanich Wells** (*see* above), on the south side of the Dee about midway between Ballater and Cambus o' May.

3. To **Lochnagar** (allow 4–5 hours). A public road on the east side of the Muick leads to the Spittal of Glenmuick (9 miles), whence a footpath crosses the glen to Alltnagiubhsaich, where the well-defined Lochnagar path commences.

4. **Glenmuick** and the **Linn of Nuick** (6 miles). Keep to the east road up Glen Muick.

5. **Clova** (19 miles), and **Kirriemuir** (34 miles). *See* p. 57.

6. **Tarfside,** 16 miles; **Edzell,** 28 miles; **Brechin,** 36 miles (*see* p. 59).

7. **The Burn of Vat** (6½ miles). Four miles of walking may be saved by taking bus to Cambus o' May, then taking a road on the left that leads to Strathdon. At the end of 1½ miles is a small bridge. Cross it and then follow the path up the stream to the "Vat," a singular granite chasm on Culblean Hill (1,567 feet).

Ballater to Braemar

As far as Balmoral, some 8 miles, there is a road on either bank of the river; the road along the north side is shorter and better, and is that generally used by motors. The view along the south road is frequently restricted by hills and woods, but at the same time the route is highly picturesque, and the round from Ballater, up the north side and down the south side, is very popular.

The north road on leaving Ballater begins by winding round the boldly-marked Craigendarroch. It crosses the *Gairn* (1¾ miles), and then lies through pleasantly-wooded country. About 3¼ miles from the starting-point is the *Coilacriech Inn.* Two miles beyond, on the opposite bank of the river, is **Abergeldie Castle.** A mile farther is **Crathie Church,** where the Queen and the royal family worship when at Balmoral, the Castle being in the parish of Crathie. It is a plain, almost austere building of grey granite, relieved only by the handsome altar and reredos in memory of Edward VII, the busts of George V and Queen Victoria (who laid the foundation-stone in 1893), and the mural monument to her son the Duke of Edinburgh.

Across the river from Crathie is –

Balmoral Castle

(From May 1 to July 31 the grounds are usually open to the public, in the absence of the Court, daily except Sundays, from 10 a.m. to 5 p.m. Admission *fee* devoted to charities. The interior of the Castle is not shown.)

It stands on a plateau nearly a thousand feet above the level of the sea, but the thick belt of trees almost completely screens it from the road.

The Castle was erected by the Prince Consort in 1854, the Prince himself designing the principal features. It is of light-coloured granite, in the Scottish Baronial style of architecture, and comprises two blocks with connecting wings, bartizan turrets, and a projecting tower, a hundred feet high, in which is a clock.

About 250 yards from the Lodge Gates the drive forks: that to the right leads to the Castle and that to the left leads to the village, passing the golf links and a number of statues and monuments.

On the south side of the main road is the *Carn na Cuimhne*, **Cairn of Remembrance.** Its Gaelic name is the slogan of the Farquharsons, and the spot is said to have been the rendezvous of the clan when summoned to battle.

A mile on (52 miles from Aberdeen) is **Inver,** with a hotel and granite quarries. On the south side of the river is **Ballochbuie Forest,** extending nearly to the summits of the lower hills. About 6 miles from Balmoral the road to Braemar crosses the Dee by **Invercauld Bridge** from which there is a fine view of the river and of the Old Bridge of Dee, a short distance

The River Dee at Braemar

downstream. Another mile brings one abreast of **Invercauld House,** away to the right—the ancestral home of the Farquharsons of Invercauld.

On the south side of the river is **Braemar Castle** (*open daily from May to mid-October*); this fine castle was built in 1628 by John Erskine, Earl of Mar, but has been in the Farquharson family since 1731.

Braemar

Angling.—The *Invercauld Arms* and *Mar Lodge* hotels have several miles of salmon-fishing on the *Dee* and fishings can also be rented by local arrangement.

Buses to Ballater and Aberdeen. There is occasional connection with Pitlochry in summer.

Early Closing.—Thursday, suspended in summer.

Distances (by road). Aberdeen, 59 miles; Perth, 50 miles.

Golf.—An 18-hole course.

Hotels.—*Fife Arms, Invercauld Arms, Braemar Lodge, Callater Lodge, Mar Lodge, Mayfield* (guest), etc. Furnished houses and apartments available (apply (S.A.E.) Secretary, Tenants' Association).

Population.—500.

Tennis.—Courts available.

Youth Hostel.—In Corrie Feragie Lodge.

Braemar, or, to give its full title, *Castleton of Braemar*, is 1,100 feet above sea-level, and is surrounded by well-wooded, lofty hills, which effectually shield it from winter winds. It has a very dry climate, and its air is remarkably pure and bracing. First and foremost of its kind, its "Gathering" or Highland Games, held in September, attracts huge crowds.

At *The Cottage*, R. L. Stevenson spent the summer of 1881 and wrote *Treasure Island*, his first great work. The Invercauld Galleries opposite house displays of traditional Scottish crafts.

70

Excursions from Braemar

Visitors must bear in mind that, where excursions into the surrounding countryside are concerned, their movements are liable to considerable restriction, especially during the stalking season (from August onwards). It should also be remembered that some of the mountain excursions are of considerable severity and that they should on no account *be attempted by indifferent walkers, especially in doubtful weather. All the routes are minutely described in* Ward Lock's "The Complete Scotland."

1. **The Ascent of Morrone Hill,** 2,819 feet above the sea, but only about 1,700 above Braemar. The summit can be reached and the descent made in three hours or less. It lies to the south-west of the village. The prospect includes a most charming view of the valleys of the Dee and the Quoich.

2. **Linn of Quoich.** The *Quoich* is a stream entering the Dee a short distance west of Braemar. The only access for cars is by a rough road from the Linn of Dee which passes the back of Mar Lodge. Pedestrians may go eastwards to the Invercauld Bridge and thence by a right-of-way track through the low ground between Invercauld House and the river. The Linn is about a mile above the confluence. The falling water has formed pot-holes in the rock; "Quoich" is the Gaelic for "cup." The falls are under 3 miles from the village in a *direct* line but two or three times as far by Victoria Bridge or Invercauld Bridge.

3. **Linn of Corriemulzie** and **Linn of Dee.** On the Dee, west of Braemar. Three miles from Braemar the Linn of Dee road crosses the Corriemulzie Burn just above its fall into a narrow wooded glen on the right of the road—the **Linn of Corriemulzie.** The **Linn of Dee** is about 3 miles farther. The river runs through a deep and narrow channel in the rocks. Both spots are extremely beautiful.

4. To **Linn of Lui.** About a $\frac{1}{4}$ mile east of the Linn of Dee on the north side a bridge crosses the Lui. Follow the stream up the east bank for $\frac{1}{4}$ mile. From this point for half a mile upstream are a fascinating series of pools, falls and narrows with several little sandy coves.

5. **Ascent of Lochnagar** (3,786 feet). Time required, four to five hours to the top. Double journey 22 miles. The route from Braemar is quite interesting but less used than either of the others (from Balmoral and Ballater), and the road is much rougher. The great features of "dark Lochnagar" are the precipices and corries on the north side, where snow lies all the year round.

6. To **Loch Builg** (13 miles), **Tomintoul** (24 miles), and **Ballindalloch** (40 miles). Road (which attains 2,200 feet) from Braemar to Loch Builg. From the Loch to Inchrory shooting-lodge, a distance of 4 miles, there is only a footpath. From Inchrory a poor road (partly private) through interesting scenery follows the course of the Avon to Tomintoul (*see* p. 42).

7. To **Blairgowrie** by Spittal of Glenshee (35 miles): one of the finest drives in the Highlands. The road climbs Glen Clunie from the level of 1,100 feet at Braemar to 2,199 at the summit at **Cairnwell Pass** (10 miles), the last 3 miles being particularly steep. The descent is also steep. At **Spittal of Glenshee** (15 miles) there are two hotels and another at *Bridge of Cally* (29). By Blairgowrie (35 miles) the level has fallen to 300 feet (*see* p. 53).

8. To **Clova** (19 miles), on foot by "Jock's Road." *See* the route in the reverse direction, p. 58.

9. To **Kirkton of Glenisla** (25 miles) and **Alyth** (31 miles). *See* p. 54.

10. To **Blair Atholl** *viâ* **Glen Tilt** (30 miles). The road passes the Linn of Dee (*see* above), beyond which to the ruined house at Bynack (12 miles) there is a rough road, impracticable for cars. There is no place for refreshment between Braemar and Blair Atholl. For further particulars, *see* pp. 30–32.

11. To **Aviemore,** in Strathspey (30 miles), or **Lynwilg** (32 miles), *viâ* the *Larig Ghru Pass.* The road up Glen Lui may be closed to all vehicles. Beyond *Derry Lodge,* 10 miles from Braemar, the traveller will pass only one house until he is within a couple of miles of Aviemore. The roads in the **Rothiemurchus Forest,** at the far end of the route, are very bewildering and it is desirable to repeat the warning given above with regard to the severity of this route (*see* p. 37).

12. To **Nethy Bridge** (31 miles), in Strathspey, by the *Larig an Laoigh.* From Derry Lodge (*see* above) the path runs north up Glen Derry and east of Ben Mheadoin (Vain), fords (*dangerous in bad weather*) the Avon below Loch Avon, climbs to 2,586 feet in the Larig beside Ben Bynac, and descends into the Nethy valley near the Revoan Pass (*see* p. 37), 7 miles from Nethy Bridge by a drivable road.

BUCHAN

The north-eastern district of Aberdeenshire is known as Buchan, the most easterly point of Scotland being Buchan Ness, 3 miles south of Peterhead. Bus services operate north from Aberdeen to Peterhead and Fraserburgh.

For the most part Buchan is flat but richly cultivated, and what interest it possesses for the tourist is mainly due to coast scenery and local and historical associations. About 17 miles from Aberdeen is **Ellon.** Near the town are the ruins of Old Ellon castle, the Fortalice of Ardgight. By Ellon (connected by bus with Aberdeen) are salmon and trout fishings, including those of the Ythan, close by (available by daily ticket to guests of *New Inn*, Ellon), its tributary the *Ebrie* (partly free), and the *Forvie* (trout; mostly free), another feeder of the Ythan. Ellon has hotels (*Buchan, Station, New Inn, Carighall Inn*) and a golf course.

Cruden Bay

Cruden Bay, 24 miles from Aberdeen, 9 from Peterhead, has a beautiful stretch of smooth, firm sand. To the north is rock scenery which can hardly be equalled in grandeur. There is good sea-fishing, boating and bathing, bowling greens and tennis courts, and the district is an attractive one for motorists and cyclists. But Cruden Bay (*Kilmarnock Arms*) is most visited for its 18-hole **Golf Course,** nearly $3\frac{1}{2}$ miles in length, and with fine springy turf. It is considered one of the finest in Britain. There are buses from Aberdeen and from Peterhead.

Adjoining the Bay is the village of **Port Errol.** Northward is the site of the demolished Slains Castle, and half a mile farther along the coast are the **Bullers of Buchan,** a huge rocky cavern open to the sky–"perpendicularly tubulated" according to Dr. Johnson. The sea rushes into the cavern through a natural arch. To the south of Cruden Bay, on the coast, are the fragments of **Old Slains Castle;** the fishing village of **Collieston,** famed for its "speldins"; the **Sands of Forvie** (a once fertile expanse now overblown by sand and where some interesting archaeological finds have recently been made) and, at the mouth of the Ythan, the village and harbour of **Newburgh.** (Bus to Aberdeen.)

Peterhead

Angling.–River-fishing can be had in the *Ugie*, within half an hour's walk of the town. There is also good sea-fishing.
Bus to Boddam; to Aberdeen; to Fraserburgh, etc.
Caravans.–Site at South Bay.
Early Closing.–Wednesday.
Golf.–The two courses at *Craigewan* are reached by a bridge across the *Ugie*; they are within ten minutes of the town. Length of 18-hole course, 6.055 yards. Sunday play.
Hotels.–*Palace, Caledonian, Royal, Waverley, Imperial* (unl.).
Population.–14,350.

Peterhead is 32 miles by road from Aberdeen. The burgh was founded in 1593 by George Keith, 5th Earl Marischal, and is built mainly of the local red granite. In its earlier days it enjoyed a reputation for its mineral springs and later it was a whaling station. Today it is one of the principal Scottish ports concerned with the white fish industry. In the bay south of the town is a huge National Harbour of Refuge, constructed largely by labour from the prison. Peterhead has a museum and art gallery, an indoor swimming pool and golf courses (18- and 9-hole).

Peterhead is 7 miles from the **Bullers** (*see* above), and within easy cycling and motoring distance are various antiquarian remains, notably the ruins of the **Abbey of Deer,** near Mintlaw (9 miles inland), Inverugie Castle (3 miles) and Ravenscraig Castle (4 miles).

Fraserburgh

Angling.—Sea angling from rocks, piers or boats. River fishing in the Ugie.
Buses to Rosehearty, New Aberdour, Banff, Aberdeen, Peterhead, etc.
Early Closing.—Wednesday.

Golf.—An 18-hole seaside course of 6,070 yards. Meals available at Clubhouse. Sunday play.
Hotels. – *Royal, Saltoun Arms, Station, Alexandra.*
Population.—10,729.
Caravan sites at beach (apply Town Clerk).

Fraserburgh was founded in the sixteenth century by an ancestor of the family of Lord Saltoun. The population is increased during the season by several thousands of fish workers, for this port is the chief centre of the white fishery on the north-east coast. East of the town is a bay with a fine sandy beach affording good facilities for bathing. On **Kinnaird Head** are the remains of a castle surmounted by a lighthouse. The castle was built by Sir A. Fraser in 1576. Near it is the Wine Tower, a building the origin and use of which are unknown. It has no outer entrance, except on the upper storey, but the wooden stair is modern. It is built over a cave called the **Selch's** (or Seal's) **Hole.**

Five miles to the south-east are **Inverallochy** and **St. Combs. Cairnbulg** and **Inverallochy Castles,** Comyn strongholds of old, are conspicuous objects.

In the churchyard of **Rathen,** 3 miles south, lie the paternal forbears of the Norwegian composer Grieg.

Buses run along the coast from Fraserburgh to **Rosehearty** (4 miles: 9-hole golf course) and **Aberdour** (8 miles: Dundarg Castle), and near the fine cliff scenery of **Pennan;** but owing to steep hills motorists may prefer the inland road to Macduff *viâ* Byth, Crudie and Longmanhill. At Rosehearty are the ruins of **Pitsligo Castle,** once the residence of Alexander Forbes, Lord Pitsligo, the original of "Baron Bradwardine," in *Waverley.* A man of eighty, after the Battle of Culloden he lived in hiding in the neighbourhood for several years. One of his haunts was the Cave of Cowshaven, or Lord Pitsligo's Cave, 2 miles west.

THE DON VALLEY

Though it enjoys no such prestige as Deeside, the Don valley is well worth exploring for its scenery, apart from its angling attractions. The *Don* rises not far from the head-springs of the Dee, to which, in its course of 80 miles, it runs roughly parallel. Good fish are to be got from the Don, which is excellent as a trout stream and has some good salmon pools.

Alford (25 miles) and Strathdon (45 miles) can be reached from Aberdeen by bus *viâ* Skene and Tillyfourie (20 miles), this (A944) being the direct road. An alternative bus route to Alford strikes westward from the main north road (A96) at Midmill, about a mile south of Kintore, and goes round to Tillyfourie by Kemnay (15 miles; *Burnett Arms Hotel*).

North of the village are **Fetternear,** once the country seat of the Bishops of Aberdeen, and the extensive **Kemnay Granite Quarries,** the depth of which is about 400 feet. The stone is a light silver-grey colour and was used for the Marischal College in Aberdeen, for the Royal Liver Buildings in Liverpool, for the Thames Embankment and the Forth and Tay bridges, and for many other important works. About 3 miles to the south is **Castle Fraser,** with a square tower probably dating from the fifteenth century. Then comes **Monymusk,** where Monymusk House stands in a finely-timbered park ("Paradise"). Rather more than a mile to the south is **Cluny Castle.**

Alford

25 miles from Aberdeen, is a pleasant little village, the centre of an important agricultural district. Alford (pronounce *Ah'ford*) is linked with Aberdeen by bus and, in summer, with Cock Bridge in Strathdon. It is a favourite resort of anglers, as the Don may be fished by hotel guests, and there are good trout burns in the neighbourhood. (*Hotels: Haughton Arms, Vale, Forbes, Muggarthaugh*).

Alford to Tomintoul

The road runs along the north bank of the Don. At the old toll of **Mossat** it joins the main road from Gartly station. Turning to the south to Kildrummy, 8 miles (*hotel*), we pass the extensive remains of **Kildrummy Castle,** once a most imposing structure, associated with the heroic defence by Nigel Bruce against the English. Thence the road lies through the narrow sylvan **Den of Kildrummy,** and **Morven** (2,862 feet) is seen right ahead. Twelve miles from Alford we reach the *Glenkindie Arms Inn,* not far from **Towie Castle,** which is on the south side of the Don and is the scene of that pathetic ballad, *Edom o' Gordon.*

We cross the *Kindie Water,* and presently come to **Glenkindie House,** an attractive modern mansion. (Beyond, in the second field on the right, is a *Pict's House,* containing two chambers.) A little farther westward we cross the mouth of the *Buchat,* which flows for 7 miles down a wild Glen, in which are the site of **Badenyon,** the dwelling of the famous ballad hero, John of Badenyon, and the remains of **Glenbuchat Castle,** the ruined seat of a Jacobite branch of the Gordons. Upper Strathdon is entered at **Bellabeg** (89 miles: *hotel*). Here are the ruins of **Colquhonnie Castle,** and nearby the **Doune of Invernochty,** a mote hill.

Beyond Bellabeg the scenery attains its climax by the blending of water, wood and hills. The scene becomes wilder and barer near **Corgarff Castle,** which contests with Towie the evil repute of being the stronghold in which, in 1571, Sir Adam Gordon burned the wife of Alexander Forbes, with her children and household. The road has risen rapidly and is here in the wild mountain region around the springs of the Don. There is a Youth Hostel at Corgarff.

From **Cock Bridge** (28 miles: 1,344 feet above sea-level) the highway leaves the Don and goes northward by a precipitous moorland route (steep gradients) across the **Lecht** into Banffshire, attaining a maximum height of 2,114 feet at a point $\frac{1}{2}$ mile south of the county boundary. Beyond the latter (2,090 feet) the road descends steeply and 6 miles farther (37 from Alford) reaches **Tomintoul.**

Cock Bridge to **Ballater** (13 miles). A rough road running in a fairly straight line.

Cock Bridge to **Braemar** (22 miles), *viâ* Inchrory, 6 miles west of Cock Bridge, and Loch Builg, 4 miles south of Inchrory—a rough but wildly beautiful route for walkers only.

Other Excursions from Alford

1. **Terpersie or Dalspersie Castle** (5 miles north). On one of the window-sills is the date 1561.

2. The ruins of **Balfluig Castle** ($\frac{3}{4}$ mile south), built 1556.

3. **Craigievar, Corse** and **Aboyne,** 18 miles (*see* Index). **Craigievar** lies 6 miles south and has a fine old castle seven storeys high, a good example of the Scottish castellated style. The hall has a very fine ceiling and a massive fire-place. Over the staircase is a coat of arms with the date 1668 and the injunction, "Doe not vaiken sleiping dogs." Not far beyond Craigievar the road from Alford joins the main road from Aberdeen. This must be followed westward to Tarland. About a mile from the junction of the Alford road the Aberdeen road passes Corse House on the right and the remains of **Corse Castle** (1581). At **Tarland** the road turns sharply to the left, and passes near the ruins of **Coull Castle,** on a rocky eminence near Coull Church.

Craigievar Castle

ABERDEEN TO BANFF AND MACDUFF VIA OLD MELDRUM

The main road to Macduff and Banff (46 miles from Aberdeen) is A947 which strikes off northwards from Bucksburn for Dyce (*see* p. 77). Old Meldrum (18 miles: *hotel*) and Fyvie (27 miles). **Fyvie Castle,** built by Lord Chancellor Seton, is "one of the noblest and most beautiful specimens of the rich architecture which the Scottish Barons of the days of King James VI obtained from France." With its five towers, its bartizan turrets, dormer windows, and high-pitched gables, it stands in beautiful grounds. Five miles lower down the *Ythan* are the ruins of **Gight Castle,** formerly the seat of the maternal ancestors of Lord Byron.

Left of the road now will be seen the square keep of the **Castle of Towie Barclay** (founded 1300), the seat of the family of Barclay, from whom descended the Russian general Barclay de Tolly, who thwarted Napoleon in the campaign of 1812. Away to the right, a mile or two farther on, is **Hatton Castle,** a red-sandstone building, with which is incorporated part of the old tower of Balquhally, once the seat of the Mowatts.

Turriff is a busy agricultural town, with a Cross (restored 1865) and a ruined church. Turriff was the seat of a Celtic monastery, of a hospital established (1273) by the Earl of Buchan, and of a Templar foundation. Here, in 1639, occurred a skirmish, known as the "Trot of Turriff," in which was drawn the first blood shed in the Civil War in Scotland.

From Turriff the road runs down the east side of the beautiful valley of the *Deveron* to Banff.

About 4 miles from Turriff is the ruin of **Eden Castle,** the ancient seat of the once powerful Earls of Buchan.

The name of **King Edward** (5 miles from Banff), a corruption of *Ceann-eader*, is pronounced *Kin-ed' art.*

Banff

Angling.—The Banff and Macduff Angling Association controls both banks of the *Deveron* from its mouth for three-quarters of a mile; the Fife Arms Hotel has beats on the *Deveron*; rock fishing.

Golf.—18-hole course in the gronnds of Duff House

(Sunday play). Tarlair Course is within easy reach.

Hotels.—*Crown, Fife Arms, Seafield, Royal Oak, Dunvegan.*

Population.—3,363.

Tennis, Bowls, Boating, Cinema.

Banff and **Macduff** are twin towns respectively on the west and east sides of the mouth of the Deveron, across which is a seven-arched bridge designed by Smeaton. Each town has its harbour, Macduff is busy with fishing and each has its golf and its residential portions.

Banff is the capital of the county of the same name and was the site of a royal castle which on three occasions was the headquarters of the English king, Edward I. James Sharp—"Sharp of that ilk"—the famous Archbishop of St. Andrews, was born in it in 1618. The present **Banff Castle,** a house erected in 1750, is now a Community centre. The old churchyard contains remains of the ancient Parish Church and interesting gravestones. The **Market Cross** is reputed to date from pre-Reformation days. Westward of the town are the links (bus service), a beautiful sandy beach, excellent for bathing, and a caravan site.

Duff House, formerly a seat of the Earls of Fife and now belonging to the nation, dates from the middle of the eighteenth century. Golf is played in the grounds.

Through the park is a path by the side of the *Deveron* to the **Bridge of Alvah,** 2 miles, where the river has scooped out a deep channel, the surface of the water being 40 feet below the bridge. **Montcoffer House,** a former residence of Princess Arthur of Connaught, on the east bank of the Deveron, overlooks the bridge.

Macduff as a town dates only from 1783, when through the influence of the second Earl of Fife with King George III the existing hamlet of Doune was made a burgh under the name of Macduff, Viscount Macduff being one of his lordship's titles.

At **Tarlair** the Royal Tarlair Golf Club has its course. About a mile to the east is the *Howe of Tarlair*—a picturesque bay enclosed on three sides by high cliffs. Within the Howe is Tarlair Spa (chalybeate); a Swimming Pool has been constructed under the shadow of the famous **"Needle's E'e" Rock.**

Eastward of Tarlair the coast is rocky and precipitous.

On **Gamrie Head** are the ruins of **Gamrie Church,** said to have been built in 1004, in fulfilment of a vow made during a Danish raid.

In a narrow bay on the eastern side of Gamrie Head is the fishing village of **Gardenstown,** named after its founder, Alexander Garden, of Troup. It is very picturesque as it slopes up from the shore and clings to the steep side of an overhanging hill.

Troup Head, a mile from Gardenstown, is the most northerly projection on this part of the coast. In the vicinity of the Battery Green a narrow opening on the slope of the hill bears the somewhat common name of *Hell's Lum.* From it a subterranean passage, nearly 100 yards in length, extends to the sea, and along this, during a storm, the spray is forced till it finds its escape by the lum, or chimney, in the shape of dense smoke. Not far from Hell's Lum is another subterranean passage, called the *Needle's Eye.*

Pennan Head protects a small harbour and the little fishing village of **Pennan.**

ABERDEEN TO INVERNESS VIA HUNTLY

The direct road route (by A96) from Aberdeen to Inverness follows for most of the way that of the railway, *viâ* Inverurie, Huntly, Keith, Elgin, Forres and Nairn. On both sides of this line are many places of interest and the motorist can make his way to Inverness by a variety of routes along first-class roads through country already described—for example by Fraserburgh (*see* p. 73) or Banff (p. 75) and the coast; by Deeside (*see* pp. 66–71) or Strathdon (p. 73) and Tomintoul (p. 42).

On leaving Aberdeen we pass through districts largely dependent on the granite and paper-making industries and proceed up the Don. The railway keeps close to the river by Dyce, while the road takes a straighter course to meet the line again at Kintore. The A947 branches off to the right for **Dyce** (6 miles) where is Aberdeen Airport. The churchyard at Dyce contains remarkable Pictish symbol stones.

Kintore (13 miles from Aberdeen) is an ancient royal burgh with a picturesque town hall. It has a 9-hole golf course. Permits for fishing in the *Urie* and the *Don* are obtainable locally. A mile to the west are the ruins of **Hallforest Castle,** said to have been a hunting tower of Robert the Bruce.

At the confluence of the Urie and the Don is **Inverurie** (16 miles: population 5,231). The **Bass,** a mound between the two rivers, was the subject of one of Thomas the Rhymer's prophecies. Inverurie has hotels (*Gordon Arms, Kintore Arms*), a 9-hole golf course, and borough waters in the Don and Urie available to anglers (day tickets). To the east may be seen **Keith Hall,** the seat of the Earl of Kintore.

A couple of miles north of Inverurie, to the right, a granite monument marks the site of the battlefield of **Harlaw,** where in 1411 Donald of the Isles, marching on Aberdeen with a Highland host, was defeated by Lowland forces under the Earl of Mar—a turning point in Scottish history. To the left rises the Mither Tap (1,698 feet), second highest of the six peaks of **Bennachie** (pronounced Benna*hee*), renowned in song.

From **Inveramsay,** road and rail pass westward through **Garioch** district to **Pitcaple** (21½ miles from Aberdeen), one of the best points from which to make the ascent of **Bennachie.**

Beyond Pitcaple the railway and A96 again part company. They do not cross each other's track until Huntly, to which the road proceeds over the Foudland Hills, rising to 900 feet.

The railway line at this point—accompanied by an alternative road to Huntly (A979), 3 miles longer but easier in some respects—swings westward by **Oyne** and then **Insch** (9-hole golf course). Oyne is on the *Gadie Burn*, which runs, as the ballad refrain reminds us, "at the back o' Bennachie." Just beyond Insch, on the right, is the conical hill of **Dunnideer,** surmounted by a fragment of an ancient fort. On the left is the hill of **Christ's Kirk** (1,021 feet), supposed to be the scene of the old poem of "*Christ's Kirk on the Green.*" Soon to the left we have the **Tap o' Noth** (1,851 feet), on the summit of which are the remains of a vitrified fort having ramparts upwards of 8 feet high. More distant is the **"Buck"** (2,368 feet), the culminating point of the sequestered district of the **Cabrach,** accessible through the upper valley of the Bogie, in which "the cauld clay hole" of **Rhynie** is the chief centre of population.

Forty miles from Aberdeen is–

Huntly

Hotels.–*Gordon Arms, Castle, Huntly, Strathbogie.*
Population.–3,900.

a neat town at the meeting-points of roads running in every direction and with golf, an indoor swimming pool, and good fishing in the vicinity. The chief sight of the town is the ruin of **Huntly Castle,** the cradle and seat of the Gordons, Earls (afterwards Marquises) of Huntly and Dukes of Gordon. The ruins are open daily, 10–7, Sundays 2–7, at a small charge. The principal feature is a large keep with a great round tower at the south-west corner and a smaller round tower at the opposite corner. Beneath the larger tower is a dark, deep dungeon.

The earliest castle here was a Norman peel built in the latter part of the twelfth century by Duncan, Earl of Fife, who, following a grant of land from William the Lion, became the first Lord of Strathbogie. In the peel Robert Bruce found shelter in 1307, but shortly before Bannockburn the then lord of Strathbogie turned against Bruce and his lands were taken from him and given to Sir Adam Gordon of Huntly, in Berwickshire, whose descendants became Lords of Huntly, Marquises and Dukes of Gordon, and were for many generations all-powerful throughout a wide district, the head of the family being for centuries known as "the Cock of the North." A successor to the Norman building was the scene of the marriage of Perkin Warbeck. It was despoiled by Mary's troops in 1562 and "cast down" by James VI in 1594; only the underground basement and dungeon of this work are left, the remainder of the ruin dating from about 1550–1600. Ordinary processes of disintegration were assisted by the builders of Huntly Lodge in 1742, who found the Castle a convenient quarry. The ruin is now under the care of the Department of the Environment.

To many Huntly is interesting as the birthplace of George Macdonald (1824–1905; a tablet marks the house in Duke Street), who sketched it in *Alec Forbes of Howglen.*

TO ELGIN BY THE COAST

Northward from Huntly we may make for the coast at **Portsoy** (*Station, Park*), a clean little fishing town with the double harbour characteristic of this part of the coast and excellent rock scenery. A beautiful serpentine, formerly quarried in the neighbourhood, is known as Portsoy Marble, some of which has a place in the Palace of Versailles. Portsoy is a favourite holiday resort with bathing, boating and fishing, bowls and tennis.

Two miles west of Portsoy is the tiny hamlet of **Sandend,** on a fine bay, and between that and Cullen are the ruins of *Findlater Castle*, perched on the cliffs and reached by a somewhat intricate path. On the south side of the main road is *Fordyce Castle* (1592), still inhabited.

Cullen House

Cullen

Distances. – Aberdeen, 60 miles; Banff, 12; Elgin. 21; Inverness, 60.
Early Closing. – Wednesday.
Hotels. – *Cullen Bay, Royal Oak, Waverley, Seafield Arms, Grant Arms, Bay View, Three Kings Inn.*
Caravans. – Municipal and private sites.

Population. – 1,296.
Sports. – Angling in the Cullen Burn (permission from Lord Seafield necessary); sea-fishing, boating, bathing; golf, 18-hole course, bowls and tennis in grounds off Seafield Place.

Cullen, a Royal Burgh since 1455, is finely situated at the eastern end of its extensive bay. The town consists of two parts – the new town on high ground and the sea-town on the shore. The road to the sands winds down above the harbour and the fishing quarter. Adjoining the sands is the golf course, and light refreshments may be obtained at the pavilion by all. The rocks on the shore are dignified by the name of the *Three Kings of Cullen.* Half a mile off the main coast road is **Cullen House,** parts of which are upwards of 700 years old. *Open June: Wednesdays, Thursdays and Sundays, 2–5; July and August: Wednesdays, Thursdays, Saturdays and Sundays, 2–5; September: Wednesdays and Sundays, 2–5. Tearoom.* The **Bin of Cullen** (1,050 feet), 3 miles south-west, commands a wide view including the distant Cairngorms.

From Cullen to Fochabers the main road runs inland, through woods and with charming views, but an even more interesting road follows the coast closely and introduces one to a number of delightfully quaint, unsophisticated little fishing villages which make excellent quarters for a quiet holiday. **Portknockie, Findochty** and **Portessie** have accommodation for visitors.

79

Buckie

Buckie (*Commercial, Marine, Highlander's, St. Andrew's, Cliff House, Rathburn House, Strathlene House*) is a noted fishing port with up-to-date facilities and interesting harbour. The Buckie vessels, with their distinctive mark "BCK," are known all along the east and west coasts. Boat-building and the manufacture of electric lamps are thriving industries. The largest town in Banffshire (population 8,000), it has an open-air swimming pool at Strathlene, two 18-hole golf courses, tennis, bowls and putting, and a cinema among its attractions. The beach is sandy and there is a caravan site.

So by the fishing village of **Portgordon** to **Spey Bay,** where the *Spey* completes its long and adventurous journey from the Monadhliath mountains beyond Kingussie and flows quietly into the Firth. The principal features of Spey Bay as a resort are the *Spey Bay Hotel* and the fine golf links. Close to the river-mouth is the *Tugnet*, head-quarters of Crown salmon fisheries. Spey Bay is 4 miles from **Fochabers,** where the river is crossed by a bridge giving fine views.

KEITH TO ELGIN BY CRAIGELLACHIE

Keith is 50 miles from Aberdeen. The town is situated on the *Isla*, a good trout stream. (Permits on application to Strathisla Anglers' Association.) Fife Keith lies on the other side of the Isla. Keith contains several hotels and is a busy agricultural centre with objects of historic interest in its Church and old Bridge. From Keith there are two rail routes to Elgin and Inverness—either *viâ* Mulben and Orton, or *viâ* Dufftown and Craigellachie. The latter, which we now take, is 25 miles in length; the route by Mulben is only 17, but the other is much the more picturesque. The main road goes to Elgin by Fochabers.

Dufftown

Buses to Elgin and Tomintoul.   **Population.**—About 1,500.
Hotel.—*Elms*, Fife Street.

Dufftown, on the *Fiddich*, is famous for its fine air and its distilleries. It has benefited by the generosity of Lord Mount Stephen (born here in 1829), and visitors are attracted by its bracing climate—its altitude is over 600 feet—the charming walks and drives among attractive scenery in the vicinity, and the many places of interest within easy reach. Dufftown also offers fishing and tennis, etc. On the north side is the old **Castle of Balvenie.** (*Admission charge,* 10–7, *Sundays,* 2–7. *Closes at* 4 *in winter.*)

Other objects of interest in the neighbourhood are—

Castle of Balvenie

The **Church of Mortlach,** at south end of town, the seat of a Pictish Bishopric, and said to have been enlarged by Malcolm II as a thank-offering for a victory over the Danes in 1010.

The **Giant's Chair,** a mile from the church, a kind of natural seat overhanging the *Dullan,* and approached by a path alongside the stream. The **Cradle,** a basin in the rock, about 100 yards from the Giant's Chair.

The high-placed ruins of **Auchindoun Castle,** 2½ miles south-east.

Ben Rinnes (2,755 feet). Distance to the summit, 7 miles. The ascent presents no difficulty. The descent may be made to Aberlour (*see* p. 82; bus service to Dufftown), or to Ballindalloch, 8 miles. The two **Convals** offer nearer and easier ascents. Buses run *viâ* Glen Rinnes to Glenlivet and Tomintoul (19 miles). (*See* p. 42).

Beyond Dufftown the route winds through picturesque **Glen Fiddich,** past Kininvie and the ruined Gauldwell Castle, emerging at **Craigellachie** (accent on the second syllable). With its level tract through which the Spey winds, its picturesque Rock and Bridge, its own high tree-clad grounds and neighbouring wooded heights, its wide prospects and fine air, Craigellachie has naturally become a popular resort. Trouting can be had on some of the neighbouring streams. Craigellachie has a good hotel.

Keith to Elgin: route continued on p. 83.

STRATHSPEY

The **Spey,** one of the most rapid rivers in Scotland, is 110 miles long, and the third of Scottish rivers in point of length, and, next to the Tay, it is the grandest river in the country. The section up from Craigellachie to Boat of Garten is one of great loveliness, the "thundering Spey" rolling wide and deep through a circumscribed valley, abundantly wooded and backed by softly-swelling hills and high mountains, a magnificent National Forest Park. The A95 road follows the course of the river with its endless twinings, at many places running on its very brink, and innumerable stretches of the stream are disclosed to view. The Spey ranks high as a salmon river, and on that account most of it is preserved. Trouting is not permitted in those parts that are let for salmon fishing. It also contains finnocks.

From Craigellachie we run along the right or east bank of the Spey to **Charlestown of Aberlour,** where a magnificent view is obtained of **Ben Rinnes** (2,755 feet), on the left. The distance to the summit from Aberlour is 7 miles. Aberlour has a 9-hole golf course; residents may fish a mile of the Spey; and permission to trout on streams in the neighbourhood can generally be obtained. Less than a mile and a quarter from Aberlour Church is the **Linn of Ruthrie,** a cataract about 20 feet high.

From Aberlour to **Carron** is 5½ miles. The Spey, flowing in broad sweeps and through birch-hung gorges, is nowhere more beautiful than in the reach here begun. So by **Blacksboat** (formerly the site of a ferry) to **Ballindalloch** (12 miles), near which the Spey is joined by the *Avon*, on the right bank of which is **Ballindalloch Castle,** one of the finest specimens of a Scottish baronial castle.

Four miles farther up the Avon, near the ruins of Drumin Castle, the *Livet* joins it. **Glenlivet** produces the whisky that bears its name.

Above Ballindalloch the scenery becomes more markedly Highland. Just beyond **Advie,** and on the south side of the Spey, is **Tulchan Lodge.** Here the valley widens, and bears great masses of birches and firs. The **Cromdale Hills** appear on the left, and not far from Cromdale are the **Haughs of Cromdale,** the site of a battle fought in 1690.

After Cromdale **Castle Grant** comes into view on the right.

Beyond Grantown the Braes of Abernethy and the range of the **Cairngorm Mountains** are on the left of the valley, and the **Monadhliath** range is visible on the right, while upstream the view is closed by the (Upper) **Rock of Craigellachie.** At **Nethy Bridge** (first-class hotel; 9-hole golf course; salmon and trout fishing) there is a fine view of **Cairn Gorm** (4,084 feet). Nethy Bridge is one of the spots from which the ascent of this mountain can be conveniently made. (For fine tramps to Aviemore and Braemar, *see* pp. 36 and 71 respectively.)

Nethy Bridge lies a little south of the main road and then comes **Boat of Garten.** The name commemorates the ferry which the bridge superseded. There are an 18-hole golf course, tennis courts and accommodation includes *The Boat Hotel* and *Craigard Hotel*.

Keith to Elgin (viâ Craigellachie): Route resumed from p. 81.

Leaving Craigellachie, we cross the Spey under the Lower Craigellachie Rock, and enter Morayshire. In 3 miles we come to the picturesquely-situated little town of **Rothes** (pronounced *roth' es*), below which the river is constricted between a ridge of **Ben Aigen** (1,544 feet) and **Finlay Seat** (861 feet). We now leave the valley of the Spey, and passing through the **Glen of Rothes,** reach **Longmorn,** a district, like Rothes and Craigellachie, abounding in distilleries. Less than 3 miles farther is **Elgin.**

Elgin

Distances.–Aberdeen, 66 miles; Inverness, 38. Forres, 12; Keith, 18; Lossiemouth, 5½.
Early Closing.–Wednesday.
Hotels.–*Gordon Arms, City, Laichmoray, St. Leonards, Tower; Thunderton House, Royal* (unl.), *Sunninghill* (unl.).
Population.–16,530.

Railway Access.–From the south *viâ* Aberdeen.
Sports.–Fishing in the upper reaches of the *Lossie* (daily bus service). Loch fishing on Millbuies Lochs (permits from City Chambers); bowls, boating, golf (18-hole course), putting, tennis, etc. Indoor swimming pool.

Elgin is an attractive little city (it claims the title as a Cathedral town of old) on the south bank of the Lossie, about 5 miles from the coast and some 38 east of Inverness and 66 from Aberdeen. It is the centre of a fertile district known as the Garden of Moray, has a mild climate and provides good educational facilities.

The ruins of the **Cathedral,** the principal object of interest, are accessible weekdays from 10–7; winter, 10–4 (*tickets at office at N.W. tower*), but at other times a very good idea of their beauty can be gained from the road skirting the enclosure. The most notable feature is the fine western doorway.

The Cathedral, the "Lanthorn of the North," was founded in 1224 by Andrew, Bishop of Moray, but of the structure then erected the remains of the transepts and the towers are the chief portions, the rest of the church as it exists today having been built after a fire in 1270.

The building again suffered from fire in 1390, through the act of Alexander, Earl of Buchan, commonly known, on account of his rapacity, as the Wolf of Badenoch, who, having been excommunicated for deserting his wife, sought to be revenged. Under compulsion by his half-brother, Robert III, who feared terrible ill might follow the outrageous sacrilege, the earl helped to repair the damage.

In 1506 the great steeple – rebuilt by Bishop Innes (1407–14), fragments of whose monument remain – fell. With the Reformation came the beginning of the final destruction of the beautiful building, for in 1568 the Regent Moray and his Privy Council, being hard pressed for money wherewith to pay their soldiers, ordered the lead to be stripped and sold for their benefit.

For nearly a hundred years the ruins lay utterly neglected, except by those who found the fallen walls a convenient quarry and, near the end of the period, by an enthusiastic antiquary, one John Shanks, who set himself the task of removing what had become mere rubbish and laying bare the ground plan of the building.

The style of architecture is the First Pointed Order, and the building is perhaps the best specimen of ecclesiastical architecture in Scotland. When entire, to quote an authority, Elgin Cathedral was "a building of Gothic architecture inferior to few in Europe." The edifice was 289 feet long. greatest breadth, 87 feet: western towers, 84 feet in height.

The best preserved portion is the early fifteenth-century **Chapter House,** at the north-east corner. In the centre is a massive pillar, some 9 feet in circumference, having the form of a cluster of sixteen slender shafts.

Between the Chapter House and the vestry is the Sacristy, containing a lavatory, the water basin of which was the cradle of General Anderson, the founder of the local institution bearing his name (*see* below).

In the Chancel is the tomb of the founder of the Cathedral, and to the right, in St. Mary's Aisle, is the burial-place of the Gordon chiefs. The first Earl of Huntly lies here and also the last Duke of the male line.

Elgin Cathedral

A portion of the Deanery has been incorporated with the house known as North College; South College is the Archdeacon's Manse, modernized. The wall at the rear of South College garden leads to *Panns Port*, the only one remaining of the four entrances to the Cathedral precincts. Close at hand is **Anderson's,** a Corinthian building "for the support of old age and the education of youth," which is also the memorial of the romantic career of Lieut.-General Anderson. At his father's death his mother was so destitute that she was forced to find a dwelling among the Cathedral ruins (*see* above). Later the boy enlisted as a drummer in the Honourable East India Company, rose to the rank of Lieut.-General and died in 1824, leaving a considerable sum for the foundation of the institution which bears his name.

In **Cooper Park,** across the road from the Cathedral, is *Grant Lodge*, the dower house of the Earls of Seafield; the mansion contains a public and rural library. The policies of the house now form Cooper Park (named in honour of the donor). Towards the eastern end of the main street of Elgin is the **Little Cross,** supposed to have marked the eastern limits of the burgh; opposite is the *Museum* of the Elgin Literary and Scientific Institution (*weekdays*, 10–12.30, 2–5; *Tues.,* 10–1). Also in this street is the **Muckle Cross,** beside the Parish Church, a large Classic building. Along High Street towards the north-west may be seen the summit of **Lady Hill,** crowned by a monument commemorating the last of the old Dukes of

84

Gordon, "a benefactor of agriculture in the North." A Charter of 1106 mentions a Castle which stood upon the hill and which was the residence of early Scottish kings. The remaining fragment is named *Duncan's Castle* (King Duncan, of *Macbeth*, is believed to have died nearby at Pitgaveny).

The ruins of an old *Greyfriars' Abbey* (founded by Alexander II) have been restored and incorporated with a chapel. For permission to view apply at Convent in Abbey Street.

The *Ladies' Walks* are an attractive series of paths beside the Lossie.

Excursions from Elgin

1. Southward from Elgin a road traverses the **Glen of Rothes** to Rothes and Craigellachie, in Strathspey. **Birnie,** to the west of this road, about 3 miles from Elgin, has "the oldest bishop's church in the diocese of Moray." It belongs to the twelfth century, and is still strong and perfect.

Rothes, a distilling centre, is commanded by a ruined Castle of the Leslies, in which Edward I quartered himself in 1296. For **Craigellachie** *see* p. 80.

2. **Pluscarden Priory,** 6 miles south-west of Elgin, was founded by Alexander II, in the thirteenth century, and restored and part of it fitted up in 1898 by the Marquess of Bute. The fittings are rich in carving and the altar is one of the finest in the north of Scotland.

The Abbey is beautifully placed in the narrowing glen of the Lochty, and the road may be followed onward to Forres, passing **Blervie Tower,** an ancient structure five storeys high, commanding a grand view.

3. The road north from Elgin to Lossiemouth passes near the remains of **Spynie Palace,** for many centuries the residence of the Bishops of Moray. It was inhabited by Roman Catholic Bishops up to 1573, and then for upwards of a hundred years by Protestant Bishops. Its extensive ruins comprise a very fine keep. *Spynie Loch* was originally an arm of the sea, but has been gradually drained or silted up and for the most part is rich meadow-land. *Pitgaveny*, near the south end, has already been mentioned.

Numerous bus excursions to places farther afield.

Lossiemouth

Access. – From Elgin, 5 miles, by the A941 road (bus service).
Early Closing. – Thursday.
Golf. – The *Moray Golf Club* has a very fine course of 18 holes, and a 9-hole relief course.
Hotels. – *Stotfield, Laverock Bank, Rock House.*
Population. About 6,349.

Lossiemouth is composed of the ancient fishing settlements of Seatown and Old Lossie, the newer settlement of **Branderburgh,** which dates from about the middle of the last century, when a new harbour was constructed, and, lastly, **Stotfield,** a district of modern villas. It is built on and around a headland rising from the Laich of Moray.

It would not be easy to find another resort in the North which has grown so rapidly and has so quickly obtained such a wide reputation. Modern Lossiemouth is almost entirely a creation of the present century. It was the birthplace of James Ramsay MacDonald (1866–1937), the first Labour Prime Minister of Great Britain (1924). He resided at "The Hillocks." A memorial plaque marks the cottage (1 Gregory Place) where he grew up.

Lossiemouth has bracing air; a low rainfall and high sunshine record; a long, broad, sandy beach; and around are extensive prospects which charm the eye. It also offers golf, bowling, putting, tennis, trout and sea fishing. The Royal Naval Air Station (H.M.S. *Fulmar*) adjoins the burgh on the west.

West of Lossiemouth, about 3 miles, is **Covesea** (pronounced *Cowsie*), with a tall white lighthouse and interesting rocks and caves. One of these caves was supposed to have communicated by an underground passage with Gordonstoun, half a mile distant, for long the seat of the Gordons and now a famous School for boys. In this direction also is **Duffus.** The few ruins of Duffus Castle are noteworthy for its well-preserved Moat. The ruins of Spynie Palace (3 miles south of Lossiemouth) mark the original extent of Spynie Loch, which once lapped the palace walls.

Westward again from Covesea are the fishing village of **Hopeman** and the busy little port of **Burghead.**

Across the neck of the elevated promontory are the remains of a triple breastwork and of inner ramparts, within which is a chamber cut in the solid rock, with a cistern and spring in the centre—the so-called *Roman Well*. All these were formerly reputed to be of Roman workmanship, but are now regarded as Celtic. On the crest of the promontory—supposed to be the "Ptoroton" of Ptolemy—the *Clavie*, a relic of ancient fire-worship, is kindled by the fishermen on New Year's Eve (Old Style, i.e. January 12), to ensure a successful year's fishing.

Burghead and Hopeman have fine bathing sands. There is golf at Hopeman.

The 12-mile run from Elgin to Forres is across the fertile *Laich of Moray*. For **Forres** *see* pp. 43–44, and for the route from Forres to Inverness, pp. 45–47.

Edinburgh or Glasgow to Oban via Callander

There is much beautiful scenery along this route.

Motorists proceeding from Edinburgh reach Callander *viâ* Linlithgow, Falkirk and Stirling; from Glasgow the general route is *viâ* Cumbernauld and Stirling, though a shorter route with finer scenery is *viâ* Canniesburn, the outskirts of Milngavie and Aberfoyle, and the Lake of Menteith.

By whichever route **Stirling** is reached, the journey thence is by way of **Bridge of Allan,** an attractive resort, **Dunblane** (with a fine cathedral, an excellent golf course, and a palatial hydro-hotel), and **Doune** (with its historic Castle). Alternatively the A84 from Stirling may be taken, a more direct route. Eight miles beyond Doune is –

Callander

Angling. – Tickets for the *Teith, Loch Vennachar* and the *Blackwater* can be obtained at the tacklemakers. There is free fishing on Lochs Achray and Lubnaig. Loch Voil is private.

Distances. – Stirling, 16; Glasgow, 42; Oban, 72; Edinburgh, 52; Trossachs, 10.

Early Closing. – Wednesday.

Golf. – An 18-hole course. Sunday play.

Hotels. – *Caledonian, Dreadnought, Crown, Bridgend House, Pinewood, Ancaster Arms, Coppice*, etc.

Post Office. – On the south side of Main Street, near the Caledonian Hotel.

Proportionately to its population (less than 1,800) Callander has a greater number of hotels and boarding-houses than any other place in Scotland. It is, of course, the "jumping-off" place for the celebrated Trossachs Tour, but it deserves attention also as a very good centre for road excursions in all directions, being equally in touch with Edinburgh and Glasgow and the finest loch and mountain scenery. The town itself needs no description. As to the surrounding country, no Guide Book can compete with the glowing pictures in Scott's *Lady of the Lake*.

At the east end of Main Street is a wicket gate at the entrance to a glacial deposit forming a long winding mound, commonly called the **Roman Camp.** It affords a fine view of the Crags, Ben Ledi and the River Teith. Excavations at Bochastle, $1\frac{1}{2}$ miles to the west of Callander, have disclosed remains of a Roman fort.

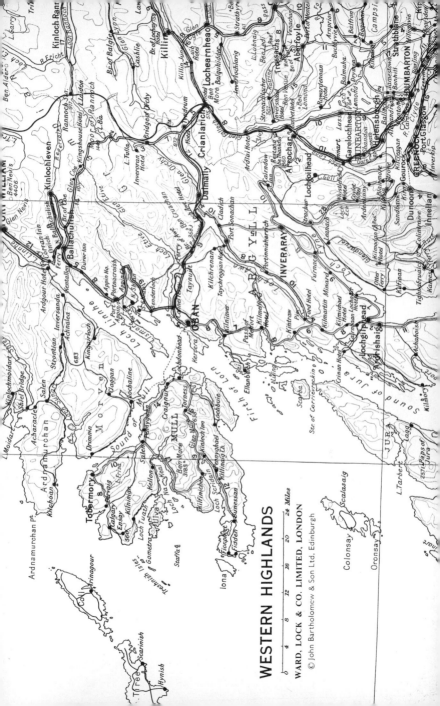

WESTERN HIGHLANDS

WARD, LOCK & CO. LIMITED, LONDON

© John Bartholomew & Son Ltd, Edinburgh

Excursions from Callander

1. To **Bracklinn Falls,** a fine cascade on the Kelty Water, 1¼ miles north of the town.

2. **Callander Crags** (2 miles) command a good view.

3. **Ascent of Ben Ledi** (2,875 feet). Distance, 5½ miles. Time required, from 2½ to 3 hours. The easiest route is by way of Coilantogle Farm, 2½ miles on the Trossachs road. A more interesting route is by the Pass of Leny. The view from the summit is exceedingly fine.

4. Walk through the **Pass of Leny** to **Strathyre,** 8½ miles, from which bus can be taken north or back to Callander. The Pass is extremely beautiful.

5. **Through the Trossachs.** This is probably the most popular excursion in the Highlands. Coach services daily.

The road (A821) follows the line of the chase described in the *Lady of the Lake* by Sir Walter Scott, who put the Trossachs on the tourist map. Commanded to the north by Ben Ledi, it skirts lovely **Loch Vennachar** (4 miles long) from Coilantogle to Lanrick (*Youth Hostel*), then passes by **Brig o'Turk** (spanning the Finglas) – a favourite haunt of artists – to wood-girdled **Loch Achray** (over a mile long: *hotel*) on the verge of the Queen Elizabeth Forest Park. Near the western end of Loch Achray is the turreted *Trossachs Hotel,* beyond which begins the famous Pass, a rugged romantic gorge leading to Loch Katrine and Trossachs Pier (9½ miles from Callander: *car park*), where the public road ends.

Loch Katrine (8 miles long) is overlooked by **Ben Venue** (2,393 feet) and **Ben A'an,** and many islands break its surface. The most interesting is **Ellen's Isle,** a short way from the pier. The Trossachs end of the loch is the most beautiful part.

The loch, which is the chief reservoir of the Glasgow water supply, contains trout, permission to fish for which must be obtained from the Glasgow Corporation.

A steamer runs between the Trossachs Pier and **Stronachlachar,** and a coach between that point and **Inversnaid** (5 miles) on Loch Lomond. Since the road over the hills from the Trossachs to Aberfoyle was rebuilt, it is possible to include the Trossachs in a circular tour embracing also Aberfoyle and the Lake of Menteith.

6. **Circular Tour** (by motor, steamer, coach and train) to the Trossachs, Loch Katrine, Loch Lomond, Balloch, and back by Glasgow and Stirling.

7. To **Balquhidder** and **Rob Roy's Grave.**

8. Trips to **Loch Earn, Loch Tay,** and **Loch Awe.** By coach.

9. To **Loch Lomond** and **Glen Arklet** *viâ* **Aberfoyle.** Motorists go from Callander either direct or *viâ* Doune to *Thornhill,* whence is a westerly road to Aberfoyle and on past Lochs Ard and Chon (*see* below) to Stronachlachar and Inversnaid. The return road may be varied by turning off at Aberfoyle over the rebuilt road to the Trossachs. **Aberfoyle** (*Bailie Nicol Jarvie, Altskeith House,* etc.) is the "capital" of a district which still largely answers to the description given in Scott's *Rob Roy.* This region's popularity has been enhanced by the creation (1951) of a National Forest Park stretching from Loch Achray to Loch Ard.

Westward of Aberfoyle the road passes **Lochs Ard** and **Chon** and the **Falls of Ledard.** On an island in Loch Ard is the ruin of Duke Murdoch's Castle. On the west side of the loch runs the Loch Katrine aqueduct to Glasgow. Up Glen Dubh is a way to the summit of **Ben Lomond** (3,192 feet). **Stronachlachar** is near the western end of Loch Katrine, and if the time-table is kind one may return to the Trossachs Pier by steamer. Or from Stronachlachar one can go down Glen Arklet to Inversnaid, on the bonnie banks of Loch Lomond: but this road is a cul-de-sac from which the only outlets are the Loch Lomond steamers, a ferry (no cars) across the loch, and the hill paths.

Callander to Killin

From Callander the A84 road runs west and then north for Killin. In about 3 miles we run through the **Pass of Leny.** A mile beyond is the farm of **Tombea,** or "birk hill,' where Tombea's Mary dwelt; and on rising ground on the north bank of the river are the ruins of **St. Bride's Chapel,** where she was married, as narrated in the *Lady of the Lake.* Then we reach **Loch Lubnaig,** the "crooked lake." Near its head, the line (which follows the western shore) runs over the site of Laggan Farm, whence Rob Roy is said to have carried off Mary MacGregor to make her his wife. Just over 8 miles from Callander is **Strathyre,** a Forestry Commission nursery. It has past associations with Dugald Buchanan, the Gaelic poet. At 11 miles **Kingshouse** (*hotel*) marks the road running westward for 2 miles to **Balquhidder,** in the churchyard of which Rob Roy is buried (*see* p. 22).

Beyond the Balquhidder turning the road runs down hill for a mile to **Lochearnhead** (*see* p. 22).

From Lochearnhead we climb stern **Glen Ogle** for over 3 miles, then descend into Glen Dochart, at the foot of which, by the head of Loch Tay, lies the beautifully situated village of **Killin** (*Killin, Bridge of Lochay, etc., and unlicensed hotels: Youth Hostel*). Killin has a 9-hole golf course and bus connections with Aberfeldy.

Loch Tay

ranks among Scotland's most beautiful lakes, long famous for its salmon fishing (obtainable through the hotels: trout fishing is free). The loch is some 15 miles in length and a mile broad. An inferior road on the south side goes to Kenmore by Ardeonaig, Ardtalnaig and Acharn.

The main road (A827) to Kenmore (*see* below) crosses the Lochay (*Bridge of Lochay Hotel*), which enters the loch at the Killin end, near the ruins of **Finlarig Castle,** and proceeds north-eastwards, past a hydro-electric power station, to Lawers (*unl. hotel*) at the foot of **Ben Lawers** (3,984 feet). This giant is largely National Trust property and boasts rare alpine plants and good ski-ing slopes.

Loch Lubnaig

From **Fearnan,** a picturesque village three miles from the eastern end of Loch Tay, a road runs due north to Fortingall, in **Glen Lyon.** (*See* p. 26).

Beyond Fearnan, **Drummond Hill** casts over the waters on the north side its broad, deep shadow, answered by the reflection from the other side of the soft-swelling hills of **Acharn.**

Quite near the lower end of the lake is a small but pretty island, containing the ruins of a Priory, founded in 1122 by Alexander I, whose first queen, Sybilla, daughter of Henry I of England, was buried in it.

Kenmore

is a neat and pretty village at the end of Loch Tay. A few yards from the pier one comes to a quadrangular space, along one side of which are the picturesque *Breadalbane Hotel* and a reading-room to which strangers may obtain admission. On the opposite side are the **Church** and one of the entrances to the grounds surrounding *Taymouth Castle* (on the site of the old Balloch Castle), formerly the chief seat of the Marquis of Breadalbane, but now no longer used as a residence. Within the grounds of Taymouth Castle is an 18-hole golf course. Some notes on the surroundings of Kenmore will be found on p. 24.

KILLIN TO OBAN

From Killin we travel westward through **Glen Dochart,** which is flanked on the south by **Ben More,** with its twin **Stobinian,** respectively 3,843 feet and 3,827 feet. Past **Luib,** on a hill above the road and marked by a placard, are two gable ends, said to belong to Rob Roy's house.

We now pass Loch Tubhair and Loch Dochart, and enter Strathfillan. One mile beyond the head of Loch Dochart is **Crianlarich** (*Crianlarich Hotel*) where the road from Glasgow *viâ* Loch Lomond-side comes in.

From Crianlarich we run through **Strathfillan** to **Tyndrum** (34 miles from Callander: *Royal Hotel*), a small village of increasing importance since the construction of the new road to Glencoe. For Oban, however, we travel westward through **Glen Lochy.** As we approach **Dalmally** (*Dalmally Hotel*), a grand view is obtained of Glen Orchy and Glen Strae, and in late afternoon in summer the views of the Glen Cruachan corries are exquisite. Dalmally is at the foot of **Glen Orchy,** and in "the loveliest spot in all that lovely glen." From it we cross the mouth of Glen Strae, once the headquarters of the wild MacGregor Clan, and turn southward to the northern shore of **Loch Awe** (p. 108).

Excursions from Dalmally

1. **Kilchurn Castle** (pronounced *Kil-hoorn*). The Castle figures in Scott's *Legend of Montrose.*

2. The **Falls of Cruachan** may be reached by the Taynuilt road, 7 miles.

3. **Loch Awe** can be traversed from end to end by boat from Loch Awe Hotel, or skirted by road (B840) along the eastern side.

4. **Glen Aray and Inveraray.** As far as Cladich the road (rebuilt) follows the shore of Loch Awe; then it climbs to a height of 675 feet at the summit by Tighnafead and falls finely through lovely woods to Inveraray.

River Tay, Kenmore

Resuming the journey to Oban, we rise to a considerable height on the side of **Ben Cruachan** (3,689 feet: *see* below). As we pass the **Falls of Cruachan,** a peep at the cascade may be obtained through the trees which line the banks of the deep ravine.

We next enter the famous **Pass of Brander,** enclosing a narrow arm of the loch. It is about 3 miles in length. Then comes the **Pass of Awe,** the upper part of the gorge through which the river rushes from the loch. About 7 miles from Loch Awe Hotel, the road crosses the stream by the **Old Bridge of Awe,** which figures so prominently in Scott's *Highland Widow.*

Hydro-electric undertakings are leaving their mark on the Awe and its surroundings.

Ben Cruachan is most easily ascended from the Bridge of Awe. From the east end of the bridge a track leads past the railway and then bears left, following the right bank of the Awe downstream. A short way beyond the railway, however, a path doubles back on the right and follows a fairly steep but obvious path eastward to the summit. Ben Cruachan is one of the highest mountains in Argyllshire. It has two crests: the eastern (or Dalmally) is 3,689 feet, the western 3,611 feet. The connecting ridge is about three-quarters of a mile long and 3,400 feet above sea-level.

A more direct route to the eastern peak is from beside the Falls of Cruachan, starting by the western bank of the Cruachan stream until a branch of the stream shows the way to a ridge on the left connecting a prominent shoulder with the main peak. When the ridge is scaled the main route lies to the right.

The two routes given above may be combined, of course; good walkers may strike eastward from the main summit along the main ridge by Drochaid Glas (3,312 feet) and Stob Diamh (3,272 feet), which is the middle peak of the three forming the "horseshoe," and descend by either of the other two peaks to the main road near the head of the loch.

Continuing on our way, we catch a glimpse of **Loch Etive** on the right, and soon reach **Taynuilt,** some 60 miles from Callander. This attractive village ($12\frac{1}{2}$ miles from Oban) has an hotel (which lets rods on the River Awe; Loch Awe and Loch Etive can also be fished).

The woody hillside behind the village is celebrated in the well-known song, *The Braes abune Bonawe:*

> "When simmer days clead a' the braes
> Wi' blossomed broom sae fine, lassie,
> At milkin' shiel we'll join the reel –
> My flocks shall be a' thine, lassie.
> Wilt thou go, my bonnie lassie?
> Wilt thou go, my braw lassie?
> Wilt thou go? say Aye or No!
> To the braes abune Bonawe, lassie?"

On the route from Taynuilt to Oban glimpses are caught first of Loch Etive and later of the Firth of Lorne. The railway touches the shore of Loch Etive at Ach-na-Cloich with its pier. Ardchattan House and church and the Valliscaulian **Ardchattan Priory** are on the opposite shore.

Three miles beyond Ach-na-Cloich is **Connel** (*Falls of Lora, Dunstaffnage Arms, Loch Etive* (unl.)), pleasantly situated on the shore of Loch Etive. Formerly there was a ferry at this point, but traffic now crosses the loch by the bridge that carries the road to Appin and Ballachulish.

The mouth of Loch Etive being narrow and the site of a reef of rocks, the tide often passes through it with great rapidity, and there is formed a cataract known as the **Falls of Lora,** situated just above the bridge. About a mile from Connel a magnificent view towards Fort William and Ben Nevis is opened up, and the ruins of **Dunstaffnage Castle** are seen on the side of the Loch. The road passes Dunollie Lodge and so to **Oban.**

An alternative road is now available for cars from Connel. A re-surfaced road leaves the main road at the Dunstaffnage Arms Hotel and wanders through the Glencruitten Hills, passing Loch Nell and Glencruitten golf course, entering Oban at the south end of the town.

Glasgow to Fort William and Mallaig

From Glasgow to Tarbet, on Loch Lomond, there is a choice of routes: one can turn north from Dumbarton and by Balloch follow the road which skirts the western side of Loch Lomond, from end to end; or those who wish for a glimpse of the Gare Loch and Loch Long should continue alongside the Clyde from Dumbarton to **Helensburgh,** a popular resort of Glasgow folk, as witness the size of the railway station. Continue alongside the **Gare Loch,** with its sailing boats, coasting vessels and, generally, a few larger vessels laid up. From the village of Garelochhead the road rises swiftly to the height of Whistlefield, and here it is well to draw aside for a few minutes for the sake of the very fine view down the Gare Loch and over the Clyde. Then we descend and follow the eastern side of **Loch Long.** This sea-loch is $16\frac{1}{2}$ miles from end to end. Beyond its western shore is a mountainous district which is ironically termed **Argyll's Bowling Green,** the elevation being over 2,000 feet. Here is the estate of **Ardgoil,** which forms part of the **Argyll National Forest Park.** The Park has a total area of 54,000 acres, of which 19,000 are reserved for afforestation and the remainder for use as a National Park.

The mouth of rugged **Glen Douglas** is crossed almost opposite **Glen Croe,** overhung by the broken summit of **Ben Arthur,** or **The Cobbler** (2,891 feet), and by **Ben Ime** (3,318 feet). **Arrochar** (40 miles), at the head of Loch Long, has hotel (*Arrochar, Loch Long, Arrochar House* (unl.)) and other accommodation, and is a handy little centre. Caravan site at Glen Loin House.

From Arrochar the road which rounds the head of Loch Long passes up Glen Croe and by way of *Rest and Be Thankful,* Cairndow and **Inveraray** provides one of the best motor routes to **Oban.**

At Arrochar we turn our back on Loch Long and cross the narrow strip of land which separates Loch Long from Loch Lomond, and at the far end of which is the village of **Tarbet** (*hotel*), on the shore of **Loch Lomond.** Bearing to the left here we run along the western shore and pass Glen Inveruglas (caravan site) opposite Inversnaid. The road skirts **Ben Vorlich** (3,092 feet) through which runs a 2-mile tunnel from gigantic Loch Sloy dam (160 feet high) to the hydro-electric generating station at Inveruglas.

The head of the loch comes into view, and we soon reach **Ardlui.** Here we enter **Glen Falloch,** which conducts us to **Crianlarich,** an attractive little place on the east-west, Killin–Oban route (*see* p. 92). All around are great hills, of which the loftiest are **Ben More** (3,843 feet) on the right and **Ben Lui** (3,708 feet) on the left. Then for some 5 miles the route is westward through **Strathfillan.**

A mile or two beyond Crianlarich, we pass the ancient **St. Fillan's Chapel.** Of the Holy Pool in its vicinity a host of stories are still current concerning miraculous cures. Two miles farther is the scene of the Battle of Dail Righ or Dalree ("King's Field"), where Bruce lost the famous "Brooch of Lorne" in 1306. About a mile beyond **Dalree,** and 4½ from Crianlarich, is **Tyndrum** (*Royal Hotel*—salmon fishing in Orchy; trout in lochs and burns), where we leave the Oban road and turn northward on to the modern highway. Another mile brings us to the boundary between Perthshire and Argyllshire, at an elevation of 1,025 feet. This high ground is the great watershed of Scotland, the streams flowing on the one side to the North Sea and on the other to the Atlantic. The way passes for miles among wild heather-clad hills. **Ben Dorain** (3,523 feet), "the mountain of storms" sung by the Gaelic bard, Duncan Ban Macintyre (1724–1812), rises on the right above **Bridge of Orchy** (*hotel*).

From Bridge of Orchy the road sweeps out across Rannoch Moor, a great morass, 20 miles square, which Robert Louis Stevenson brings into *Kidnapped* as the scene of the escape of young David Balfour and Alan Breck from the dragoons. On the left is seen **Loch Tulla,** famed for its salmon and trout.

From here road and railway take completely different routes to Fort William, the West Highland line cutting boldly north-eastward across the moor, amid scenery of the wildest, to lonely **Rannoch** Station; then on to Corrour (*Youth Hostel* at Loch Ossian, a mile away), along the side of Loch Treig into Glen Spean, and down by Roy Bridge to Spean Bridge, to enter Fort William from the east.

In a series of curves the road attains the highest point of the Moor, and then ahead are seen the twin peaks of **Buachaille Etive,** guarding the entry into **Glencoe.** Beyond the *Kingshouse Hotel* (a rendezvous of fishers, climbers and skiers) the road falls swiftly into the Glen, which is described on p. 114.

At **Carnach,** at the foot of Glencoe, the Fort William road swings to the right to round **Loch Leven,** at the head of which is the industrial townlet of Kinlochleven, but an alternative is to continue westward as far as **Ballachulish** and to cross the loch by the ferry—a saving of a dozen miles or more. The Ballachulish ferry takes cars and operates daily through the year.

From prettily-placed **Onich** (*see* p. 113) we have our last backward view of Glencoe, and turn our attention to **Loch Linnhe,** whose waters splash the road in rough weather. From **Corran** the road runs beside the loch to Fort William.

Fort William

Access. – *Rail.* – From *Glasgow* by Crianlarich and Spean Bridge. From *Mallaig* direct.
    Road. – From *Glasgow* as on foregoing pages. From *Stirling* by Crianlarich as on pp. 87 92. and thence as above. From *Kingussie viâ* Loch Laggan (*see* pp. 33 34). From *Inverness viâ* Fort Augustus.
    Steamer from Oban. Pier adjoins station.
Distances. – London, 524 miles; Glasgow, 122 (by rail), road (*viâ* Luss and Loch Lomond) 103; Oban, 33 by water, 48 by road (*viâ* Ballachulish Ferry), 67½ *viâ* Kinlochleven; Inverness, 64¾ by road; Fort Augustus, 32 by road.
Early Closing. – Wednesday.

Hotels. – *Alexandra, Croit Anna, Cruachan, Grand, Imperial, Highland, Nevis Bank, Milton, Station, West End; Commercial* (unl.).
Bus services. – Between Fort William and North Ballachulish, calling at Onich and Corran; to Inverness; and to Inverlochy, Caol, Banavie and Corpach. Coaches daily in summer to Glencoe, Glen Nevis, Achnacarry, Gairlochy, etc.
Information Centre in Cameron Square.
Population. – 4,012.
Recreation. – Boating and bathing, good sea and loch fishing, bowls, tennis and mountain-climbing. *Playhouse* cinema.

The town originated in a fort built by General Monk, during the Commonwealth, to overawe the Highlanders, and was reconstructed in the time of William III, from whom the place derives its name.

The fort was unsuccessfully besieged during the rebellions of 1715 and 1745, was garrisoned until 1860, and dismantled in 1866. The only part now standing is the north-west rampart and governor's house, the rest having been levelled for the railway. The gates now serve as the entrance arch to the Craigs burial ground.

The introduction of the railway led to the development of the town as a tourist resort, and the motor and the rebuilt roads have added to its claims upon visitors, while the huge hydro-electric undertakings in the neighbourhood have done much to secure an all-the-year-round prosperity for a place which ordinarily would have enjoyed only a brief summer season.

The **West Highland Museum,** in Cameron Square, contains antiquities and Jacobite relics, tartans, and replicas of an old croft interior and of the Governor's room at the Fort. (Admission charge.) Opposite in the square is a cinema.

At Fort William the River Lochy terminates its brief life of 8 miles by flowing into the head of **Loch Linnhe.** The loch itself has a westward continuation in **Loch Eil,** and in the angle formed by the two lochs are **Corpach** (*Corpach Hotel*) and **Banavie,** of some importance as the southern terminal point of the Caledonian Canal and, with the large villages of Inverlochy and Caol, ranking as satellites of Fort William in the eyes of tourists.

Excursions from Fort William

1. **The Ascent of Ben Nevis,** the highest mountain in the British Isles (4,406 feet), is, for the hardy, the chief event of a visit to Fort William or Banavie. It is most easily ascended from Achintee Farm (2½ miles from Fort William), which can be reached by car by *crossing* the Bridge of Nevis at the north end of the town and then turning sharp to the right up a fair road which follows the north bank of the River Nevis. There is a rough path to the summit (7½ miles from Fort William), but in spite of this there is some stiff climbing to be done after the first mile or so, and strong boots, preferably nailed, are needed on account of the rough rocks. It is essential to take some food and warm clothing. Four hours should be allowed for the ascent and two to three for the descent. The stone building at the summit was, until 1904, a meteorological observatory. Hardy walkers often ascend in the evening and spend the night

Loch Shiel, Glenfinnan

on the mountain for the sake of the glorious view at sunrise, but mists are apt to cause disappointment.

2. **Old Inverlochy Castle,** 2 miles north of Fort William, is a large quadrangular structure, probably erected in the thirteenth century–possibly by Edward I–and partially restored by James Lord Abinger.

A mile or so from the old stronghold is the **New Castle of Inverlochy** (1866–92). Inverlochy has attained to importance as a seat of an aluminium manufacturing industry (British Aluminium Co., Ltd.). Here, as also at Kinlochleven and Foyers, alumina is reduced to yield aluminium, a process requiring electricity. The power for this is obtained by an extensive system of engineering works whereby the waters of Lochs Treig and Laggan, and even part of the head-waters of the Spey, are led through a 15-mile tunnel, the outlet pipes of which can be seen emerging from the northern shoulder of Ben Nevis.

3. **Neptune's Staircase,** a series of eight locks in that part of the Caledonian Canal lying between Corpach and Banavie. Each lock has a drop of 8 feet.

4. **Glen Nevis.** The Glen is wildly picturesque and contains two fine waterfalls. Other objects of interest are the remains of the vitrified fort of **Dun Dairdill** (pronounced *Jardill*), on the summit of a hill about a mile above Glen Nevis House, and a curious rocking stone at the foot of the hill. The route passes but does not cross Nevis Bridge, at the northern end of the town. The distance there and back is 16 miles. In Glen Nevis is a popular Youth Hostel.

5. **Glencoe** (*see* pp. 112–113) by coach during the season.

6. **To Glenfinnan, Glenfinnan Monument and Arisaig.** This tour can be accomplished by the Mallaig branch line (*see* below) or by road from Fort William. The approach to Glenfinnan presents points of surpassing beauty and grandeur.

7. **Achnacarry and the Dark Mile.** Motors make trips embracing Achnacarry and the Dark Mile. **Achnacarry,** for centuries the seat of "Lochiel, the Chief of Clan Cameron," is a modern residence at the foot of **Loch Arkaig,** a long, narrow sheet of water connected with Loch

Lochy, adjoining the Caledonian Canal. Near by stood the old Castle, burnt by the Duke of Cumberland in 1746. The public road from Clunes, on Loch Lochy, to the foot of Loch Arkaig runs through the **Dark Mile,** formerly lined with gigantic birch-trees. Near it is a cave, in which "Bonnie Prince Charlie" hid in his flight from Culloden.

8. **The Falls of Monessie** and the **Parallel Roads of Glen Roy.** By road (bus) or by train to Roy Bridge station.

9. To **Onich** and **North Ballachulish Ferry,** by the shores of Loch Linnhe (bus service).

10. **Loch Shiel Circular Tour.** A favourite round is by, coach to Glenfinnan, steamer down Loch Shiel, and coach back to Fort William *viâ* Corran Ferry.

11. **Steamer Cruises.** These can be taken on Loch Linnhe to **Oban,** or among the lovely lochs on the west coast in the vicinity of **Mallaig,** which is easily reached by train from Fort William. Weekly day trip to Iona.

For a fuller description of the many excursions from Fort William, *see* our *Guide to Western Scotland.*

FORT WILLIAM TO MALLAIG

Road and rail run side by side through a beautiful district that is also of considerable romantic and historical interest, as Prince Charles landed upon its shore in 1745 and fourteen months later re-embarked from it as a fugitive after the failure of his attempt to drive George II from the throne.

From Fort William we cross the Lochy and Corpach Moss to **Banavie** and **Corpach** (at the south-western end of the Caledonian Canal), beyond which we follow the northern shore of **Loch Eil,** an inlet of the sea, 10 miles long.

Leaving Loch Eil, we traverse a strath alongside the Callop River and after crossing the head of **Loch Shiel** come to historic **Glenfinnan. Loch Shiel** is a fresh-water lake 20 miles in length, and everywhere less than a mile in width. There are no roads along the lochside other than the one built by the Forestry Commission for timber-carrying from Glen Huirich forest to the pulp mill at Corpach. At its head stands **Glenfinnan Monument,** a column surmounted by a statue of a Highlander. It marks the spot where his ill-fated standard was unfurled on August 19, 1745. There is a boat service to Acharacle. Six miles down the loch, on the right, is **Glenaladale,** old family residence of the Macdonalds.

Beyond Glenfinnan, where there is an hotel, known as *Stage House Inn,* the shores of **Loch Eilt** are skirted, the River *Ailort* is crossed and **Kinloch Ailort** (*hotel*) reached. Then we cross the narrow peninsula of **Ardnish,** separating the salt waters of **Loch Ailort** and of **Loch nan Uamh** ("Loch of the Cave"). In the latter the ship which brought Prince Charlie and his seven followers from France cast anchor on July 25, 1745. After the battle of Culloden, Loch nan Uamh was entered by two French frigates, with arms and 40,000 louis d'or, in a vain attempt to rally the scattered Jacobite forces. From **Borrodale,** on Loch nan Uamh, also, the Prince bade his last farewell to Scotland, on September 20, 1746.

The district is inseparably associated with the final wanderings of Prince Charlie. After Culloden he fled to Glen Beasdale, where he waited till a boat could be obtained to convey him to the Outer Isles, hoping to find a ship there that would carry him to France. But from South Uist he returned to the mainland, piloted part of the way by Flora Macdonald. He landed near Mallaig, was conducted through the military cordon by his friends, and after many wanderings farther east came back to Borrodale, where he stepped on board the ship which carried him to France.

Magnificent views are obtained from **Arisaig** (34 miles from Fort William; *Arisaig Hotel*), a hamlet in a charming spot, indented by inlets of the sea that are sprinkled with rocky islands, and that afford fine sea-fishing. Six miles farther we come to the outlet of **Loch Morar,** 12 miles in length, and "the deepest hole in Europe"–164½ fathoms. Escaping from the loch, the river tumbles over a series of falls in a short course of a quarter of a mile, and plunges into the salt water, fringed by snow-white sands, of Outer Loch Morar. At **Morar,** as at Arisaig, there is an hotel and youth hostel; and the views across to Skye are entrancing.

Mallaig

(42 miles from Fort William), a small town busy with fishing and shipping. It has a pier and breakwater and there are hotels (*Marine, West Highland*). The **Sound of Sleat** separates Mallaig from **Skye,** less than 4 miles distant. During the fishing season many fishing boats may be seen in its harbour, where their freights are landed for dispatch to southern markets.

Now a popular resort, Mallaig offers exceptional facilities for visiting other ports. Mail steamers call at its pier, and at all seasons there is daily communication (Sundays excepted) between Mallaig and **Kyle of Lochalsh,** and **Portee.** There are also daily sailings to and from **Stornoway,** and to Armadale (for Mallaig–Armadale ferry, *see* p. 134), and on certain days, to and from the Outer Isles. Small motor cruisers run day trips to many of the lochs and islands in the vicinity.

Also served by steamer from Mallaig are the islands of Eigg and Rhum. **Eigg** (pronounced egg), about an hour's sail south-westward from Mallaig, is principally inhabited by crofters and fishermen. It has a bold and striking appearance, due largely to its basaltic *Scuir*, described by Hugh Miller as "a tower 300 feet in breadth by 470 feet in height, perched on the apex of a pyramid like a statue on a pedestal." To the south is the small island of **Muck,** occupied as a sheep and dairy farm. **Rhum** is a beautiful island with shapely peaks, the highest of which is **Askival** (2,659 feet).

Glasgow to Oban via Loch Lomond and Crianlarich

The full beauty of the Loch and its surroundings can best be appreciated from the steamer; but the road alongside Loch Lomond makes this a fine route also for motorists going to Oban or to Fort William from Glasgow. The customary bus route from Glasgow to Oban is *viâ* Helensburgh and Garelochhead, Tarbet and Crianlarich as already described on pp. 95–96. (A favourite circular motor run from Glasgow is the "Three Lochs Tour" skirting Loch Lomond, Loch Long and Gare Loch.)

The journey to **Balloch,** at the southern end of Loch Lomond, takes about an hour by rail. (Balloch is also connected with Glasgow by bus.) By road the route is *viâ* Dumbarton and Vale of Leven. (Balloch hotels include *Balloch, Glenroy, Loch Lomond, Tullichewan, Woodbank*.) Loch Lomond Youth Hostel, with 400 beds, is 2 miles up the west bank.

Loch Lomond

is about 23 miles in length, and its greatest width is 5 miles. For its beauty it justly deserves the title of "Queen of the Scottish Lakes," and for the sport its fish affords them it is in high repute among anglers. Its waters yield salmon, sea-trout, loch trout, pike and perch. The Loch Lomond Angling Improvement Association, from whose Secretary at 86 St. Vincent Street, Glasgow, C.2 (Tel. Central 6822), full information can be obtained, protects and controls the fishing in Loch Lomond, the Gare Loch, the Clyde Estuary, and in the rivers Leven and Fruin, and parts of the rivers Endrick and Falloch. The Association issues day and season permits to the general public.

A lovely road follows the western shore, affording fine views across the loch of Ben Lomond and later of Ben More. The loch contains many islands. The largest, as well as the first to be passed in the voyage up the loch, is **Inchmurrin** (the grassy island). On **Inch Cailleach** (Nuns' Island) is an ancient graveyard. **Inch Moan** is a gull sanctuary. Between **Balmaha,** the first calling-place, and Luss, **Ben Lomond** (3,192 feet) comes more fully into view on the right shore, and **Ben Vorlich** (3,092 feet) may be seen at the northern end of the loch. **Luss** is a favourite little resort, and a good centre for anglers, as are also Balloch, Rowardennan, Tarbet, Inversnaid, Ardlui, and (within easy reach of the loch) Arrochar, at each of which they

Views of Loch Lomond

find comfortable accommodation and can have boats and boatmen. **Rowardennan** pier is the best landing-place for those who desire to climb Ben Lomond, the ascent on this side being quite gentle. It can be made in from to-and-a-half to three hours. There is an hotel at Rowardennan.

A Diversion

From **Tarbet** (*see* p. 95) a road runs through **Arrochar,** the old seat of the Macfarlane clan, pleasantly situated at the head of **Loch Long,** and thence through the wild pass of **Glen Croe** to Inveraray, on the western shore of Loch Fyne. The last mile of the old road up Glen Croe is carried in zigzag fashion to the summit (860 feet), where is a seat inscribed "*Rest and be thankful,*" an invitation to which Wordsworth alludes in one of his sonnets. A modern road eases the ascent. By turning left instead of right at "Rest and be Thankful," the motorist can make his way to beautiful **Lochgoilhead.** The main road continues past Loch Restil and then turning west descends Glen Kinglas to Cairndow on the shore of Loch Fyne. (Just before reaching Cairndow a road branches off to the left and leads down the eastern shore of Loch Fyne to Loch Eck, Kirn, Dunoon and various popular Clyde resorts in the Cowal peninsula otherwise attainable only by steamer.)

Inveraray presents an imposing appearance from across the water, but actually it consists of little more than a single street. Though small, it has most of the adjuncts of modern resorts (including a cinema and fishing), and is the centre for lovely woodland walks. (*Argyll Arms, George, McBride's, Torrsdown, Temperance.*) The town Cross is a tall Celtic burial-cross removed from Iona. Those who leave the main route at Tarbet can regain it at Dalmally by turning north, after visiting Inveraray, up delightful **Glen Aray** to the shores of Loch Awe at Cladich.

From Tarbet the Loch Lomond steamer completes its journey by crossing the loch to **Inversnaid,** an important point on the Loch Lomond-Trossachs tour (*see* above).

Just before Inversnaid is reached, its waterfall comes into view. About a mile north of the pier, and on the same side of the loch, is **Rob Roy's Cave,** near the water's edge. Both road and rail from Tarbet follow closely the lochside to **Ardlui** at the head of the loch and then on to Crianlarich.

From Crianlarich to **Oban** as described on pp. 92–94.

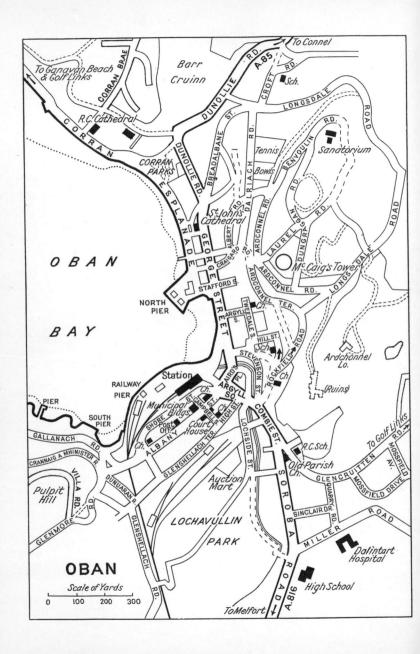

OBAN

Scale of Yards

0   100   200   300

Oban and District

Oban

Access. – From Glasgow *via* Loch Lomond, *see* p. 101: *via* Inverary. p. 103: from Perth and Killin. *see* pp. 87 94.

By Rail: From Glasgow *via* Dumbarton, Helensburgh, Ardluie, Crianlarich and Dalmally.

Distances by road. – Ballachulish, 36 miles: Edinburgh (*via* Callender and Crianlarich), 124; Fort William (*via* coast and Ballachulish Ferry) 48, (*via* Kinlochleven) 68, (*via* Dalmally, Bridge of Orchy and Glencoe) 80; Glasgow (*via* Tarbet, Arrochar and Inveraray) 100, (*via* Tarbet and Crianlarich) 93½; Loch Awe Pier, 22; Taychreggan, 20.

Early Closing. – Thursday.

Fishing. – Good sea-fishing and trout and salmon abound in neighbouring hill lochs.

Golf. – Pitch and putt course at Ganavan, adjoining Bathing Beach, 9 holes. *Glencruitten* course, half-mile from Oban Railway Station, 18 holes. Excellent club-house.

Guide Book. – See the Ward Lock *Guide to Western Scotland.*

Hotels. – *Caledonian, Kings Arms, Argyll, Great Western, Alexandra, Royal, King's Knoll, Marine, Park, Columba, Balmoral, Commercial.* Unlicensed: *Claredon, Palace, Burnbank,* and numerous others. Full list available from Information Bureau.

Population. – 7,000.

Post Office. – Albany Street.

Sports. – Bathing, boating, yachting, bowls, fishing, golf, tennis. Indoor entertainments comprise cinema, occasional concerts, etc.

Youth Hostel.

Oban occupies a natural amphitheatre facing a sheltered bay across the mouth of which is stretched the island of Kerrera. It is little more than a century old – a not unpleasing medley of large modern buildings of no particular style jostling smaller shops and houses which contrive to suggest a greater antiquity than is strictly justifiable. On the slopes behind the town are some splendidly situated residences; the skyline is broken by an imposing tower which a local banker, McCaig, financed to aid unemployed masons, and by the even less picturesque remains of an abortive hydropathic establishment. Towards the southern end of the town are the railway station and the Pier, the Post Office, and the Municipal Buildings; running northwards through the town is **George Street,** the principal business thoroughfare, and parallel to that the **Esplanade** curves round the bay and is continued past Dunollie Castle to **Ganavan,** where is Oban's bathing beach. The climate is mild, equable and healthy.

Oban is very well provided with hotels and boarding-houses of all kinds, has golf links, tennis courts, bowling and putting greens, etc., and it is a splendid centre from which to tour the Western Highlands, but its interests on the water are even greater. Standing on the Pier, one has a rare sense of being at the edge of beyond, and even those unable to indulge in any of the steamer trips can derive endless enjoyment from the contemplation of the arrival and departure of the numerous steamers which maintain communication with the islands whose shadowy forms can be discerned far to the westward.

The foundation-stone of the **Scottish Episcopal Cathedral of St. John the Divine,** in George Street, was laid in 1910. The reredos is a memorial of Bishop Chinnery-Haldane of Argyll and The Isles. The **Free High Church,** in Rockfield Road, behind Argyll Square, was designed by Augustus Pugin and won Ruskin's praise.

On the Esplanade is **St. Columba's Roman Catholic Cathedral,** a noteworthy building designed by Sir Giles Scott.

Oban Bay, being remarkably safe through the protection afforded by the island of Kerrera, is a favourite yachting station, there is a Sailing School, and instruction is available in skin diving.

It is during the Oban Highland Games Week at the end of August that the bay and the town present their busiest and gayest aspect. During this Week is held the Argyllshire Highland Gathering, an event which attracts many thousands of people. Throughout the season, however, Oban is never dull and between excursions delightful hours can be spent in all manner of enjoyment, including the admiration of glorious sunsets, feeding the swooping gulls on the esplanade, visiting a seal island, listening to the Oban Pipe Band, attending a fish auction and many other pursuits.

Excursions from Oban

1. To **Dunollie Castle,** an enjoyable walk along the Corran Esplanade. The Castle (*not open*) is about a mile north of Oban, overlooking Loch Linnhe.

Standing near the road, about a quarter of a mile from the Castle, is a huge upright mass of conglomerate, called the "Dog Stone" from a tradition that Fingal used it as a stake to which he bound his dog Bran. The principal remnant of the Castle is the donjon or keep. Dunollie, which is believed to date as far back as the twelfth century, was the principal seat of the Macdougalls, Lords of Lorne.

2. To **Dunstaffnage Castle,** less than 4 miles north-east of Oban, and $3\frac{1}{4}$ miles west of Connel station. The ruins stand on a promontory, almost an island, jutting into Loch Etive. The Castle is said to belong to the thirteenth century, but the oldest portions remaining are believed to date only from the fifteenth century. Dunstaffnage was a seat of government of the Dalriadic Scots from about 500 till the middle of the ninth century, when Scone became the capital.

3. To **Glenshellach and Gallanach,** south-west of Oban. The route passes **Lochavoullin,** a marshy piece of ground on which a lake dwelling was discovered. The return is made by the road alongside the seashore.

4. To the **Island of Kerrera.** By ferry from the southern shore beyond Kilbowie Lodge (2 miles from Oban). The Sound there is half a mile wide. The remnant of the **Castle of Gylen,** an ancient stronghold of the Macdougalls, is the principal object of interest in the island. The route to it from the ferry landing-place on the island is southward by road and path. Motor boats cruise round the island, the excursion occupying a couple of hours.

5. **Loch Awe Tours.** Loch Awe may be visited on the way to or from Glasgow by road, or may be made the object of a special excursion from Oban. Various circular tours are in operation in the season. From Ardrishaig and along the eastern or Portsonachan side of Loch Awe there is a good road.

6. **Easdale and Seil Island,** reached by a so-called "Bridge over the Atlantic"—a favourite run. Easdale (16 miles south-west of Oban) is famed for its slate quarries.

7. **Loch Nell,** a lovely loch 5 miles to the south-east, where tradition places the grave of the Ossianic hero, Cuchillin.

Oban from Pulpit Hill

OBAN TO LOCH AWE

(a) The Melfort Route

The road route leaves Oban by Combie Street and Soroba Road, with a fine view of the Pulpit Hill on the right, and after ascending to about 300 feet descends to Loch Feochan, the south shore of which is skirted to Kilninver at the entrance to Glen Gallain, which has wooded sides rising on the right to a height of 700 feet above sea-level, and on the left having an elevation of 1,110 feet. The road used to run alongside the river *Oude* and through the Pass of Melfort, one of the most picturesque bits of country in the Western Highlands, but owing to the danger of falling rocks this part of the road was closed and a new road constructed which runs over a hill above the Pass, commanding a fine view of Loch Melfort. It descends to the village of **Kilmelfort** or Kilmelford (*Cuilfail Hotel*) at the head of the loch (15 miles).

The road then skirts the side of Loch Melfort for about 4 miles, crosses the hills to the head of Loch Craignish, and enters the narrow and steep **Pass of Kintraw,** and beyond that is the **Pass of Craigenterive.** The road to Ardrishaig, by Kilmartin, is left at Carnassarie. A little way short of Ford (30 miles) is the pretty **Loch Ederline.**

Loch Awe

(Hotels in locality: *Loch Awe, Carraig-Thura, Portsonachan* (by Dalmally), *Taychreggan*). Loch Awe is one of the largest and most beautiful of the lochs of Scotland. It is 23 miles in length, with a breadth not exceeding three-quarters of a mile; maximum depth, 307 feet. It is surrounded by finely wooded mountains and is studded with islands.

The loch abounds in salmon, trout and other fresh-water fish; the sport is good, and the hotels on and near the shores provide boats and men for their guests.

The ruin of **Fincharn Castle** is a couple of miles from Ford, on the east side of the loch. **Inverliever** Estate, along the opposite shore, is a pioneer State forest. At Dalavich a new village (with a school) came into being in 1952 for workers in the Inverliever forest and that of Inverinan adjoining. About half a mile north of **Portinisherrich** is the islet of **Innis Chonnell,** on which are the ruins of the **Castle of Ardchonnell,** once the chief seat of the Campbells. Two miles farther is the stream in which is the **Blairgour Waterfall,** 90 feet in height. The loch is at its narrowest between **Taychreggan** (west bank) and **Portsonachan** (east bank).

Beyond Portsonachan the loch becomes wider, and in 2 miles we pass the **Priests' Isle.** In another 2 miles the loch attains its greatest width, and the view increases in grandeur. On the east is the beautiful peninsula, **Inistrynich,** and in the foreground is the **Island of Inishail,** the site of a nunnery containing many ancient monuments. Close to the northern shore, under the towering mass of **Ben Cruachan,** is **Innis Chonain,** with its wood-surrounded mansion and the restored Church of St. Conan. Near Loch

Awe pier, which is immediately beneath the hotel, is the ruin of **Kilchurn** (*Kil-hoorn*) **Castle.**

(b) Glen Nant and Taychreggan

The Glen is a favourite objective. It is entered *viâ* Taynuilt, which those wishing to explore Glen Nant on foot can reach by train or bus.

From **Taynuilt** the road runs up the right bank of the Nant, past **Tailor's Leap,** at the junction of a tributary and the main stream. A mile beyond, a small stream called *O'Harrigan's Burn* marks another charming spot. Where the Glen is left the road ascends **Barrachander Hill** (515 feet). About a mile short of Taychreggan, is the village of **Kilchrenan,** where is the tomb of Sir Colin Campbell of Lochawe–Cailean Mor, or Great Colin, from whom the Chief of Clan Campbell (the Duke of Argyll) takes his Gaelic name of Mac Cailean Mor.

A rough road runs 8 miles along the west shore of Loch Awe from Kilchrenan, and then 10 miles over by Loch Avich to Kilmelfort (*see* p. 108).

At Taychreggan the road comes to an end beside Loch Awe. The homeward journey is by the same road.

THE ISLAND OF MULL

Daily throughout the year, Sundays excepted, the car ferry service sails between Oban and Craignure in Mull. There are coach connections at Craignure for Tobermory and other parts of Mull.
Air service connections Glasgow–Oban–Mull.

Mull is one of the largest islands of the Hebrides. In shape it is extremely irregular, and its coast-line is so much indented that it measures quite 250 miles in circumference, while the longest walk in a bee-line across the island would be but 30 miles, and the shortest only 3.

The southern and eastern part is mountainous, the peaks varying from 1,500 to over 3,000 feet in height. The northern portion of the island is hilly, but no eminence attains an elevation of 1,500 feet.

The greatest indentation of the island is **Loch na Keal,** on the western side. It is a favourite resort of seals, and at its head is a beautiful sandy beach. Coal is found at Ardtun, on the shore of the loch, and the leaf-beds here are rich in fossils.

The columnar shores and promontories of Loch na Keal and the Sound of Ulva are clothed with ivy and with oak and ash copses. The shores of Loch na Keal, the long promontory called the Ross of Mull, and some other portions of the island, are particularly interesting to geologists.

The island abounds in lochs, most of which contain brown trout. The rivers also provide sport for anglers. The residents at some of the hotels have the right of fishing in certain waters, and the proprietors of preserved waters will occasionally give permission for a day's fishing when application is courteously made.

Those who desire to climb **Ben More** (3,169 feet) should set out from **Salen,** which commends itself to visitors by its central situation. (Postal address, Aros, to avoid confusion with Salen on Loch Sunart.) The village is connected (4 miles) by a good road, through Glen Aros, with **Loch Frisa,** providing good fishing. An easy road runs from Salen south-eastward to **Glen Forsa,** some 3 miles distant. In the woods of the glen and in the corries of the adjacent hills are many red deer.

Tobermory, "the Well of Mary," is the chief town in the island of Mull. It stands on the shore of a bay which affords safe and spacious anchorage and is protected by the small island of Calve, much in the same way as Oban Bay is by Kerrera. (Hotels: *Western Isles, Mishnish, Macdonald Arms.*)

One of the ships of the Spanish Armada was sunk in the bay in 1588 by Donald Glas MacLean who, retained as a hostage, set fire to the magazine. Some of her timbers, brass and iron guns, shot, silver plate and other relics have been recovered at various times. Diving operations are still carried on, from time to time, for the recovery of treasure and divers of the Royal Navy located a hulk in May 1950.

For a fuller account of the island *see* the *Red Guide to Western Scotland.*

Iona Cathedral

OBAN TO STAFFA AND IONA

This excursion, the most popular sea trip from Oban, includes (except on Wednesdays) the circuit of the island of Mull.

Steamer leaves about 9 a.m. and is due at Oban again about 6 p.m. On certain days the steamer goes by the Sound of Mull, and returns along the south of the island. On other days the route is reversed.

The voyages covers about 120 miles.

Crossing the Firth of Lorne, the steamer bears for **Lismore Lighthouse,** nearly opposite which is the **Lady Rock,** the scene of a legend recorded in Campbell's *Glenara*. On the nearest point of Mull is **Duart Castle,** the seat of the chief of the MacLeans, and near **Duart Point** is a lighthouse in the form of a castellated tower, of interest as it was erected to the memory of William Black (1841–98), the novelist, by his literary friends and admirers all over the world. The first place of call is Craignure. Then the steamer passes on the Morven, or mainland, side, the ancient keep of **Ardtornish,** the scene of the opening lines of Scott's *The Lord of the Isles*, and west of that touches at the mouth of **Loch Aline,** the "beautiful loch." Next comes **Salen,** in **Mull,** after which the ruin of Aroc Castle is passed and then the steamer glides into the harbour of **Tobermory,** the chief town in the island. North-west of Tobermory is Ardmore Point which the steamer veers gradually round until we are steaming due south. We pass near the **Dutchman's Cap,** one of the **Treshnish Isles,** after which we may see off the coast of Mull the closely adjacent islands of **Ulva** and **Gometra.**

Then at length we reach—

The Island of Staffa

In form it is roughly oval. Its length is 1 mile; its breadth a quarter of a mile. The southern cliffs are 135 feet in height.

The chief object of interest in the island is **Fingal's Cave,** named from the great Gaelic hero, whose achievements have been made familiar by the *Fingal* of Macpherson. It is entered by a majestic arch, domed over, and resting on basaltic pillars. It is 60 feet high by 42 broad, a width which gradually decreases to about one-half at the end of the cave, 227 feet from its entrance. The harmonies called forth by the billows inspired Mendelssohn's overture "Die Fingalshöhle." The composer visited it in 1829.

Separated from the **Causeway** by a narrow channel is **Buachaille,** or the Herdsman. It is a very regular and symmetrically conical, columnar pile, rising to the height of 30 feet, and lying on a bed of curved horizontal columns, visible only at low water.

A staircase at the end of the Causeway gives access to the top of the cliffs, from which is obtained the best view of the **Clam-Shell** or **Scallop Cave,** which cannot be entered either by boat or on foot. There are many other deep caves in the island, but they are not visited. The island is, for the greater part of the year, uninhabited. An ancient chapel has been discovered on it.

Eight miles from Staffa is—

The Island of Iona

3 miles long by 1½ wide. To it, in 563, came St. Columba, an Irish monk of kingly descent. With his twelve companions he founded a monastery and kindled the light of Christianity in the Western Islands. From Iona these missionaries of the faith carried the message in later years to the mainland of Scotland, and even to England, and the continent of Europe. Iona became the tomb of the Royal line of Scotland, and although church and monastery were repeatedly burned by the Norsemen, they had successive restorations, and in the beginning of the thirteenth century a Cathedral was founded, which fell into decay after the Reformation, when many crosses and other sculptured stones were heaved into the sea.

For a full description of Iona *see* our *Guide to Oban and Western Scotland.* Here we have space for only a few brief details.

Iona is the property of the Duke of Argyll. A guide conducts visitors to the most revered spots. These include the ruins of the **Nunnery, McLean's Cross, St. Oran's Cemetery,** "the Westminster Abbey of Scotland," reputed to be the oldest Christian burial-place in Scotland, and said to contain the graves of forty-eight Scottish, two Irish, one French, and two Norwegian kings, besides that of numerous other powerful chieftains and ecclesiastics; **St. Oran's Chapel;** and, finally and chiefly, the **Cathedral,** with **St. Martin's Cross** opposite the west door and **St. Columba's Tomb** near the west entrance.

In 1899 George, eighth Duke of Argyll, conveyed the ruinous cathedral to a public trust in connection with the Church of Scotland, and that has restored the building and fitted it for worship. Restoration work is carried on by the *Iona Community,* a fellowship of ministers and laymen who live and work together here in summer.

On the way from Iona back to Oban the chief objects of interest are the **Carsaig Arches,** on the coast of Mull (Carsaig is the *Castle Dare* of William Black's novel), and **Gylen Castle,** on Kerrera.

OBAN TO BALLACHULISH AND GLENCOE VIA APPIN

By road from Oban to Ballachulish. From Ballachulish by motor up and down the Pass of Glencoe and to and from Kinlochleven.

A round trip may be made by motor all the way from Oban, going by Benderloch and Appin, and returning by Glencoe and Dalmally—or *vice versa*.

From **Connel,** where the bridge is now converted for vehicles and pedestrians, the route is northward through the district of **Benderloch,** rich with legends of Fingal and Ossian, the king and the bard of early Gael tradition. Beyond the Castle of **Barcaldine** is **Loch Creran,** on whose low islets white sea-swallows (terns) make their nests and seals often bask. The road makes a detour round the head of the loch, by Glasdrum. A little farther northward, on an islet near Appin, stands the square restored tower of **Castle Stalker,** built by Duncan Stewart of Appin as a hunting-lodge in which to entertain James IV. In those days the Stewarts of Appin, "the gallant, devoted old Stewarts of Appin," as the Ettrick Shepherd calls them, held the whole region of "Green Appin" as far as Ballachulish, to which the way runs by the shore of Loch Linnhe.

Ballachulish (*Ballachulish, Laroch*; 39 miles by road from Oban) is a slate-built village on the Argyllshire side of Loch Leven. It was formerly busy with the export of roofing slates, large slate quarries (now closed) being in its neighbourhood. It stands in the midst of magnificent scenery, and offers facilities for boating and sea-fishing. Not far from the hotel, in the wood of **Leitir Mhor,** on the lower slopes of **Sgurr Dhonuill** (3,284 feet), took place (as told in Stevenson's *Kidnapped*) the shooting (1752) of Campbell of Glenure or the "Appin Murder," for which "James Stewart of the Glens" was convicted and executed.

From Ballachulish the road runs eastward to the little clachan of Carnach (*Hotel*), beyond which it begins to ascend—

Glencoe

which maintains its air of wild grandeur, despite the broad highway and its increasing stream of traffic.

The Glencoe road strikes off from the loch-side at Carnach, a mile or so to the east of Ballachulish. The alternative older road carries on to quickly cross the *Coe*, by Bridge of Coe, and passes a monument commemorating the "Massacre of Glencoe" (February 13, 1692). Nearby is Glencoe House, now a hospital. A mile or two up the Glen on the same side clusters of green mounds and grey stones mark the sites of the ruined townships of the clan. At the head of the wider part of the Glen rises the **Signal Rock,** which owes its name to the tradition that it was the spot from which the signal for the massacre was given. A footbridge connects it with the main road. Close above this spot stands the *Clachaig Inn,* 6 miles from Ballachulish Ferry. Beyond Clachaig the two roads join, the *new road* having thus far kept to the left bank. In front is the precipice of the **Black Rock** of Glencoe, with the lonely tarn, **Loch Achtriochtan,** at its foot. High in the face of the Black Rock—one of the "Three Sisters of Glencoe"—is a narrow but deep recess known as **Ossian's Cave,** and **Ossian's Shower Bath** may be seen in a corrie close by. A precipice high on the left has been called the **Chancellor.** At the head of the Pass is a parapet known as the **Study** (i.e. the anvil). From it the best view of the Glen can be obtained.

Beyond the summit of the Pass, a track on the left, known as the **Devil's Staircase,** climbs over to the head of Loch Leven. The path was the route taken by the two young sons of the chief of the Macdonalds in escaping from the massacre of their clan—and by two navvies in Patrick McGill's *Children of the Dead End.*

The whole upper part of Glencoe is the property of the National Trust for Scotland, the boundaries of the **National Park** so formed being—the north ridge of Glencoe (Aonach Eagach) from above Clachaig to Altnafeadh, the River Coupal to its junction with the River Etive and along the latter to Dalness, thence north-west by the ridge of Bidean nam Bian to Clachaig. The total area is about 12,000 acres. The surrounding mountains provide some of the finest rock-climbing in Scotland.

The excursion can be prolonged by road from Ballachulish to the head of **Loch Leven** (*not* the Loch Leven that held the prison of Mary Queen of Scots), which, to its farthest extremity, presents an unbroken succession of grand and romantic landscapes. Opposite the slate quarries is the **Isle of St. Munda,** the burial-place of the Macdonalds of Glencoe.

Glencoe

Kinlochleven (Kin = "head") in 1900 was merely a pair of houses; now at the head of this romantic loch there are the factories of the British Aluminium Company and a town for the workpeople. The factories produce aluminium and carbon electrodes. The power for the works is supplied by the water stored in the Blackwater Reservoir, 8 miles long, by means of a huge dam, three-quarters of a mile long, over 60 feet wide at the base, and with an average height of 80 feet.

OBAN TO FORT WILLIAM BY STEAMER

Distance: Steamer (*Summer only*) from Oban to Fort William, 38 miles.

On leaving the pier at Oban passengers see the Dog Stone and Dunollie Castle on the right, and soon there can be obtained a glimpse of Dunstaffnage Castle. On the right is Loch Nell, "the lake of swans," with Loch Nell Castle on the western side. On the left is the long island of **Lismore,** for a time the seat of a bishopric. (The *Book of the Dean of Lismore* is a valuable sixteenth-century collection of Gaelic and English verse.) The narrow channel between the island and the mainland is called the **Lynn of Lorne.** Before the steamer gets through it passes, on the right, the narrow entrance to **Loch Creran,** and then **Airds Bay,** with a fine natural arch at the western extremity. Shortly afterwards the steamer sails past the tiny village of **Appin** and then enters the main channel of **Loch Linnhe.** On a rocky islet stands the ancient bulk of **Castle Stalker.** At the southern extremity of the island of **Shuna** is another castle. From the north of Shuna we catch the first glimpse of Ben Nevis. Forty minutes after leaving Appin the vessel passes, on the right, **Ardsheal House,** frequently the residence of young Walter Scott.

Then comes the mouth of **Loch Leven,** with Ballachulish on the southern shore, and on the northern side **Onich** (*Hotels: Craigdhu, Onich*). Onich Manse was the residence of the Rev. Alex. Stewart, LL.D., the enthusiastic and literary Celt known by his *nom de plume* "Nether Lochaber." From Onich the route is through the **Corran Narrows** and past **Ardgour** (Corran), where are a hotel and a ferry, which carries cars.

A quarter of an hour later we pass, on the left, **Inverscaddle Bay,** on the shore of which is **Conaglen House,** the seat of the Earl of Morton. Ben Nevis, which has been lost to sight, appears again on the right, and straight in front is the Great Glen, through which runs the Caledonian Canal. A few minutes later the pier at **Fort William** is reached.

113

The Great Glen

FORT WILLIAM TO INVERNESS

Motoring.–A fine modern road (A82) runs through the Glen all the way from Fort William to Inverness (66½ miles).

There is a regular bus service between Fort William and Inverness (time 2¾ hours) *viâ* Spean Bridge (where is connection with trains from and to the South) and Fort Augustus all the year round.

The **Great Glen** is a deep natural depression extending north-eastwards across Scotland from Fort William to Inverness; from Loch Linnhe to the Moray Firth. The Glen provides the route of the **Caledonian Canal.** The total length of the passage from Corpach to Muirtown, the northern terminus, is 60½ miles, of which only 22 or 23 miles are Canal, the remainder consisting of the lochs which the Canal connects. The Canal is 50 feet broad at the bottom, and 110 feet at the top, and can take vessels with draught not exceeding 14 feet. The natural portions of the waterway are Loch Lochy (10 miles), Loch Oich (4 miles), and Loch Ness (24 miles). There are altogether twenty-eight locks in this singular waterway. The Canal was begun by Telford in 1804. Buses have superseded the passenger service by steamer and likewise the railway to Fort Augustus.

As the road leaves Fort William there is a good view of the western end of the tunnel 15 miles long and 15 feet in diameter, bringing water from Loch Treig for the production of electricity. It is hardly picturesque, but demands some respect as a monument to modern engineering skill and resource.

Then, on the banks of the *Lochy*, stands old **Inverlochy Castle,** and beyond it the famous Nevis Distillery and the modern Inverlochy Castle. Nine miles from Fort William is **Spean Bridge.** On a hillock at Spean Bridge is the fine **Commando Memorial** (by Scott Sutherland). It was unveiled by Queen Elizabeth the Queen Mother in 1952 and commemorates the commandos who trained at Achnacarry.

The road to the right is that by Roy Bridge and Tulloch to **Kingussie** and **Strathspey** (*see* pp. 33–34).

Roy Bridge is the starting-point for the excursion up **Glen Roy,** of the highest interest to geologists and to all with an interest in the evolution of scenery.

114

The **Parallel Roads** are shelves or terraces formed by the waters of a lake that once filled the intervening glen. They begin about 2 miles north of the hotel, and extend to Brae Roy shooting-lodge (10 miles), to which there is a road. An excellent view of them is obtained from a point about midway. The highest "road" is, of course, the oldest, and those below it were formed in succession as the waters of the lake decreased in depth. The lake not only filled Glen Roy, but also some of the valleys adjoining it on the west. The water was held by a glacier in the glen and in the valley of the Caledonian Canal. The latter was apparently filled to the brim with ice, which blocked the mouths of Glens Roy and Spean.

From *Turret Bridge*, 10 miles up Glen Roy, strong walkers have three routes: (1) Cross the ridge westward to the head of Glen Gloy, the foot of which is at Glenfintaig, on the Spean Bridge–Fort Augustus road: (2) follow the track to the *col* at the head of Glen Roy (14 miles from Roy Bridge) and 4 miles farther join the *Corrieyairack route* (p. 116) at Melgarve, thence either eastward to Laggan Bridge or (3) north-westward to Fort Augustus.

At Spean Bridge the Inverness road swings to the left and climbs to a moorland from which there are magnificent views of Ben Nevis (4,406 feet). Then it runs down through woods and for many miles keeps along the shore of **Loch Lochy.** Across the loch are Glengarry deer forest and **Ben Tee** (2,957 feet), and near the south-western end is the opening of **Loch Arkaig** (*see* p. 98). At the northern end of the loch a short length of Canal connects it with Loch Oich. Here are the Laggan Locks, and here the road crosses from east bank to west. A Youth Hostel lies between the two lochs.

Loch Oich is a beautiful loch forming the summit level of the Canal. Steep mountains fringe it on the south, and pretty islets dot its bosom. Near the south end of the loch is a strange monument, overlooking a spring called Tobar nan Ceann—the **Well of the Heads.** It was erected as a memorial of the vengeance inflicted on the murderers of some members of the family of Macdonald of Keppoch. The heads of the seven murderers were presented to the chief of the clan after having been washed in this spring.

Invergarry stands in the middle of the west side of the loch, amidst lovely scenery. On a rocky headland are the ruins of a Castle long the home of the MacDonells of Glengarry. Prince Charles spent part of the night of August 26, 1745, within its walls, and also took shelter in it the first night after the battle of Culloden. A little to the right is *Glengarry Castle Hotel*, erected in 1869. In the village is a good hotel (*Invergarry*) and the *Garry*, which there flows into the loch, is one of the earliest salmon rivers in Scotland.

Invergarry to the West Coast.—This road is through scenery of great grandeur and beauty. The first portion is through woods and for about 2 miles along the north side of **Loch Garry** (*Tomdoun Hotel* is at the far west end of the loch). The road then strikes north over by the foot of Loch Loyne to meet the Glen Moriston road below the east-end of Loch Cluanic. Thence the road is westward through **Glen Shiel** to **Shiel Bridge,** at **Loch Duich,** and on to Dornie and Kyle of Lochalsh. Hydro-electric schemes at Glen Garry and Glen Moriston, with a drainage area of 300 square miles, have involved considerable damming and road reconstruction in the district.

From *Tomdoun Inn*, the westward road follows the course of the Garry to **Loch Quoich** and the head of **Loch Hourn,** a distance of 17 miles. This area has been the scene of great hydro-electric development. At the eastern end of Loch Quoich is the largest rockfill dam in Great Britain, being 1,000 feet in length and 120 feet high.

A stretch of the Canal 5 miles in length connects Loch Oich with Loch Ness, at the southern end of which is—

Fort Augustus

Access.—Buses to and from Inverness and to and from Spean Bridge station in connection with the trains.

Hotels.—*Lovat Arms, Inchnacardoch, Caledonian, White Gates.*

The Fort built here between the Jacobite rebellions of 1715 and 1745 was called after the Duke of Cumberland. Its remains now form part of the charmingly situated Benedictine Abbey, so created in 1882. A conspicuous feature of the village, which provides visitors with boating, fishing, golf (9-hole course) and attractive walks, is a series of locks leading the Caledonian Canal from Loch Ness.

A Wade road from Fort Augustus over the **Corrieyairack Pass** (2,507 feet) to the upper Spey was used by Prince Charlie's army in 1745. By the nineteenth century it had degenerated into a very rough track for hardy walkers only—25 miles to Laggan (*see* p. 34) with no inns or shelter but with glorious views and, for company, hydro-electric pylons striding alongside.

Loch Ness. The second largest freshwater loch in Scotland, Loch Ness is 22½ miles long, from a mile to a mile and a half wide, and 754 feet at its deepest. Devoid of islands and never freezing, the loch is famed for an elusory, if not illusory "Monster."

Along each side an excellent road runs north-east for Inverness. That on the eastern side (A862) is hillier, but it compensates by more extensive views. From Fort Augustus it climbs abruptly up past romantic **Glen Doe** and **Loch Tarff** (3 miles) to nearly 1,300 feet before descending to **White-bridge** (9 miles), whose hotel offers anglers a choice of lochs. The main road continues by Loch Mhor, but an alternative road (B852) runs down to **Foyers** (*hotel*)—aluminium works have robbed the Falls here of some of their former appeal—and keeps along Loch Ness by **Inverfarigaig** to join A862 at Dores (8 miles from Inverness) near the foot of the loch. (Fort Augustus–Inverness by A862, 34 miles. Bus service from Inverness to Foyers and to Whitebridge.)

The usual road (A82) to Inverness—the bus route—hugs the western shore of Loch Ness. At **Invermoriston** (6 miles from Fort Augustus) the road to Kyle of Lochalsh branches off westward. At **Alltsaigh,** 3 miles beyond Invermoriston, is a much-frequented Youth Hostel, commanded by the dome-shaped **Mealfuarvonie** (2,284 feet).

At the mouth of the rich Highland vale of **Glen Urquhart,** on the western shore of Loch Ness, are the picturesque ruins of **Urquhart Castle,** originally built in the twelfth century. The first castle was besieged by Edward I, in 1303, and in its place he erected this formidable-looking fortress. It peers down on the loch, which is here 750 feet deep (*Admission charge*).

The road here makes a loop round the mouth of the Enrick, passing through Lewiston (*hotel*) and Drumnadrochit (*hotel*), amid charming scenery. Drumnadrochit is 19 miles from Fort Augustus, 15 from Inverness. (Bus service to Glen Urquhart from Inverness.)

A good road runs up Glen Urquhart, passing Loch Meiklie, a mile long, to **Invercannich,** in Strathglass (about 14 miles), whence one may go northward to Beauly; and a pretty road goes northward from Milton and through to Beauly. Some 2 miles south-west from Drumnadrochit are the **Falls of Divach,** higher than Foyers.

From the northern end of Loch Ness near wood-screened **Dochfour,** emerge the River Ness and the Caledonian Canal which makes its way between the road and the river to the outskirts of Inverness, to join the Beauly Firth at Clachnaharry.

Invermoriston to Glenelg and Kyle of Lochalsh (60 miles). The road has been much improved in connection with the Glen Moriston hydro-electric scheme with the result that there is a good surface for the 25-mile stretch to Cluanie (*inn*), a popular headquarters of hikers, etc. Hence the way is down through **Glen Shiel** to **Shiel Bridge,** at the head of Loch Duich (*hotel*). Here the main road swings to the right: that continuing straight ahead proceeds to climb the **Mam Ratagain Pass,** which by a series of sharp elbows with a general gradient of 1 in 7 carries one in 3 miles to 1,116 feet above sea-level. The road is safe, but an awkward place for cars towing large or heavy caravans. The views are glorious. It then runs westward to **Glenelg** (*Barn Hill*) beyond which it is narrow and hilly, leading in about 10 miles to Arnisdale, on Loch Hourn.

The **Kintail Estate,** at the head of Loch Duich, is National Trust property and includes Ben Attow and the "Five Sisters."

From Shiel Bridge the main road rounds the head of Loch Duich and then, after a steep climb at Keppoch, descends to Dornie, with good views of **Eilean Donan Castle,** once a ruin, but now restored. At **Dornie** (*hotel*) a bridge (free of toll) has been built to carry traffic over Loch Long to **Ardelve,** superseding the ferry.

Three miles west of Ardelve (*Loch Duich Hotel*) the road from **Strome** comes in on the right, and then we reach **Kyle of Lochalsh,** a small town, with hotels (*Lochalsh, Kyle*), banks and shops and glorious views across to Skye. It is the terminus of the railway line from Inverness and the South and MacBrayne steamers connect it with Armadale and Portree in Skye, with Stornoway and the Outer Hebrides, and with Mallaig. It is of principal importance as the starting-point of the ferry across to Kyleakin, but is also a splendid centre for fishing and for sea trips.

Eilean Donan Castle, Loch Duich

Inverness to Northernmost Scotland

From Inverness the road and the Highland line of the railway run due west for 10 miles through pretty country on the shores of the Beauly Firth to Beauly, crossing the Caledonian Canal a mile from the city. **Clachnaharry** (the "watch stone") is the site of a memorable clan battle (1454), recorded on an adjacent monument, between the Munros and the Mackintoshes. Near Clunes are **Moniack Castle and Glem,** and **Kirkhill,** in which is shown the grave of Simon Fraser, Lord Lovat.

Beauly (*see* p. 50) is the starting-point for grand excursions. Running from it in a south-westerly direction is the beautiful **Strathglass,** off which branch the magnificent glens, **Glen Farrar, Glen Cannich** and **Glen Affric.**

Three miles north of Beauly is **Muir of Ord,** a small village beside the stance of an old cattle fair, now a golf course. (Hotels: *Tarradale, Ord Arms.*)

Half a mile before the village a road runs off to the right into—

The Black Isle

The **Black Isle,** or *Eilan Dhu,* is neither black nor an island, but the pleasantly pastoral peninsula between the Beauly and Cromarty Firths. Just over a mile north of Redcastle is **Kilcoy Castle** (restored in 1890), and to the south, on the shore of the Beauly Firth, is **Redcastle** (3¾ miles from Muir of Ord), a good specimen of mediaeval architecture. It is said to have been built by William the Lion in 1179. **Munlochy** is a charming village on Munlochy Bay, which is guarded on the north by **Ormond Hill,** a reputed stronghold of Macbeth, and on the south by the haunted crags and cave of **Craigiehowe.** Then comes the village and fishing harbour of **Avoch** (pronounce *awch*).

Fortrose (*Royal Station, Oakfield* (unl.)) was once a famous seat of learning and cathedral town of the Bishopric of Ross. Only a fragment remains of the Cathedral—the south transept, containing the tomb of "Rory Mor" and other Mackenzie chiefs, and the chapter house, the upper storey of which is used as the council chamber of the combined burgh of Fortrose and Rosemarkie. The Cathedral, founded on a Pictish monastery, dates from the first half of the thirteenth century and was not completed until 1485. Its destruction is attributed to Cromwell, who utilized its stones in the construction of a fort at Inverness.

Rosemarkie, half a mile distant, is much frequented for sea-bathing. In the parish church-yard is a stone with fine Pictish sculpture. There is an 18-hole golf course on Chanonry Point, at the end of which is a lighthouse.

Cromarty (*Royal*), at the eastern extremity of the Black Isle, is a small town picturesquely situated on a promontory. The entrance to the Cromarty Firth lies between two headlands called the Sutors. Cromarty was the first home of Hugh Miller (1802–56); a monument to him overlooks the little burgh; his birthplace, a thatched cottage, has been converted into a

Hugh Miller Museum. His first geological researches were made in the Ethie burn and the rocks facing the Outer Firth. Sir Thomas Urquhart, translator (1653) of Rabelais, also came from Cromarty.

The Black Isle can be reached by bus from Inverness or Dingwall, and more directly by *Kessock Ferry,* at the entrance to the Beauly Firth.

For a fuller description of the Black Isle see the Guide to Inverness in this series.

The direct road from Inverness to the west coast *viâ* Achnasheen (*see* p. 129) strikes north-west from Muir of Ord, avoiding Dingwall, to which the main railway line proceeds due north. From Muir of Ord this road–which is also the shortest route to Strathpeffer–runs by Ord distillery, Urray Kirk, Marybank (cross-roads), and Moy Bridge (over the Conon), to Contin, where the main west-bound road from Dingwall and Strathpeffer is joined.

For Dingwall and the North both railway and road cut across the neck of the Black Isle to **Cononbridge,** where the **Cromarty Firth** comes into view, and then on to Dingwall, 18 miles from Inverness. Prominent in the view is a tower erected as a *Memorial of General Sir Hector Macdonald,* distinguished by his services in the Sudan and South Africa. **Dingwall,** an ancient burgh dating from 1226, is the county town of Ross-shire, and has a population of just over 3,800. Through its Academy it is an educational centre for the north and west (Hotels: *National, Royal, Lisliard*). It has an old town hall and cross, tennis courts, bowling green, boating pond, large sheep and cattle markets and is the focal point of a wide agricultural county. It is an excellent centre, but to tourists it is chiefly important as the junction of road and rail routes to the west and north coasts.

Strathpeffer

Angling.–The *Conon* and its tributary, the *Blackwater,* are excellent salmon-streams. Several of the hotels have fishings.

Bowls in Pavilion grounds; **tennis** at Highland Hotel.

Distances.–Inverness, 23 miles; Oban, 122; Aberdeen, 131; Edinburgh, 215; London, 610.

Early Closing.–Thursdays in winter. In season some shops remain open between 8–10 p.m.

Golf.–There is a course of 18 holes on high ground within ten minutes' walk of the town square.

Hotels.–*Ben Wyvis, Holly Lodge, Highland, Strathpeffer.* Unlicensed: *Ravenscroft, Rosslyn lodge.*

Strathpeffer is quite a small town–or a large village–which made its name as a spa in the latter part of last century. Now "the Strath" is chiefly known as a centre for tours in Northern Scotland. A glance at the map will show how conveniently placed it is for runs into the West, and it is equally handy for Dingwall and the roads to John o' Groats or southward to Inverness.

Strathpeffer is an open-air resort. But during the season popular dances and concerts are arranged in the Pavilion.

Excursions from Strathpeffer

1. **Knockfarrel** (720 feet) and the **Cat's Back** (882 feet). The shortest ascent of Knockfarrel is by a pathway from the Ben Wyvis Hotel. On the summit is one of the best preserved vitrified forts in the country. The Cat's Back is the western end of the same ridge. To the summits and back is about 4 miles. In the valley behind them are the wood-fringed shores of **Loch Ussie.**

NORTHERN HIGHLANDS

WARD, LOCK LIMITED, LONDON

© John Bartholomew & Son Ltd, Edinburgh

0 4 8 12 16 20 24 Miles

C. Wrath

Sandwood L.

Oldshore More
Kinlochber
Loch Inchard
Bade
Loch Laxford
R
Lax
Scourie
ddrachillisch.
Eddrachillis
Bay
Pt. of Stoer
Oldany
Drumbeg
Clashnessie
Stoer Ch.
Achfarr
Kylestr
Bearr
Culkeir
Unapool
813
Lochinver
2779
Inverkirkaig
Canisp
Suilven
542
Rubha Coigeach
Enard
Bay
Knockan
12
Cul Beag
Summer I.s
Achiltibuie
Strathkanair
Ardmair
Loch Broom
Ullapool
Greenstone Pt.
Gruinard Bay
Lit.Loch Broom
Ardchar
Rubha Réidh
Laide
Gruinard
Ho.
Dundonnell
Inverla
Melvaig
Loch
Ewe
Aultbea
Tuirnaig
L.Sheallag
6
falls
Braen
Poolewe
Fionn Loch
1110
Glasca
Gairloch
Hotel
ROSS A
L.Fannie
Red Pt.
Res.
Hotel
L.Fada
Shiant I.s
10
Ben Fionn
3060
Achnase
Scalpay
Kinlochewe
L.Torridon
10
815
Achnas
Rubha Hunish
Duntulm
Kilmaluig
Torridon
L.Rosque
Scardroy
Quiraing
Staffin
Shieldaig
Strath
Kilvaxter
Inn
833
32
Damh
Craig
Achnashellach
Uig
Craig
Vig
Coulags
L.Monar
Loch
Snizort
Hinnisdal Br.
Applecross
L.Carron
Strathcarron
Stein
fairy Br.
Bernisdale
Kensaleyre
Res.
Joscaig
L.chearron
Hotel
Edinbain
Carbost
Attadale
Dunvegan
Roag
Gearymore
Plockton
Crowlin I.s
Stromeferry
L.Mullardoch
Glen
PORTREE
L.Long
Gl.Elchaig
Glen
Bracadale
Coillore
Raasay
Kyle
Lochalsh
Balmacara
Mam Soul
3862
Lodge
Struanmore
SKYE
497
Crossal
Scalpay
Dornie
Affric
L.Bracadale
Carbost
Inverinate
Morvich
Glen
A
Talisker
Sconser
Lui
Balmacara
Kyleakin
Kylerhea
Shiel Bri.
Ben Attow
3383
Sligachan
Broadford
Kylerhea
Glenelg
L.Eynort
Cuillin
Hills
Coruisk
Glen
Glenbrittle

2. **Raven Rock** (874 feet), a good viewpoint about 2 miles north-west, and best reached by walking along the railway from Achterneed.

3. **View Rock** (500 feet) is picturesquely situated 2 miles from Strathpeffer *viâ* **Loch Kinellan.** (From it Loch Achilty and the Falls of Rogie can be conveniently visited.)

4. **Falls of Rogie,** 3 or 4 miles west, on the Ross-shire Blackwater. They are seen to most advantage from a chain bridge which spans the river below them.

5. **Loch Garve.**—About 4 miles beyond the Rogie Falls. The road lies through mountainous and romantic scenery.

6. **Loch Achilty** (5 miles) is a beautiful sheet of water surrounded by birch- and fir-clad hills, including the wooded pyramid of **Tor Achilty.** West of the new power station is **Loch Achonachie** in which there is salmon and trout fishing.

7. **Circular Tour by Brahan and Dingwall** (16 miles).—This excursion lies through varied and beautiful scenery. The road is by Contin (or Kinnahaird) to within a short distance of Moy Bridge. Instead of crossing the bridge it keeps straight on and passes up a hill-road from which there are wide views of the colourful countryside and of **Brahan Castle,** the former stronghold of the Earls of Seaforth, Chiefs of Clan Mackenzie.

8. **Ascent of Ben Wyvis** (3,429 feet).—The summit is about 10 miles from Strathpeffer, and the ascent is easy.

From Dingwall the route to the North skirts Cromarty Firth. From Evanton village the **Black Rock**—a fine gorge—can be visited, and there is a track up beside the Glass river to Loch Glass. Crowning Knock Fyrish is a representation of the Gates of Negapatam—erected (to give employment in bad times) by Sir Hector Munro of Foulis (1726–1805), who won distinction as a General (and a fortune) in India.

About 2 miles beyond Evanton a good, though hilly, road, A836 (bypassing Alness, Invergordon and Tain, saving 13 miles), branches off to the left and strikes almost due north across the hills, past lonely *Aultnamain Inn,* and the Struie hill, to the Dornoch Firth at Wester Fearn. This road reaches a height of 782 feet above sea-level and commands magnificent views, particularly towards the northern mountains. The main road, A9, continues by **Alness** to **Invergordon** (Hotels, *Royal, Marine, Rhua* (unl.)), a large town on either side of a wide main street. There is a swimming-pool, golf links and facilities for tennis, bowls and boating.

On by **Saltburn** – a waterside village in marked contrast to its great Yorkshire namesake–and by the shore of Nigg Bay. In Nigg churchyard is a fine Celtic sculptured stone. At **Shandwick,** 2 miles to the north, is another Celtic stone.

At Barbaraville the road turns inland and crosses the promontory to **Tain,** an ancient and thriving town on the southern shore of the Dornoch Firth. (Hotels: *Royal, St. Duthus, Balnagown, Mansfield House.*) Tain has a particularly good golf course of 18 holes. The turf is excellent and the situation ideal.

A massive tower forms the entrance to the Court House and County Buildings, but the architectural treasure of Tain is the restored ruin of **St. Duthus' Chapel.** The saint, often known as St. Duthac, is said to have been born on the site of the building. He became known as "the godly Bishop of Ross," and was reburied within the precincts of the chapel in 1253. The church, as now restored, was built in 1487. The Papal Bull authorizing its erection is in the archives of the burgh. The pulpit was presented by Regent Moray in recognition of the zeal of the inhabitants for the Reformation.

Four miles south-east, not far from Fearn station, are the remains of the **Abbey of Fearn,** a portion of which is still used as the parish church. Ten miles east of Tain, not far from Tarbat Ness Lighthouse, is Portmahomack, a fishing village.

There is no way across the Dornoch Firth and one needs must go westward to Ardgay and Bonar Bridge (some 12 miles) in order to cross the Firth.

Like the main road, the railway runs up the Dornoch Firth from Tain to Ardgay and Bonar Bridge station, whence the line continues northward and inland by Culrain, past **Carbisdale Castle** (a palatial Youth Hostel) into Sutherland at Invershin (*hotel*) and Lairg, returning by Strath Fleet to the coast at Golspie.

At **Bonar Bridge** (*Dunroamin, Bridge, Caledonian Hotels*), an excellent centre with fishing, the main highway (A9) turns eastward in the direction of Dornoch, passing **Skibo Castle,** once owned by Andrew Carnegie.

Main route resumed on p. 124.

BONAR BRIDGE TO LOCHINVER

The first few miles are along the northern shore of the Kyle of Sutherland. At **Inveran** ($4\frac{1}{2}$ miles) cross the River Shin and strike up Strath Oykell to **Oykell Bridge** (*hotel*: 18 miles), where are some fine falls. Hence the road continues to climb, past Loch Craggie, reaching its highest point about 2 miles farther. It now descends through increasingly grand scenery to **Loch Borralan** (*Altnacealgach Hotel*), beyond which the road from Ullapool comes in on the left. (*Hence* as on pp. 129–131).

Five miles north of Inveran and 11 miles from Bonar Bridge is **Lairg** (*Sutherland Arms*), an important link between the railway and the road services. It stands at the southern end of **Loch Shin,** a fine sheet of water, $17\frac{1}{4}$ miles long, containing trout. The loch can be fished by visitors at the hotels at Lairg and **Overscaig** (at the far end of the loch), or by permit from Lairg Angling Club.

Road Routes from Lairg

1. **Lairg to Tongue** (37 miles). – The route is up Strath Tirry, over the **Crask** (870 feet) to the foot of **Ben Klibreck** (3,154 feet), and winds round the western side of that hill to the *Altnaharra Hotel*, at the upper end of **Loch Naver**, a sheet of water 7 miles long. The loch contains salmon, sea and brown trout. It can be fished by guests at the *Altnaharra Hotel*. Half a mile north of the hotel a road leads along the north side of Loch Naver and then down Strath Naver to Bettyhill. The Tongue road strikes north and after rising to about 750 feet makes for the southern end of **Loch Loyal.** The loch is about 5 miles long, and is surrounded by high hills. One of these, **Ben Loyal** (2,504 feet), has a curiously splintered summit. The loch contains splendid trout and may be fished (on permit) by residents at the Tongue Hotel, as can also the neighbouring Loch Craggie and other lochs. The road skirts the western shore of Loch Loyal and then runs due north to the village of **Tongue** (*hotel*), on the east side of the **Kyle of Tongue,** and in the neighbourhood of much mountain scenery of a grandly picturesque character. Near the village are the ruins of **Castle Varrich,** an old feudal keep. The *Borgie Lodge Hotel* between Tongue and Bettyhill offers exclusive fishing (on five lochs), and shooting.

From Tongue there is a good road eastward (50 miles) to Thurso, by **Bettyhill** and **Melvich,** at both of which places there are hotels.

A road runs westward from Tongue to **Durness** (about 37 miles: *see* p. 124) skirting the deep sea-loch Eriboll.

2. **Lairg to Scourie** (44 miles). – The first portion of the road is along the northern side of **Loch Shin.** Then the road skirts **Lochs Griam** and **Merkland,** both of which can be fished by

guests at the Overscaig Hotel, 16 miles from Lairg. Beyond Loch Merkland is **Reay Deer Forest,** of which **Ben Hee** (2,864 feet) is the highest point. Then comes **Loch More,** at the far end of which, 31 miles from Lairg, is **Achfary.** Soon afterwards the road reaches **Loch Stack,** under the cone of **Ben Stack** (2,364 feet), and the river *Laxford* that flows from it. The loch is one of the most famous in Scotland for its fish, and it is now open to the public. The Laxford, a fine salmon river, is strictly preserved. At 37 miles from Lairg is **Laxford Bridge.** From it a road runs northward to **Durness** and one south-west for 7 miles to **Scourie,** a straggling village on the coast, with a good and comfortable hotel, visitors at which may fish on several lochs.

At the end of 5 miles from Laxford Bridge the road to Durness reaches *Rhiconich.* Six miles to the west lies *Kinlochbervie,* a thriving fishing port. Scourie, Kinlochbervie and Durness are connected with Lairg by bus services. Two miles short of Durness, on the left, is *Cape Wrath Hotel.* Those wishing to proceed along the road to **Cape Wrath** must first make arrangements for crossing the Kyle of Durness, there being no regular ferry service. **Durness** is the most north-westerly parish on the British mainland. There are fine sands and either in or near the village are good hotels (*Cape Wrath, Smoo Cave: Parkhill* unl.); *Morvada* (guest), *Seaview* (guest). One mile east is *Smoo Cave,* which goes 150 feet into the limestone rock. Close to **Balnakiel** (1½ miles) are some ancient stones and the ruins of a church.

3. **Lairg to Lochinver** (47 miles). – From Lairg to **Rosehall** (11 miles), thence by the side of the *Oykell* to **Oykell Bridge** and hotel (16 miles), and thence over the watershed of Sutherland, with mountain peaks pricking the skyline in all directions, and numerous lochs within easy reach, all containing trout, to *Altnacealgach Hotel* (26 miles), a good resting-place, close to **Loch Borralan.** Hotel guests can fish Loch Borralan and the *Ledbeg* river, and also numerous nearby lochs and trouting streams. *Inchnadamph Hotel* (35 miles) is a favourite centre with anglers and geologists. From Skiag Bridge (37½ miles) a popular tourist road goes north by free car-ferry to Scourie.

Lochinver is described on p. 130.

Main route resumed (from p. 123).

BONAR BRIDGE TO JOHN O' GROATS

Having crossed the Dornoch Firth at Bonar Bridge, the road now runs seaward again along its northern side to **Dornoch,** a few miles short of which Skibo Castle is passed on the right. Dornoch, created a Royal Burgh by Charles I in 1628, is the capital of Sutherland and almost the smallest county town in Scotland (population nearly 1,000). It has a Cathedral, erected in the first half of the thirteenth century; its ancient castle used as a bishop's palace is now an hotel; good hotels (*Dornoch, Dornoch Castle, Royal Golf, Burghfield House*) and boarding-houses; miles of links with two golf courses (18 and 9 holes); and good sea-bathing. Salmon and trout fishing can be had in the county. But it is as a "Golfers' Paradise" that Dornoch most strongly appeals. Golf at Dornoch dates back to 1616, and the Dornoch golf links are the third earliest mentioned in history. Visitors are welcome. Close to the beach is a good caravan and camping site.

North of Dornoch lies **Loch Fleet,** almost landlocked, and the main road crosses its head by an embankment known locally as the *Mound.* Hence to the left a road goes up Strath Fleet to **Lairg** (p. 123); but the main route swings eastward once more.

A colossal statue of the Duke of Sutherland, erected by the Sutherland tenantry, comes into sight on the left. **Golspie** (84¼ miles from Inverness, 70 by using A836) is a pleasant village with an 18-hole golf course, and an

Dunrobin Castle

excellent beach for sea-bathing. Visitors at the *Sutherland Arms Hotel* may fish Loch Brora, which contains trout averaging one pound. Also available is the fishing in Lochs Lundie and Horn. At a short distance are two of the best-preserved *brochs* or Pictish towers in the Highlands. Golspie is a mile and a half from **Dunrobin Castle,** where the Countess of Sutherland has established a school. Admission to the grounds is readily granted, but the house can be seen only by special order.

Beyond Golspie comes **Brora** (*Links, Royal Marine, Grand, Sutherland Arms*), situated on a beautiful bay, stretching for miles, and perfect for bathing or boating. The river *Brora,* containing brown and sea trout, is free for fully half a mile from its mouth, and visitors at the two latter hotels may fish **Loch Brora,** 4 miles distant. The golf course extends along the seashore for more than 3 miles.

Just under 100 miles from Inverness is **Helmsdale** (*Bridge, Belgrave, Navidale*), a white-fishing centre. Overlooking the harbour are the ruins of a castle, formerly a hunting seat of the Sutherland family.

From Helmsdale the main road, which is now in first-class condition, follows the coast and immediately after leaving Helmsdale climbs steeply up to a maximum height of 747 feet in order to surmount the **Ord of Caithness,** the beginning of a long chain of mountains running north-westward. The sea-views from the road as it climbs are extremely fine and maintain their interest for many miles. The road then descends steeply into

125

the picturesque village of **Berriedale,** just before reaching which there is a very fine view to the left up the **Langwell Glen** to the conical mountain of **Morven** (2,313 feet), with **Scaraben** (2,054 feet) to the right. (For permission to climb these two hills apply at the Factor's Office at Berriedale.)

Beyond Berriedale the road climbs up very steeply with hairpin bends and then follows the coast through not very interesting country past **Dunbeath** (*hotel*), **Latheron** (*hotel*), and **Lybster** (*hotel*) to Wick, 37 miles from Helmsdale.

The railway and a good road turn north-westward from Helmsdale through Strath Ullie, a bare valley, having little to interest the traveller after the first few miles. Near **Forsinard** is an hotel, visitors at which may fish several neighbouring lochs. The road reaches the north coast at **Melvich** (p. 128). The railway, from Forsinard, turns off north-eastward across moorland for **Halkirk** (*Ulbster Arms Hotel*) and **Georgemas Junction,** whence a branch goes north to Thurso, while the main line runs south-east to its terminus at Wick (161 tortuous miles from Inverness).

Wick

Airport.—The most northerly on the mainland. Flying times: Inverness, 25 minutes; Orkney, 12 minutes.	**Early Closing.**—Wednesday.
	Golf.—18-hole course at Reiss Links, 3 miles distant.
Angling.—May be arranged for in the river *Wick* and neighbouring burns and lochs.	**Hotels.**—*Station, Mackay's, Nethercliffe, Queen's, Rosebank.*
	Population.—About 7,500.

Wick is the county town of Caithness. It was at one time a busy herring fishing station, but this has now given way to a thriving business with white fish which are iced at a factory here, boxed and sent to the South.

In the neighbourhood are several interesting ruins, including Castles Sinclair and Girnigoe, and an ancient tower called the **Old Man of Wick,** on the edge of the cliffs a mile to the south of Wick Bay. There are also some of the finest specimens of brochs in the North, several of which, at **Keiss,** have been opened up. Near the Old Man of Wick is magnificent rock scenery, especially at the spot called the Brig o' Tram.

From Wick to John o' Groats the road, about 16½ miles, for the most part runs along the coast. There is a daily bus service. Objects of interest *en route* are the modern **Keiss Castle** and the ruined ancient castle; **Bucholie Castle,** once a stronghold of Swayne the Pirate; **Freswick Castle;** a magnificent panorama from **Warth Hill** (412 feet).

John o' Groats (*hotels*) is not, as is popularly supposed, the most northerly point of the mainland; for that it is necessary to go to Dunnet Head, nearer Thurso. John o' Groats is, however, 876 miles from Land's End in the very far south-west, and even the facility of modern motoring cannot banish altogether some feeling of achievement on the part of those who have come thus far. There are grand views across to **Stroma** island and to Ronaldsay and Hoy in the Orkneys. The beach is thickly strewn with shells, particularly with a kind of cowry, known as Groatie buckies.

According to tradition, John de Groot was one of several Dutch brothers who settled in Caithness in James IV's reign, and prospered until fratricidal strife threatened over the question of precedence at the annual family banquet. The wily John averted the danger by designing a house with eight walls, eight windows and eight doors, and a table with eight sides, so that each of the eight claimants could enter by his own door and assert that his was the seat of honour – like the Highland chieftain who haughtily declared "Wherever the Pherson sits, that's the head of the table!" A room in John o'Groats Hotel commemorates this legend. Another explanation of the name is that the ferryman to Orkney, proving extortionate in olden days, the magistrates fixed his fee at one *groat* (fourpence); hence he became known as Johnny Groat or John o' Groats.

A mile and a half east of John o' Groats is **Duncansby Head** (210 feet), the most beautiful headland in the North of Scotland. About a mile south of the Head are two immense pillars of rock, called the **Stacks of Duncansby.**

Castle of Mey

ALONG THE NORTH COAST

The roads are easy and comfortable for motorists and cyclists to reach a number of places with great potentialities as holiday resorts. None of them is large – few are more than hamlets – but for cliffs and sands with fine mountain backgrounds this coast is very well worth exploration.

From John o' Groats the way is by **Canisbay Church** – outside which is a large inscribed slab *said to be* the gravestone of the veritable John o' Groats – and through relatively uninteresting country, passing on the right, Mey, where is the sixteenth-century **Barrogill Castle** (Castle of Mey) which belongs to Queen Elizabeth the Queen Mother and is used by her as a summer residence. On next to Dunnet, at the southern end of **Dunnet Head,** which is the most northerly point of the mainland. **Dunnet Bay** (*hotel*) has a splendid stretch of firm sands divided from the road by dunes of almost mountainous proportions. Sand yachting is a well-established sport. *Youth Hostel* at Castletown.

Thurso (*Royal, Pentland, Holborn, St. Clair, Park*) is the most northerly town on the mainland. Steamers to and from the Orkney Isles (Scapa and Stromness) call at **Scrabster Harbour,** 2 miles north of the town. **Thurso Castle,** near the town, occupies the site of the old seat of the Sinclair family. Other objects of interest are the house of Robert Dick, baker, botanist and geologist, whose life was written by Smiles, and the Museum, with a notable herbarium, bequeathed to the town by Dick.

Though the town will not long detain the visitor, Thurso has excellent natural advantages as a seaside resort. The bathing is good and the long stretch of firm sands one of the finest in the North. There is an 18-hole golf course and an indoor pool.

At **Dounreay,** 8 miles from Thurso, is the United Kingdom Atomic Energy Authority's Experimental Atomic Station. A striking central steel sphere 135 feet wide houses the reactor. This station, the most advanced of its type in the world, began producing small amounts of electricity towards the end of 1962, although its main purpose is the development of what is called the fast breeder reactor, which should lead to the building of very efficient nuclear power stations in future years. In the old airfield control tower near the main Thurso–Tongue road is a most interesting museum set up by the Atomic Energy Authority and which is open to visitors during summer months.

Two miles farther west is **Reay,** a hamlet near the head of the aptly named **Sandside Bay,** and then comes **Melvich** (*hotel*), a collection of small houses, overlooking Melvich Bay, into which the Halladale river flows. There are good sands in the bay; there is plenty of fishing–sea and freshwater–and all along the coast are rocky coves well worth visiting. **Strathy, Armadale, Farr** (with a noteworthy Celtic cross) are representative of other places along this coast–humble hamlets, yet in splendid holiday surroundings.

Bettyhill, with a modern hotel, is a growing village at the mouth of the Naver river, which here flows into Torrisdale Bay.

From **Borgie Bridge** (*Borgie Lodge Hotel* half a mile to the north) to **Tongue** there are magnificent views of **Ben Loyal** and this most shapely mountain dominates the southward prospect as the road rounds the Kyle of Tongue, and makes for the bridge at the northern end of **Loch Hope.**

Loch Eriboll is a fiord-like inlet of sea, surrounded by great grim mountains, so that even in summer one can appreciate the twist given to the name by Naval men stationed here. "Loch 'Orrible," they called it!

At the entrance to Loch Eriboll is **Rispond** (*hotel*) and from there the rocky coast runs up to **Durness** and **Fairaidh** (*see* p. 124).

Inverness to the West Coast

There are four important road routes between Inverness and the west coast and at least two well-used walking-routes. Of the roads the most important has long been that accompanied by the railway by Garve and Achnasheen to Strathcarron whence a new road has superseded the former Strome Ferry to complete the journey to Kyle of Lochalsh. A popular alternative is via Invermoriston and Cluanie and so crossing Loch Long by the bridge at Dornie.

Branching from the Strome Ferry route at Achnasheen is the lovely road by Loch Maree to Gairloch and Poolewe and thence to Gruinard Bay, and leaving the same road at Garve is the main road to Ullapool.

The two walking-routes referred to are that from Struy in Glen Cannich to Lochcarron and that through Glen Affric to Dornie. They are described on p. 52.

The road from Inverness to Beauly and Muir of Ord has been described on p. 118.

Motorists bound for the West or the North turn *sharp left* in Muir of Ord and cross the railway, just beyond which there is a choice of routes. The road straight on winds by Urray and **Moy Bridge** to **Contin,** where it is joined by the somewhat longer main road swinging to the right at Muir of Ord for **Dingwall** (*see* p. 119).

Three miles or so farther our road passes Rogie Falls, climbing through birch woods, then descends to run alongside **Loch Garve,** at the western end of which is the village of **Garve**–the hotel, the station and a dozen houses.

To Ullapool and Lochinver

Bus service (twice daily mid-June to mid-September, 3-hour run) between Inverness and Ullapool *viâ* Contin and Garve: also between Garve and Achiltibuie.

The road which branches right about a mile beyond Garve runs through one of the wildest districts in the North of Scotland, the scenery being grand and varied. It first traverses the pretty **Strathgarve,** and at the end of 10 miles reaches **Aultguish** (*inn*) where hydro-electric activity includes a dam and the new Loch Glascarnoch, five miles long, beside the Ullapool road. The road skirts this reservoir flooding the Strath Dirrie. The summit level is reached at **Loch Droma,** 15 miles from Garve. On the right is **Beinn Dearg** (3,547 feet). About 21 miles from Garve a sudden bend round a shoulder of Beinn Dearg provides a startling change in the immediate scenery, sombreness giving place to marvellous brightness.

A road goes off on the left for **Dundonnell, Poolewe** and **Gairloch** (pp. 132–133).

At this point, too, the river forms the **Falls of Measach.** The uppermost fall is difficult to see well owing to the narrowness of the ravine (Corrieshalloch Gorge) in which it roars: a gate on the left of the road about 100 yards below the bridge leads to a viewpoint, and one can gain a glimpse of the fall by walking down the left bank from the bridge. In spite of recent tree-felling the scenery all along the gorge is very fine. The land is now Scottish National Trust property.

From Braemore to Ullapool the road commands a succession of beautiful views, and the eye gratefully rests upon cultivated fields, patches of woodland, and the grass-clad hills of **Loch Broom,** a fine sea loch. The name signifies "the lake of showers."

Ullapool (*Caledonian, Royal, Argyll, Morefield*), on a peninsula running into the loch, is a village established by the British Fisheries Association in 1788. The vicinity is very beautiful, and there is good and safe bathing, sea-fishing, trouting, etc. The district is popular with campers. Ullapool is connected by bus services with **Garve,** on the Dingwall–Kyle line. By the ferry (no cars) at Ullapool there is ready, if steep, access to Little Loch Broom and to **Dundonnell** hotel at its head, whence the ascent can be made of **An Teallach**–the "Red Forge" (3,483 feet).

On the northern shore of the inlet rises **Ben More Coigach,** and at the mouth of the loch are the **Summer Isles,** favourite resorts of picnic parties. **Achiltibuie** (*hotel*), overlooking the Summer Isles (Youth Hostel at Achininver), is connected by bus with Ullapool.

Northward from Ullapool a wild and adventurous road, with magnificent scenery, makes its way by **Inchnadamph** (*hotel*), at the head of **Loch Assynt,** from which **Ben More Assynt** (3,273 feet) can be ascended.

The scenery along the road from Inchnadamph to Lochinver is among the loveliest in Scotland. The road runs along the shore of Loch Assynt, nearly 7 miles long, with **Quinag** (2,653 feet) and **Glasven** (2,541 feet) in its vicinity. From the side of Loch Assynt a road strikes off northwards, rising to a height of some 850 feet between Quinag and Glasven; it leads *viâ* the Kylesku Ferry (cars carried; daily service, free; delay at low tides) to **Scourie,** whence a road goes to Laxford Bridge and it is possible to make a way through grand and wild scenery to Cape Wrath and eastward to Thurso.

The Lochinver road from Inchnadamph continues by Loch Assynt and the banks of the *Inver* to **Lochinver** (at pier, *Culag Hotel; Achmelvich Youth Hostel,* 4 miles north-west), at the head of the sea loch of that name. The village is popular with all classes of tourists, but the chief attraction is the angling on numerous lochs in the neighbourhood. There are no fewer than 280 named lochs in the parish. The sea-fishing is very good, and there is much trout fishing in the neighbourhood, available through the Assynt Angling Club (*charge*). The **Falls of Kirkaig** (2 miles) are well worth a visit. Striking features of the scenery of the district are the mountains, and notably Suilven, Canisp, Ben More and **An Stac** or Stac Polly, which, in the words of Macculloch, "seem as if they had tumbled down from the clouds, having nothing to do with the country or each other in shape, material, position, or character, and which look very much as if they were wondering how they got there."

INVERNESS TO LOCH MAREE AND GAIRLOCH

Four miles beyond Garve (*see* p. 130) we run along the northern end of **Loch Luichart,** the source of the river *Conon*. The loch is about 5 miles in length by 1 mile in breadth. Hydro-electric work has necessitated raising the level of the water. Beyond that we cross the river *Grudie*, pass close to the Falls of Grudie, and enter **Strath Bran,** bare and bleak, through which we travel to **Achnasheen** (46 miles from Inverness, 27½ from Dingwall). Even in summer Achnasheen is a lonely hamlet, consisting of little more than a station (the nearest station to Loch Maree and Gairloch), an hotel, a shop, a petrol station and one or two cottages.

For the first half of the journey from Achnasheen the road is on the rise, then it runs alongside **Loch Rosque,** a rather tame, river-like lake, some

Slioch across Loch Maree

3 or 4 miles in length. From the farther end may be seen, on the left, a hill shaped like a recumbent face, and called **Cairn-a-Crubie.** The watershed is reached about 6 miles from Achnasheen. It has an altitude of 815 feet, and from it there bursts upon the view beautiful Loch Maree. From this point the route is full of interest. Descending **Glen Docherty,** a wild and narrow ravine, bounded by steep mountains and extending for about 4 miles, during which the road falls 700 feet, we enter **Kinlochewe,** a scattered hamlet, with an hotel. A couple of miles beyond Kinlochewe begins—

Loch Maree

one of the finest lochs in Scotland. It is about 12½ miles long and from 1 to 3 miles broad. The river Ewe flows from it and enters the sea at Poolewe and the road runs for 10 miles along the south shore. Across the loch are **Slioch** (3,217 feet), which may be ascended either from Kinlochewe or (crossing the loch) Loch Maree Hotel, **Ben Lair** (2,817 feet), and **Ben Airidh Charr** (2,593 feet). On the southern side **Ben Eighe** (3,309 feet), one of the Torridon Hills, attracts attention by its peak of white quartz rock and its beautiful form.

The surface of the loch is broken by no fewer than twenty-four islands. They are partially wooded with pine, birch and holly, and are the habitat of many species of fern.

The most celebrated island, Isle of Maree, lies near the northern shore, directly opposite the Loch Maree Hotel, and contains a primitive burying-ground and the scanty ruins of an ancient chapel, dedicated to the Virgin, and said to have been erected in the seventh century by St. Maelrubha, after whom the loch and island are named.

Two miles beyond Loch Maree Hotel the road leaves the loch side and strikes westwards across the hills to the river Kerry, alongside which it runs through very beautiful scenery to **Flowerdale,** just beyond which we reach—

Gairloch

This Ross-shire village, at the head of the sea loch of the same name, is the centre of a beautiful district, and enjoys popularity as a summer resort. Bathing, boating and fishing may be enjoyed in the bay, which abounds with a great variety of fish. Excellent trout fishing, free to visitors at the *Gairloch Hotel*, may be had on several lochs within an easy walk, and there is a 9-hole golf course. *Youth Hostel* at Carn Dearg, 4 miles.

GAIRLOCH TO ULLAPOOL

From Gairloch the main road continues eastward to **Poolewe** (*hotels*), on the strip of land separating Loch Maree from Loch Ewe. Thence by **Aultbea** (*hotel*), a small village on a bay in **Loch Ewe** (*Inverewe House* is famed for its gardens), and across to **Gruinard Bay**, descending by a very steep hill (average gradient 1 in 7·8) with a sharp turn at the foot. The thrill of this road is the suddenness with which, as we turn between the rocks, the expanse of Gruinard Bay is revealed with its background of mountains. The hamlet of Laide is on the left, and the road skirts the bay for several miles, finally passing through woods and beside the tumbling river to Gruinard House.

Leaving Gruinard Bay the road crosses another promontory and proceeds to skirt the southern shore of **Little Loch Broom.** Here and there the hillsides spout fine waterfalls, but the scenery calls for no special comment; one is too close to its flanks to appreciate the rugged red mountain, An Teallach ("The Forge"). The loch is left at the *Dundonnell Hotel* at its head and thence the road winds through the hills to the Garve–Ullapool road at Braemore, 45 miles from Gairloch. **Ullapool** is about 10 miles westward.

TO LOCH CARRON AND KYLE OF LOCHALSH

At the western end of Achnasheen bear to the left over the Bran and follow the valley of its tributary, the *Ledgowan,* and the shore of **Loch Gowan,** in the midst of wild moorland scenery. Then come pretty **Loch Scavan,** or Sgamhain and a fine run down the valley of the *Carron.* We pass **Achnashellach,** with station and Youth Hostel. **Loch Doule,** or Dughaill, is over a mile in length. The grand Torridon mountains are here well in sight. We approach the salt-water **Loch Carron** about a mile before which a left turn leads to **Strathcarron** (*hotel*). Now rail and a new road follow the eastern shore of the loch to touch South Strome from which a road turns south to connect with the Ardelve road for Kyle of Lochalsh.

Beyond the Strathcarron turn the main road continues along the northern shore of Loch Carron a few miles down which is **Lochcarron** village, or Jeantown (*hotel*) whence a road runs to Shieldaig or to Applecross (*see* below).

LOCHCARRON TO SHIELDAIG AND APPLECROSS

Bus service Strathcarron station to Shieldaig.

From Lochcarron village a road strikes sharply up the hillside and for some miles runs through grandly rugged scenery to **Kishorn** (*Youth Hostel*) and **Tornapress,** at the head of Loch Kishorn (where the Applecross road – *see* below – diverges on the left). The Torridon road continues northward through the romantic **Glen Shieldaig,** with its overhanging cliffs from four to five hundred feet high. Near the centre of the pass is a fine waterfall. The final portion of the road (18 miles) is through lovely woods to **Shieldaig** (*hotel*) on Loch Shieldaig, a branch of **Loch Torridon,** which is surrounded by scenery of great grandeur and beauty with the very ancient red Torridonian sandstone much in evidence. There are hill roads (now available for cars) to the village of **Torridon,** at the head of Upper Loch Torridon, whence a road runs to Kinlochewe. Loch Torridon, running for 20 miles into Western Ross, opens out some of the wildest scenery in the West Highlands. The mountains around its upper portion rise to over 3,000 feet, the finest of them being **Ben Alligin** (3,232 feet), **Liathach** (3,456 feet), and **Ben Eighe** (3,309 feet). Youth Hostels at Craig (Diabaig) and Inveralligin.

At Tornapress the road to Applecross by the *Bealach nam Bo* strikes off to the left. This road, which reaches a height of 2,053 feet, is one of the steepest – and yet grandest – in Scotland. It is emphatically *not* a route for caravans or large or overladen cars, not merely on account of the gradient (the road rises from sea-level to over 2,000 feet in just over 5 miles), but because the final stages of the ascent include a series of hairpin bends of such sharpness that very few cars can negotiate in "one go." Once over the summit the route is somewhat easier and in the course of the descent one has opportunity for admiring the really magnificent view across the sea to Skye.

Applecross (*hotel*) is placed at the head of a small bay and is served by boat from Kyle daily. The seventh-century Celtic missionary St. Maelrubha made his headquarters here. The principal occupations are boating and fishing, but there are some splendid walks – particularly that across country to Loch Shieldaig.

Skye

Access. * – There are two main approaches to Skye from the mainland, viz. from Mallaig on the west coast of Inverness-shire and from Kyle of Lochalsh on the west coast of Ross-shire. Mallaig is reached by rail and road from Fort William, the routes to which are given on page 97. Kyle of Lochalsh is reached by rail from Inverness (*see* page 49), and by road either from Inverness *viâ* Achnasheen or Invermoriston, or from Invergarry *viâ* Shiel Bridge. From the south a convenient route is *viâ* Fort William, Spean Bridge and Invergarry.

From *Mallaig* there are several routes to Skye: (1) By MacBrayne car ferry or motor launch to Armadale across the Sound of Sleat; (2) by MacBrayne steamer to Kyle of Lochalsh (thence by ferry to Kyleakin); (3) by MacBrayne steamer to Portree.

There are bus services from Armadale and Kyleakin for Broadford, Sligachan, Portree, etc., but here again the use of a current time-table is essential, though as a general rule buses connect with steamer arrivals.

Ferries. – MALLAIG – ARMADALE. Car ferry, 25 mins.

KYLE OF LOCHALSH TO KYLEAKIN. There are continuous crossings of the motor-car ferry between the hours of 7 a.m. and 11 p.m. (Tel.: Kyleakin 13). Operates throughout the year. Sunday service from June to September only.

GLENELG TO KYLERHEA. Small ferry with accommodation for six cars between Glenelg (30 miles south of Kyle by road) and Kylerhea in Skye. Service operates from 8.30 a.m. to 9 p.m. or dusk, daily except Sundays, early May to end of September.

Notes – (1) There is no public communication in Skye on Sundays. (2) Pier dues may be charged in some places. (3) There is no air service with Skye except in special emergencies.

As many may think not all the attractions of Skye are solely for climbers. Most of the roads are in good condition, and almost every one of them commands grand views, so that motorists can enjoy fine scenery without any physical effort. Moreover, the traffic-stream is not so heavy as to make either cycling or walking along these roads unpleasant, and in addition there are innumerable byways leading to outlying corners of the island which are well worth exploration. Mountain-climbing in the Cuillins is perhaps the chief holiday attraction, but Skye has boating of all kinds, bathing, fishing, golf, tennis, while the Games are an important fixture. "Skye Week," held in late May or early June, is an annual period of "festivities and typical Hebridean celebrations" – Highland games, ceilidhs, piping competitions, etc.

The island is some 50 miles from end to end, with a width varying from 4 to 25 miles, and of such extremely irregular shape that no part is more than $4\frac{1}{2}$ miles distant from the sea. As the map shows, it consists of a central nexus, on which are Portree and the Cuillins, and a number of long peninsular arms intersected by wild sea-lochs. The principal places on the island are the village of Portree, and the villages of Broadford, Kyleakin, Dunvegan, Staffin and Kilmuir.

* See footnote, p. 10.

Skye has a long history, mingling with prehistory (of which there are relics) and legend. St. Columba visited the island in the sixth century, and for four centuries and more it was under the sway of the Norsemen, as many place-names testify. Clan warfare went on through succeeding centuries, to be followed by no less dire struggles against economic difficulties, largely of an agrarian nature. For over a century depopulation and emigration have left vacant many a "lone shieling of the misty island" and many of Skye's best sons have sought (and made) their fortunes afar. Things are perhaps not as bad as they were, but the battle goes on. Most of the people are still crofters, eking out a living by other means where possible. Fishing is carried out and cattle and sheep are sent to the markets on the mainland. Of growing importance is the tourist industry; the island has some excellent hotels, many good boarding-houses, and five Youth Hostels (much frequented in the season). Electricity is available in most parts and practically every house has water, while the island's bus services are quite excellent.

Visitors who cross from the mainland by the Kyle of Lochalsh ferry land at—

Kyleakin

(**Hotels.**—*King's Arms, Marine, Triton, White Heather, Dunringell.*)

a pleasant little village bordering the broad strip of green turf through which the road runs and with grand views across the Kyle, up Loch Alsh to the Five Sisters of Kintail and (from the northern end of the village) a long way up the north-east coast of Skye. Kyleakin (the name, by the way, is pronounced "kyle-akin") for fishing and boating is a splendid spot.

Overlooking the pier is the ruined **Caisteal Maol** (the turretless castle), reputed to have been built by a Danish princess nicknamed "Saucy Mary," who stretched a chain across the Kyle and allowed no ship to pass without paying toll.

From Kyleakin to Broadford is a matter of 8 miles along a road commanding wonderful views across the sea and up the coast and, above all, of the incomparable Cuillins. Seaward a variety of islands are in view on a clear day, Raasay being noteworthy by reason of the prominent truncated cone of Dun Can (1,456 feet). At Lusa the steep and narrow mountain road from **Kylerhea** comes in on the left.

A few miles west of Lusa is—

Broadford

Buses.—To Kyleakin, Portree, etc.
Distances.—Kyleakin, 8; Armadale, 16½; Elgol, 15; Portree, 26.

Hotels. — *Broadford, Dunollie,* and many guesthouses.
Youth Hostel.—North shore of the bay.

Broadford is the second largest community on Skye, though here as elsewhere on the island the term "parish" would be more aptly descriptive than "village," the houses and hotels being spread over a considerable area. The main portion overlooks Broadford Bay, where boating and fishing can be enjoyed. Broadford is a good centre for exploring Skye, for from the village roads go to Armadale and to Elgol on Loch Scavaig and to the north end of the island.

The Coast near Staffin Bay, Skye

Broadford to Loch Scavaig (15 miles).—This is one of the finest excursions on Skye, amply demonstrating the fallacy of the belief that the island has nothing to offer those who are not mountaineers. Immediately beyond the Broadford Hotel the Red Cuillins spring into view, looking very shapely and forming a horseshoe suggesting a nice walk. One could ascend the southern end of the horseshoe and from it carry on over **Beinn Dearg** (2,323 feet) to **Beinn na Caillich** (2,403 feet) and down the latter; but walking on the Red Cuillins is not quite so easy as it looks from a distance, and a little exploration will show there is more remunerative outlet for energies close at hand. Go, for instance, a mile or so farther along the Elgol road, past the ruined church of Kilchrist and the neighbouring loch, and you will have a fine distant view of the Black Cuillins. The road winds past the loch and through hilly pastoral country and then again springs a surprise in the shape of a full-length view of **Blaven** (3,042 feet), its eastern face riven with corries. The beauty of the view is intensified by **Loch Slapin**, in the foreground.

From **Torrin** (or **Torran**) the road runs round the head of Loch Slapin (from which a path leads northwards through Strath Mor to Luib (3½ miles) on the coast road from Broadford to Portree), and then follows the western side of Loch Slapin past the entrance to Strathaird House and finally drops down to Elgol on the shore of Loch Scavaig.

Walkers who intend to make for Coruisk should leave the Elgol road by a path which starts a few hundred yards beyond Strathaird and goes nearly due westward, keeping well up on the hillside to avoid the boggy ground below, and in four or five miles arrives at **Camasunary,** on a wide bay. Camasunary is an important meeting-point of routes: northward through Glen Sligachan to Sligachan Hotel; southward down the coast to Elgol (but this walk should be taken in the reverse direction, for the sake of the views) and westward to Loch Coruisk. This last walk is one of the excursions for which Skye is famed, though it may be well to warn strangers that the only ways out of the Loch Coruisk basin are over the mountains (*see* below) or by the path from Camasunary or by one of the boats bringing visitors from Elgol or Glenbrittle. From Camasunary take the narrow path on the far side of the stream, working round the steep and rocky headland at a considerable height above the sea. The distance is not more than four miles, but the walk is extremely rough and is not recommended to those who dislike narrow and exposed paths. The worst portion of all is at the notorious **Bad Step,** where the rocks over which one passes shelve steeply to the sea. There are various ways of crossing the Bad Step, some more dignified than others. The most common error is to get too high up on the rock: the actual path is about 15 feet above high-water level.

The road from Broadford ends at **Elgol,** a small and very scattered upland village (boarding-house and cottage accommodation) from which there is a steep descent to the beach. Everyone should descend to the beach, for it commands what is probably the finest sea and mountain view in Britain–that up Loch Scavaig to the heart of the Cuillins. In the rocky amphitheatre beyond Loch Scavaig lies Loch Coruisk.

LOCH CORUISK

Boats take parties from Elgol (and Mallaig) at prices varying according to the number of passengers on board. Time is usually allowed for an exploration of Loch Coruisk and its immediate surroundings, but special arrangements should be made for a longer stay. A landing is made during the weekly steamer excursion from Fort William.

The real grandeur of this incomparable scene–the quintessence of Skye– is only to be appreciated in the course of the approach to it across the waters of Loch Scavaig. Loch Coruisk itself is not visible, but the great rocky amphitheatre in which it lies is mirrored in the waves and the whole picture is so satisfying that even the most daring artist would not require to take liberties with any detail of the grouping or colour. The identity of the various peaks can best be obtained from a map: they are formed of great slabs of black "gabbro"–rock so rough and reliable and so broken into handholds and footholds that the Cuillins offer some of the best rock climbing in Europe.

From the landing place a few minutes' walk brings us above the end of **Loch Coruisk** ("Coroosk") and the view from this point is such that most people decide to have their picnic here and to explore the loch-side afterward.

The path to Sligachan is by the east side of Loch Coruisk as far as the Big Burn (say about half a mile). Here turn to the right and (keeping the burn and Loch Choire Riabhaich on our left) an easy climb brings one to the summit of **Drumhain** (1,038 feet–a grand viewpoint). Here is a large cairn. The view of the Cuillin ridge from Drumhain is most impressive; unfortunately it is often blotted out by mist and rain. By walking along the summit of Drumhain in a north-west direction for about a mile a very fine view into **Harta Corrie** may be obtained. This is one of the wildest corries in the Cuillins, hemmed in by steep black rock peaks extending from Sgurr nan Gillean on the right to Bruach na Frithe and Bidean Druim nan Ramh on the left.

The direct descent from Drumhain to Harta Corrie is not easy and one should therefore retrace one's steps to the cairn at the pass. From the cairn a fair track leads northwards across an eastern shoulder of the hill and then descends into Glen Sligachan and joins the Camasunary path at a point about 1 mile north of Loch an Athain. From here the long and tedious walk down Glen Sligachan begins, and it will take one and a half to two hours' steady walking to reach Sligachan.

For the Cuillins, *see below*.

Broadford to Armadale. Armadale is situated in the southernmost point of Skye in the district known as Sleat. The run is interesting on account of the many beautiful views of the mainland after the first 6 or 7 miles have been covered, the mountains around Loch Hourn showing up particularly well. Between 8 and 9 miles from Broadford is **Isle Ornsay** (*Isle Ornsay, Duisdale*), the name applying to the village as well as to the island off the coast. Two miles farther the road passes *Loch nan Dubhrachan*, locally said to be habited by a "monster." Beyond Knock and Kilmore we pass Armadale Castle and so come to **Ardvasar,** a small village with an hotel (*Ardvasar*) and a pier at which boats call. (For Armadale–Mallaig Ferry, *see* p. 134.

Broadford to Portree. – This is one of the most interesting roads in the island, the views changing continually and being almost throughout of a high order. The islands off the coast are **Scalpay** and **Raasay,** the latter some 15 miles long, 3 miles broad, and marked by the curious truncated cone of **Dun Can** (1,456 feet). Inland, as the road rounds Loch Ainort and then runs up the southern shore of Loch Sligachan, there are innumerable glimpses of the Cuillins, and from time to time there are fine distant views up the coast to the Storr Rock, beyond Portree. Walkers who prefer to get off the motor road will find a short cut between Strollamus (4 miles from Broadford) and Luib, on Loch Ainort. This rejoins the coast road at **Sconser** on the southern shore of Loch Sligachan (9-hole golf course).

About 19 miles from Broadford is the **Sligachan Hotel,** famous as a headquarters for climbs in the Cuillins. The road straight ahead continues to Western Skye, but for Portree we turn right. From Sligachan Bridge the views of the Cuillins are magnificent: another good viewpoint is the top of the rise on the Portree Road about half a mile from the hotel. For Portree, *see* p. 140.

THE CUILLINS

The Cuillins (or Coolins) undoubtedly provide the most splendid mountain scene in Britain. It is not a question of height or extent (the highest point is some 3,300 feet above the sea and the main group measures only about 8 miles by 6 in extent) but of proportions, as a result of which the peaks seem to soar to a much greater height than they do in fact and possess a sublimity which is not encountered elsewhere in Britain.

Walking and climbing about the Cuillins is dangerous for those unaccustomed to such conditions. The steepness of the routes is such that in several cases there is no feasible alternative route, so that if one misses the right path one is almost bound to get into difficulties which might trouble even experienced climbers. The one path which is quite safe for novices is that up to Bruach na Frithe; almost anyone with sufficient energy can manage this in safety given clear weather; as for the rest, one should take an experienced companion, a water-flask and an "iron ration" of, say, chocolate or biscuits in case of delay. The compass, owing to the magnetic nature of the rock, especially on the ridges, is quite unreliable, so that a sudden envelopment in mist may make descent a matter of some difficulty and danger.

The best known and most popular of the Cuillins is undoubtedly **Sgurr nan Gillean** (3,167 feet) – "the peak of the young men" – all in all, probably the most difficult "tourist" mountain in Scotland. The easiest way up it has some steps, especially nearing the top, that are distinctly trying to the uninitiated, and several people have lost their lives on it because they did not treat the mountain with the care and respect it deserves.

The ascent from Sligachan will take three to four hours, and the descent two to three hours. From the hotel follow the Dunvegan road for a third of a mile; then turn off on the left by the track leading to Cuillin Lodge. Cross the Red Burn by the stepping stones half a mile farther up (or a footbridge half a mile lower down) and then keep southward over the moor. Loch a' Choire Riabhaich is passed on the left, and the Coire nan allt Geala is gained by a rough, steep, stone shoot. Progress up this corrie is over a wilderness of boulders and screes to the ridge which extends south-eastwards from the summit. This ridge is struck at a point about 300 feet below the top. From this the route lies along and up the ridge, dipping over to the left-hand side in places where the direct ascent up the ridge is too steep. Hands as well as feet will here have to be constantly used, and a sharp look-out kept for the small cairns which indicate the right route: the nail marks on the rocks, too, are a useful guide. A little short of the summit a gap has to be crossed, which at first sight seems a bit sensational; but the rock is firm and good, and the handholds and footholds are excellent. The top is a very narrow one, with precipitous cliffs all around.

The view is remarkably fine, the extraordinary boldness and grandeur of the rock scenery in the immediate foreground forming such a magnificent set-off to the moors below and the "wine-dark" sea in the distance. Notice, too, the play of light and shade on the ridges and tops of the other Cuillin peaks to the west and south. The descent is exactly by the way you came up. A possible alternative is along the western ridge and over its tooth and then down a vertical chimney into Coire Bhastier; but this route is very difficult (it requires the use of a rope) and must not be attempted except by a party accompanied by a good guide.

Coire na Creiche (6 miles) is one of the wildest corries in the Cuillins. From Sligachan follow the Dunvegan road for a third of a mile, and then strike off to the left along the rough road to Cuillin Lodge. Hence a path (narrow and awkward at first) follows the left bank of the burn to the summit of the **Bealach a' Mhaim** (pron. *Vaim*), a pass 1,132 feet above sea-level. The corrie lies over this pass to the left, and to obtain the best view you must descend some distance towards Glen Brittle, on the farther side of the pass. Coire na Creiche signifies in Gaelic "the corrie of the spoil," the spot having been in the old days a rendezvous for freebooters with their booty. An easy half-day's excursion, but well worth a whole day.

Farther south, behind the shoulder of Sgurr Thuilm, is Coire a' Ghreadaidh, the stream flowing out of which has a number of very beautiful pools, one of which has a natural arch. The next corrie, Coire na Banachdich, has, quite low down, one of the finest waterfalls in Scotland.

Bruach na Frithe (3,143 feet)—"the ridge of the forest"—is not so well known as Sgurr nan Gillean, but the view from it is, if anything, finer than from Sgurr nan Gillean, and it is much more easily scaled; in fact, as we have said, there is nothing to prevent any tourist with mountain experience, from ascending Bruach na Frithe. Owing to the unreliability of the compass the ascent should be attempted only in clear weather. Time, about four hours up and three hours down. Proceed to the Bealach a' Mhaim by the Red Burn path as described above and from there turn south up over the long grassy slope for about 1,000 feet, and then over easy screes and rock to the summit. On nearing the summit keep below the ridge a little to the right, and so avoid all difficulties. The descent can be made by the east ridge towards Sgurr nan Gillean and then down into Fionn Choire where the walking is smooth and pleasant. It is worth while when on Bruach na Frithe to go round the head of Fionn Choire to the Bhasteir and Tooth.

To **Glen Brittle** (14 miles).—Either by the good but hilly road from Drynoch, on the Dunvegan road, or *viâ* the Bealach a' Mhaim, a delightful and easy walk of three hours or so from Sligachan (*see* under Coire na Creiche, above). The track becomes somewhat indistinct on the other side of the Bealach, until it joins the road near the head of Glen Brittle, but the view of the Cuillins from the top of the pass before descending into Glen Brittle is unsurpassed.

Coire Lagan.—The route up the burn which comes down just beside Glen Brittle House, near the foot of the glen, leads in about two hours into **Coire Lagan,** a scene of supreme grandeur. It is a rock basin, hemmed in by the cliffs and screes of Sgurr Dearg, Sgurr Mhic

Choinnich, and Sgurr Alasdair, and containing some of the finest examples of glaciated rock in the kingdom. Cross the burn by a plank bridge a little above the house, and then, after keeping the burn beside you on your left for a short distance–say 200 or 300 feet–bear away to the right until you reach a fair-sized loch–Loch an Fhirbhallaich = "the loch of the spotted folk" (i.e. trout). Skirt along the side of the loch, and a little way on in the same direction Coire Lagan will come into view. Bear round to the left a little, and continue straight up, making for part of the corrie. Hereabouts a judicious selection of the route will be necessary, but by looking about carefully, small direction cairns will be noticed, and here and there a slight track, and the nail marks on the rocks, which will all help one to hit off the easiest route. After a little scramble up some extraordinary glaciated rocks you find yourself at the side of a small loch, amid a scene of the wildest grandeur (**Loch Coire Lagan**, 1,845 feet). The descent should be made by precisely the same way as you came up. Visitors to Coire Lagan should make a point of seeing the Cioch, a curious pinnacle projecting from the face of Sron na Ciche, on the south side of the corrie, and a favourite objective of skilled rock-climbers.

Sgurr Alasdair (3,251 feet)–"Alexander's Peak"–is the highest peak in the Cuillins, and in every way worthy of its reputation. It is climbed from Glen Brittle. The best route of ascent is *viâ* the Sgumain Boulder Shoot from lower Coire Lagan and thence over Sgumain and along the intervening ridge between the two peaks. A "bad step" on this ridge can be avoided lower down on the Coire Ghrundda side. The descent may be made by a scramble down the Stone Shoot. The Stone Shoot is not easy to find and a guide is essential for all but thoroughly experienced climbers. Time from Glen Brittle, five to seven hours.

Full details of the ascents and climbing routes in the Cuillins will be found in the Scottish Mountaineering Club's *Guide to Skye*.

Harta Corrie is another wild corrie, also well worth seeing. The route lies up Glen Sligachan, and then up into the corrie by the bed of the stream. Time, five or six hours. At the entrance of the corrie is the famous "Bloody Stone," scene of the massacre (1601) of the Macleods by the Macdonalds.

PORTREE

Access.–By road from Kyleakin, etc. (*see* above). Daily steamer service to and from Kyle of Lochalsh and Mallaig.

Distances.–Sligachan, 9 miles; Broadford, 26; Kyleakin, 34; Staffin, 17; Uig (*viâ* Staffin). 32.

direct, 14½.

Hotels.–*Royal, Pier, Portree, Rosedale, Caledonian, Coolin Hills.* Unlicensed: *Viewfield House, Ose Farm.*

Tennis.–Courts near the Post Office.

Although its population numbers only about 1,500, Portree is the most considerable community on Skye. The name means "The King's Harbour" and commemorates a visit of James V. It is a compact little place on a hillside partly enclosing its Harbour–a bay on the picturesque Portree Loch. The best views of the town are from one of the steep headlands forming the narrow gateway through which this loch is entered from the sea. The immediate neighbourhood of the town is well wooded, a few minutes away are heather-covered hills and beyond them on the one hand are the glorious Cuillins and to the north the extraordinary Storr Rock. Portree is an excellent centre for a holiday on the island, with plenty of facilities for excursions by bus, steamer and motor-boat. Golf, tennis, fishing and various social functions are additional attractions. At the end of August (usually) the Games bring visitors from the mainland as well as from all parts of the island, and there are balls.

Prince Charlie's Cave (5 miles by boat; motor-boat trips run from the Harbour; otherwise a bargain should be struck before starting) is unremarkable in itself, and it is doubtful whether it ever sheltered the Prince. The boat trip along the coast to it, however, is very interesting, though the view is narrowed to the width of the Sound by the adjacent hills all the way. The *Cave*, blocked by a stone and bearing an inscription outside, lies to the north of the harbour and on the way to the foot of the Storr Rock, to which the boat may be taken, but the ascent from the shore is very severe.

The Cuillins

Apart from the obvious walks around the loch and the claims of the Cuillins, the first excursion from Portree is usually that to –

The Storr Rock

which lies beside the Staffin road about 7 miles from the town.

It should be understood that the climb to the top (2,360 feet) is not quite the leisurely stroll it looks to be from the main road. At least two hours should be allowed for the ascent, and almost as long for the descent, and in each case the journey from and to Portee has to be taken into consideration. Many, however, to whom such an excursion is barred can, and do, walk across the road to the Old Man: a walk which presents no difficulties.

From Portree follow the Staffin road for 5 miles past **Loch Fada** and to the northern end of **Loch Leathan** – the "Storr Lochs" of one of the hydro-electric undertakings. The Storr itself is in full view with its square-cut top and its Needle Rock, the so-called **Old Man of Storr** (a basalt monolith, 160 feet high), on the right. The upper cliff of which the Storr itself forms the crown is best climbed by leaving the road at the far end of Loch Leathan and making away to the left over a succession of grassy humps for a stony little ravine, whence the ridge of the cliff begins to rise steeply for the mountain-top. A scanty rill flows down this ravine, and into Loch Leathan. The final climb is short and steep, but its roughness makes it quite feasible. Once on top you have only to mount the long grass slope which bends round the tremendous black precipices forming the seaward front of the hills.

For good walkers there is an alternative route *viâ* Snizort. on the Portree–Uig road (bus route): this is a long and continuously uphill walk rather than a climb.

141

Portree to Uig via Staffin

If possible choose a clear day for this excursion, as one of its features is the magnificent series of views across the sea, first beyond the islands of Raasay and Rona to the mainland and then to Lewis and Harris.

For the first few miles the view is dominated by the Storr Rock, with the Old Man of Storr standing away to the right of the main mass.

Onward the views are ever-changing and always interesting. A few miles from the Storr the road crosses the head of the **Lealt Falls,** where a burn falls into a black chasm with fine effect, and then, rising high above the cliff, is seen **Dun Dheirg,** a natural formation which looks exactly like a fortification buttressed with pillars of stone. A little farther and **Loch Mealt** comes in sight: like Loch Leathan, this loch spills its water into the sea by a fine cataract, but the noteworthy sight hereabouts is the rock-formation composing the cliffs, its alternate horizontal and vertical bands having given it the name of the *Kilt Rock*. There are good views from the cliff edge a short way beyond Dun Dheirg.

Staffin (*Staffin House*) is a scattered parish of small-holdings, which seem particularly colourful, set out on the slopes at the foot of –

QUIRAING

one of the strangest and most fascinating mountains in Scotland. So broken is it into ridges and pillars that it resembles a mountain group in miniature rather than a single mountain. To describe its form briefly and accurately would be almost impossible, so confused is this mass of cliffs and pinnacles. The former Staffin road through the Quiraing is now impassable for vehicular traffic and is only suitable as a footpath. The direct road to Uig strikes due west from Staffin and ascends steeply, with many sharp bends to a high *col* (about 850 feet) between Quiraing and Bioda Buidhe. From the col it is a clear and fairly easy walk along the top to Meall na Suiramach (1,779 feet), but this route misses the most surprising feature of Quiraing– *The Table*–an area of smooth green turf sunk, as it were, into the solid rock until it is surrounded on almost every side by huge cliffs. There is a fair path from the col to the Table along the eastern side of the mountain. It runs just below the scree and passes between the main mass and the projecting rock known as The Needle. It is at least probable that the newcomer to Quiraing will find neither the right route nor the Table at the first attempt, but he will certainly come to appreciate the extraordinary manner in which the mass of rocks is broken up.

Beyond Staffin Bay the coast road squeezes between the Quiraing mass and the sea and then comes to **Flodigarry,** where the *Flodigarry Hotel* occupies the residence built by a descendant of Flora Macdonald (*see* below), who herself spent the earlier part of her married life in the adjacent cottage (the cottage is courteously shown to interested visitors). The views of the mainland from this corner are exquisite.

From Flodigarry we continue by a moorland road from which the land slopes gently down to the sea and affords magnificent views of Harris and Lewis. Inland the scenery is of little account, Quiraing looking its tamest from this side. The west coast of this–the Trotternish–part of Skye is reached at **Duntulm,** where the scanty remains of the castle rise gauntly above the cliff edge. Rather more than 2 miles southward a lane on the left of the road leads to the burying ground of **Kilmuir,** where is the large cross forming the Flora Macdonald Memorial.

Flora Macdonald (1727–90) was the daughter of a small farmer at Milton, in South Uist. Even as a child she showed unusual talents and was taken with the family of Sir Alexander Macdonald of the Isles to Edinburgh, so that she might there finish her education.

While she was visiting the Clanranalds in Benbecula, Prince Charles Edward landed there in the course of his flight after Culloden (1746), and after some persuasion Flora agreed to help in his escape. On the pretence of going to visit her mother (who had been abducted and married when Flora was only 6 years old, by Hugh Macdonald of Armadale), she obtained a passport for herself and a party which included "Betty Burke, an Irish spinning maid." Betty, of course, was the Prince in disguise. After a very rough passage, the party proposed to land at Vaternish, in Skye, but on seeing militia there they landed instead at Monkstadt, the home of that Sir Alexander Macdonald who had befriended Flora. Militia were at Monkstadt also, but arrangements were made for the Prince to spend the night at Kingsburgh, and next day he left by boat from Portree to Raasay.

Unfortunately Flora's part in the escape became generally known and she was arrested and sent to the Tower of London, whence she was released under the Act of Indemnity. Returning to Skye, she married Alexander Macdonald of Kingsburgh and the pair settled down at Flodigarry. Here they lived for over 20 years, subsequently moving to Kingsburgh, where she was visited by Dr. Johnson. In 1774 the family emigrated to North Carolina, but Flora returned in 1779, her husband having been taken prisoner in the War of Independence. On his release they lived at Kingsburgh until Flora died there in 1790.

In front as we continue, **Loch Snizort** appears, with Vaternish beyond— actually a part of Skye but seemingly so distant as to form part of a separate piece of country. The next few miles, however, will show increasingly how indented is the coastline of Skye, particularly the point just beyond the rise from Totscore where the whole of **Uig Bay** and many of the ramifications of Loch Snizort come into view. Parts of the scenery hereabouts bear a striking resemblance to that in Norway—incidentally several of the rivers flowing into Loch Snizort Beag have names ending in "dal." The road turning sharp back to the left at the top of Uig hill is that crossing the Quiraing col from Staffin (*see* p. 141). We, however, keep to the right and as the road descends have splendid views of **Uig** village, spread out along the shores of its bay and looking very green and pleasant after the bare moorlands we have traversed. Uig is in fact a good place for a quiet holiday, with fishing, boating (Uig pier boasts of being the longest in Scotland) and walking and other excursions. It has an hotel (*Uig*) and a Youth Hostel.

Beyond Uig the fjord-like ramifications of Loch Snizort are seen to the right as we approach an area of flat-topped hillocks which give one the curious sensation of being much higher than one is in fact. On the right is Kingsburgh, with its memories of Flora Macdonald (*see* above), and then the road runs steadily down through Romesdal to Snizort and Borve and so to Portree.

Portree to Dunvegan (22 miles). The outward journey on the Dunvegan round should be made by Borve and Carbost, at the head of Loch Snizort; travelling in the other direction (outward *viâ* Sligachan) one misses the magnificent views of the Cuillins which are the feature of the run between Bracadale and Sligachan. Little calls for comment on the route between Portree and Dunvegan: it is pleasantly diversified with crofts, views across Loch Snizort and, as Dunvegan is approached, of the flat-topped mountains known as the Macleod's Tables (*see* below). About midway is **Edinbain** (*Edinbain Hotel*), a quiet little place at the head of Loch Greshornish and at the Fairy Bridge, 3½ miles short of Dunvegan, a road goes off on the right for **Stein** and **Trumpan** (on the Vaternish peninsula) and affords lovely views of Loch Bay (an opening from Loch Dunvegan) which appears to be land-locked by the long natural breakwater ending in Ardmore Point and the islands of Isay and Mingay. To the south-west lies the peninsula of Duirinish, terminating in the north in Dunvegan Head, a few miles from which, on Loch Dunvegan, is Boreraig, where of old the MacCrimmons, pipers to the Macleods, had their famous school of piping. In the distance Harris closes the view: a pretty spot is Loch Bay.

Dunvegan (*Dunvegan, Misty Isle, Ose Farm* and other occommodation) is on the shore of Loch Dunvegan, with boating, fishing and golf, but is mainly visited on account of its Castle, for centuries the seat of the Macleod chiefs. It stands to the north of the village on a rock having the sea on three sides, and formerly could be reached only by a boat and a subterranean passage, but access is now obtained by bridge. The Castle and grounds are open to the public April-mid Oct., every afternoon, except Sundays, 2–5.

It is said to have been founded in the ninth century, its high tower being added four hundred years later, and a third portion being built in the reign of James VI. In recent years it has been put into thorough repair. It is among the houses that claim to be "the oldest inhabited castle in Scotland." Johnson, Boswell and Sir Walter Scott are among those who have been entertained within its walls. One of the treasures of the castle is a "Fairy Flag," which on being waved will bring relief to the chief or any of his clan. The charm was to act three times and has twice been employed. There are relics, also, of the famous chieftain, "Rory More."

Prominent across the loch are two isolated hills, called on account of their curious flat summits **Macleod's Tables.** Each is about 1,600 feet in height.

The first part of the run from Dunvegan to Sligachan is of great interest on account of the views of **Loch Bracadale**—its coast extremely irregular and its surface sprinkled with islands large and small. Some of the cliffs are magnificent. At the southern extremity of Duirinish are **Macleod's Maidens,** three basaltic columns, the tallest 200 feet high. They rise sheer out of the sea, and are backed by cliffs from six to seven hundred feet high. Towards the southern end of the Harlosh peninsula is a Youth Hostel (*Balmore House*). Beyond Bracadale village we round the long and narrow **Loch Beag** (walkers and cyclists can use the ferry) and then have before us the first of the magnificent series of views of the Cuillins which provide such a splendid culmination to the run—with, however, some steep hills to be climbed. Down below on the right is Loch Harport. At its entrance, on the far side, is Portnalong, where weaving immigrants from Lewis and Harris set up their trade in 1923; nearer its head is Carbost with the famous *Talisker Distillery*. At the head of Loch Harport is **Drynoch** whence a road leads southward to Glen Brittle (*see* p. 139). From Sligachan to Portree is a matter of 9 miles.

The Hebrides

Of the four distinct groups into which the islands of Scotland may be divided, in treating of tours in Northern Scotland and the Western Highlands, three are included here. These are the Hebrides, the Orkneys, and the Shetlands. The omitted group, the islands in the Firth of Clyde, are described in our *Guide to Glasgow and the Clyde*.

The **Hebrides,** or Western Isles, are commonly divided into two portions, the *Outer Hebrides* and the *Inner Hebrides*. The former, often called the Long Island, lies from 30 to 50 miles west of the mainland and comprises the islands of **Lewis** and **Harris, North Uist, Benbecula, South Uist, Eriskay, Barra, Vatersay, Mingulay, Berneray,** and a large number of smaller islands. The total length of the group from the Butt of Lewis in the north to Barra Head in the south is about 130 miles. Fifty miles to the west of Harris is the small island of **St. Kilda,** now owned by the National Trust for Scotland and leased to the Nature Conservancy. The Inner Hebrides are scattered along the west coast of the mainland, the largest being **Skye, Rhum, Eigg, Coll, Tiree, Mull, Colonsay, Jura,** and **Islay** (for descriptions *see* Index).

THE OUTER HEBRIDES

Access. – MacBrayne steamers run to the principal places, viz. – Stornoway in Lewis reached by steamer from Mallaig and Kyle of Lochalsh in connection with the evening trains from London and the early morning trains from Edinburgh and Glasgow; Castlebay in Barra by early morning steamer from Oban. Car ferry from Uig to Tarbert and Lochmaddy. B.E.A. operate a daily service, Sundays excepted, between Renfrew, Benbecula and Stornoway and between Stornoway and Inverness. There is a daily bus service between Stornoway and Harris.

Hotels. – **Lewis:** *County*, Francis Street; **Stornoway:** *Royal*, Cromwell Street, *Park Guest House, Caledonian*, South Beach, *Crown*, North Beach. **Harris:** *Tarbert; Rodel*.

The islands as a rule are flat, with few elevations rising higher than 500 feet. With the exception of a large area of red sandstone at Stornoway, they are composed almost entirely of ice-worn gneiss. There are practically no trees anywhere other than in the neighbourhood of Stornoway. Generally the islands consist of bleak stretches of moorland and bogs, the scenery only being saved from monotony by innumerable freshwater lochs, inlets from the sea, many of which are of great extent, the picturesque mountains of Harris and South Uist, and the magnificent cliffs on the Atlantic side of the islands south of Barra. Excellent salmon and trout fishing is to be had on the lochs and rivers and is a great attraction to fishermen.

Lewis

Stornoway, with a population of 5,300, is the only important town in Lewis (*hotels, see* p. 145). It is an important fishing centre and the Harbour is an interesting sight during the herring season, and the centre of an extensive Harris Tweed industry on the island. The town is placed on the east side of the harbour, on the other side of which stands Lews Castle. The late Lord Leverhulme, a former proprietor of Lews, presented the Castle to the Burgh along with its picturesque grounds, which now form a public park of considerable beauty and extent. A pleasant walk is to cross over to the castle and go through the grounds southwards and then along the shore to Arnish Point, which was the northernmost point reached by Prince Charlie during his wanderings in the Outer Hebrides in 1745–46. On the northern outskirts of the town stands the War Memorial, a prominent tower 85 feet in height. Buses run from Stornoway in all directions and also maintain daily connection with Harris. A golf course (18-holes) has been laid out in the castle grounds. The castle itself now houses a technical college.

An interesting short excursion is by bus eastward along the Eye Peninsula to **Tiumpan Head Lighthouse.**

One of the best excursions from Stornoway is to the **Standing Stones of Callanish** (or Callernish) at the head of East Loch Roag and 15 miles distant. They form one of the largest and best preserved stone circles in Scotland. Eight miles west of Callanish, near the entrance to East Loch Roag, is the small township of **Carloway** with its famous broch, Dun Carloway, one of the best preserved in Scotland. Beyond Carloway the north road follows the west coast of Lewis pretty closely, passing Barvas and numerous other small townships, to the Butt of Lewis. From Garynahine a winding and narrow road runs along the west side of West Loch Roag and through the narrow defile of Glen Valtos to **Uig Bay,** with its beautiful sands and rugged hills.

A good road leads south from Stornoway to **Harris.** A few miles from town was the *Macaulay Institute Experimental Farm* for the reclamation of the peat lands, a scheme which unfortunately fell through. Beyond the scenery is rather uninteresting until the head of **Loch Erisort** (16 miles) is reached, a narrow inlet from the Minch 10 miles in length. Three miles farther the road reaches the head of **Loch Seaforth,** a narrow strip of water 4 miles long running east and west, although Loch Seaforth itself runs due south for about 8 miles, to East Loch Tarbert. The Harris hills are now well seen, those of Park to the east of Loch Seaforth and Clisham, etc., to the west. The road skirts Loch Seaforth for several miles and then strikes inland, to the east of Clisham, and descends to the shore of West Loch Tarbert, and along its northern shore to **Tarbert** (*Tarbert Hotel*), 35 miles from Stornoway.

Tarbert is a small town at the head of East Loch Tarbert and is partly placed on the narrow neck of land which separates the two lochs. It is a centre for the famous Harris tweed, and has a pier from which MacBrayne's steamers run to Lochmaddy in North Uist and Uig in Skye. The ascent of **Clisham** (2,622 feet) is worth while and may conveniently be made by

Standing Stones of Callanish

driving about 4 miles along the Stornoway road to near Loch a'Mhorgain and then climbing up the south-east slope of the hill. In clear weather there is a magnificent view from the summit, comprising a long stretch of the mountains on the mainland, Skye, and, in the far west just on the horizon, the islands of the St. Kilda group 65 miles distant. The ascent of **Toddun** (1,731 feet) near the entrance of Loch Seaforth is also interesting.

From Tarbert the main road strikes south for a few miles and then cuts across the hills, passing at the summit a remarkable group of funeral cairns, to the west coast of South Harris, at Luskentyre Bay, which is followed closely to Leverburgh and **Rodel** (*hotel*) at the southern end of the island, and 24 miles distant from Tarbert. Nearby are the remains of an ancient church dedicated to St. Clement which is "the one considerable architectural monument in the Outer Hebrides."

North Uist, the third largest of the Outer Hebrides, contains a number of low hills, but in the vicinity of Lochmaddy has so many lochs that it is at times difficult to say whether land or water predominates. **Lochmaddy** (*hotel*) is the principal place and is a port of call for MacBrayne's steamers. It is in effect the county town for the portion of the Outer Hebrides from North Harris southward, which form a part of Inverness-shire. From Lochmaddy a road leads across the island to **Carinish** (*hotel*) at the south end of the island and situated at the north side of the *North Ford*, which connects North Uist with Benbecula. This causeway, about 4 miles across, was built recently. With the completion of the North Ford causeway the four isles of North Uist, Grimsay, Benbecula and South Uist are linked by road.

Benbecula is very flat–the highest point, and the only hill in fact–Rueval–being only 409 feet. There is no seaport on the island, which is traversed by a road 5 miles long from north to south, with an hotel at Creagorry at the South Ford. The South Ford is about three-quarters of a mile wide and is now spanned by a long single-track bridge.

South Uist is about 21 miles long and is the second largest of the Outer Hebrides. It is a narrow island, its features being a wide stretch of flat "machair" land alongside the Atlantic, and a fringe of mountainous country running parallel to the east coast. A fair road runs along the west side of the island from **Carnan** (*hotel*) at the South Ford to **Pollachar** (*inn*) at the south end of the island. Near the west side of the road, between the sixth and seventh milestone, are the ruins of the Birthplace of Flora Macdonald (*see* p. 142). A cross-road leads to **Lochboisdale** (*hotel*), where is a pier at which MacBrayne's steamers call. The hotel is a favourite with anglers, who obtain excellent fishing in some of the freshwater lochs. The principal hills on the island are **Ben More** (2,034 feet) and **Hecla** (1,988 feet). The ascent of the former is worth doing. The most convenient route is to drive to near the Post Office at Loch Dobhrain (11½ miles from Lochboisdale) and ascend by Maola Breac and the north-west shoulder of the hill to the summit. There is a very fine range of precipitous crags on the north-east face of the hill. If time permits the excursion could be continued over Feaveallach (1,723 feet) to Hecla and thence back to the Post Office. Geologists will note with interest that while the rocks in the saddles between the hill are highly glaciated, the summits of the three hills are not ice-worn.

Immediately to the south of South Uist is the small island of **Eriskay**, of note as being the first place in Scotland on which Prince Charlie set foot. The actual beach is called Coilleag a'Phrionnsa (the Prince's bay). The island is also celebrated as having been the principal source from which the late Mrs. Kennedy Fraser obtained "The Songs of the Hebrides."

On **Barra**, the next island, is **Castlebay** (*hotel*) which is served by MacBrayne's "Inner Islands" steamer from Oban. On a small rocky islet in the bay is the ancient Kisimul Castle, a stronghold of the McNeils for many centuries, now restored and inhabited by Macneils. **Heaval** (1,260 feet) is the highest hill on the island and may be easily ascended from Castlebay in an hour or so. It commands a good view of the southern islands. These latter are small and many of them are uninhabited. Their best features are the magnificent cliffs on the Atlantic side of **Mingulay** and **Berneray.** Biulacraig on the former is almost vertical and has a height of 753 feet. The lighthouse at Barra Head on Berneray is perched almost on the edge of a high cliff and shows its light at a height of 683 feet above sea-level.

The Orkneys and Shetlands

THE ORKNEY ISLES

Access. – Steamer between Scrabster (near Thurso) and Stromness every weekday, and on Sundays in July and August, the crossing taking just under 3 hours.

From Leith and Aberdeen by steamer about twice weekly in summer; less frequently in winter. For current details apply *North of Scotland, Orkney and Shetland Shipping Company*, Matthew's Quay, Aberdeen.

Air services from Aberdeen and Inverness, *viâ* Wick.

The Orkney Isles number sixty-seven, of which twenty-nine are inhabited, and they extend northward for upwards of 48 miles.

The western coasts present to the Atlantic an almost unbroken front of lofty cliffs, the abode of innumerable sea-birds. Everywhere the coast teems with fish; and seals, otters, whales, and porpoises are by no means uncommon.

Kirkwall and Stromness, the largest towns in the Orkneys, are on **Mainland,** sometimes erroneously called Pomona. At each there is an 18-hole golf course open to visitors, including Sunday.

Kirkwall

Kirkwall (Hotels, *Kirkwall, Albert, Ayre, Queen's, Royal, West End* (unl.)) stands at the head of a fine bay which indents the centre of the north side of the island. Its narrow streets and lanes, and its houses, with thick strong walls and small windows, which turn their crow-stepped gables towards the street, seem to speak of its Norwegian origin. The grand old **Cathedral** was begun in 1137 and dedicated to St. Magnus. (*Admission, free, in summer every weekday,* 10 *a.m. to* 6 *p.m.; winter* 10 *a.m. to* 4 *p.m.*). Its architecture resembles that of Trondheim in Norway. The oldest parts are the transepts and three bays of the choir; the first five bays of the nave are only slightly later. The nave is interesting on account of its massive Norman pillars. It is less than 50 feet wide, but this very narrowness gives an impression of height. Note the various tombstones, each with name of the deceased and various symbolic designs. The whole of the Cathedral has been thoroughly restored.

The view from the top of the tower is interesting, and useful to those who find difficulty in getting their bearings in this island of extremely irregular coastlines.

Close to the Cathedral are the remains of the Bishop's and Earl's palaces; the latter a fine specimen of sixteenth-century domestic architecture.

Wideford Hill (741 feet), in the neighbourhood of the town, commands an uninterrupted view of all the Orkney Isles. Across a narrow isthmus where the main island is nearly cut in two, and nearly 2 miles from Kirkwall, is **Scapa Pier,** well known as a base of the Grand Fleet. It is on the wide expanse of **Scapa Flow.**

A winding road, about 15 miles long (bus service), connects Kirkwall and Stromness, at the south-west corner of the island. There is an inn at **Finstown,** about half-way.

A little beyond the ninth milestone is the far-famed **Mound of Maeshowe,** a large, chambered barrow, which can be explored by visitors. (Key at the neighbouring farm of Tormiston.) Close to Maeshowe, where two large lochs, Harray and Stenness, open into each other, are the greater and the lesser circles of the **Standing Stones of Stenness,** objects of supreme archaeological interest, although "The Stone of Odin," mentioned in Sir Walter Scott's novel, *The Pirate,* no longer exists. The principal circle, the *Ring of Brogar,* has a diameter of over 120 yards and is surrounded by a deep trench. Twenty-seven of the stones still stand, the average height being about 10 feet. Nearer the road and the hotel three stones, between 15 and 18 feet high, and a table-stone are all that remains of another circle.

Stromness (*Royal, Scott's, Stromness*), the "Venice of the North," contains much that is of interest; as does **Birsay** (*hotel*), at the north-west corner of the island, where are the ruins of the Earl's Palace.

Midway between the two, on the west coast of the island and at the southern edge of the Bay of Skaill, is the exceedingly interesting prehistoric village of **Skara Brae.** Active excavations since 1928 have revealed a group of stone huts connected by covered passages, besides furniture, implements, ornaments, and one or two skeletons of the former inhabitants. The settlement probably belongs to a Stone Age later than that of the Scottish mainland.

Two miles south-west of Birsay is **Marwick Head,** off which sank on June 5, 1916, H.M.S. *Hampshire,* while conveying Lord Kitchener and his staff to Russia. On the headland is a monument to their memory.

The island of **Hoy** comes next in size to Mainland. Its steep, dark-tinted hills are the highest in the group, and its cliff scenery the most imposing in the British Isles. It is, however, difficult of access, and lacking in accommodation for travellers, at least in the northern end, where most of the wonders of its cliffs, mountains and antiquities are situated. It contains the **Dwarfie Stone** and the **Carbuncle** (a mass of sandstone) on Ward Hill, the legends attached to which play an important part in the plot of *The Pirate.* But the most noteworthy feature of the island is the **Old Man of Hoy,** an isolated pillar of rock, 450 feet high, facing the Atlantic about two miles south of St. John's Head. The latter is 1,141 feet high and is probably the loftiest vertical sea-cliff in the British Isles.

The isle of **Egilsay,** one of the most interesting of the group, contains the ruins of *St. Magnus Church,* in which the patron saint of Orkney and Shetland, St. Magnus, was murdered by his colleague in the government of the two archipelagos, in the early part of the twelfth century. It possesses a round tower. On **Eyn-hallow,** the Holy Isle, in the strait between Rousay and Mainland, are the remains of an ancient monastery.

South Ronaldsay, the most southern of the group, has an area of about 18 square miles. It contains the little village of **St. Margaret's Hope,** near which is the Broch called the **Howe of Hoxa.** Other islands deserving mention are Burray, Shapinsay, Stronsay, Sanday, Eday, **Westray** (on which is the ruined Castle of Noltland) and North Ronaldsay. A good road connects South Ronaldsay with Burray and the Mainland. **Stroma,** in the Pentland Firth, belongs to Caithness.

THE SHETLAND ISLES

Access. – Communication between the mainland and Shetland is maintained by the *North of Scotland and Orkney and Shetland Shipping Company, Ltd.*, whose steamers run between Lerwick and Aberdeen twice weekly. Current particulars respecting fares and times of sailing may be obtained from the Manager, Aberdeen.

By Air, see pp. 10 and 149. The airport is at Sumburgh.

The Mainland of the Shetland (or Zetland) group lies 48 miles to the north-east of the Orkneys. Midway between but forming part of the Shetlands lies the **Fair Isle,** a lonely island battered beneath the assaults of the Atlantic and the North Sea, which gives its name to the patterned knitted wear for which Shetland is famous. The isle is now in the hands of the National Trust for Scotland. An Observatory has been set up for the study of bird migration and over 270 varieties of birds have been recorded there. There is a hostel on the island.

The Shetland group (population 17,371) consists of about a hundred islands; less than a score are inhabited. Their total area amounts to 551 square miles. The surface of the larger islands is hilly, the hills covered to their summits with moorland, their dark surface contrasting strongly with the deep green of the valleys and cultivated coast lands, their monotony intensified rather than relieved by numerous small lochs. The highest point in the islands is **Ronas Hill,** a mass of red granite, 1,486 feet high. From its summit a magnificent panorama of the whole islands may be obtained, and at midsummer the sun may be observed to sink slowly below the horizon, reappearing in an hour or two a little to the east. In June and July it is never really dark; indeed it is this aspect of the islands, the "simmer dim," the long twilight with its ever-changing shadows, that lingers longest in the memory.

The coastline is broken and rugged. Long winding sheltered voes or inlets of the sea, bordered by cultivated fields, run far inland. Bold headlands jut out into the ocean, rising at times into lofty cliffs that for grandeur and sublimity have few rivals. The Noup of Noss (592 feet), Fitful Head (928 feet), the Kame of Foula (1,220 feet), all sheer cliffs, form conspicuous landmarks. Lofty stacks, natural arches and deep caverns abound along the coast; some caves run far inland and may reach the surface as pit-like openings, known locally as "kirns," at the bottom of which the sea foams and swirls. The Hole of Scraada at Esha Ness is a well-known example, the Round Reeva in the Fair Isle, another. The small island of Papa Stour, owing to the columnar jointing of its rocks, is honeycombed with caves.

Mainland

the largest of the islands, is 54 miles long, but of very irregular outline. On it is **Lerwick,** the capital, a busy town and somewhat cosmopolitan fishing port. (Hotels, *Queens', Grand, Lerwick, Hayfield, Kveldsro*). On the last Tuesday in January is held the festival of "Up-Helly-A" when a model Norse galley is drawn through the streets in a torch-lit procession.

At **Scalloway** (*Scalloway Hotel*), formerly the chief town, are the ruins of a castle, built in 1600 by Earl Patrick Stewart. Road bridges connect with Trondra and Burra Isle, and there are motor-boat trips to Foula ("The edge of the World").

To the east of Lerwick is **Bressay,** with the adjacent islets of **Noss,** a Nature Reserve, and the smaller **Holm of Noss** formerly reached by a rope bridge, the Cradle of Noss. A pleasant excursion, when the weather is suitable, is the circuit of these islands by motor-boat from Lerwick: the cliff scenery is magnificent.

South of Lerwick is **Mousa,** which contains the most perfect specimen of a Pictish broch in existence. This, known as Mousa Castle, is about 40 feet high and 158 feet in circumference at the base. It gradually decreases in width till within about 10 feet of its top and then again expands–an arrangement which effectually prevented an attacking force scaling its walls, while the small size of the doorway, which could be built up in case of attack, rendered access in that way impossible. Upwards of eighty of these brochs, all in ruins, occur in Shetland, occupying strategic positions on headlands or in lochs. That of Clickimin, near Lerwick, ranks next to Mousa.

On the west coast about 30 miles from Lerwick **Hillswick** (*St. Magnus Hotel*) is placed near some magnificent rock scenery and the fantastic ship-like stacks known as the Drongs. To the north of it is **Ronas Hill** (1,486).

The most northerly spot in the British Isles is a conical rock, the **Muckle Flugga,** rising nearly 200 feet out of the sea off the coast of Unst. On it stands a lighthouse, which in spite of its height–250 feet above the water– is sometimes swept by the waves. At the other extremity of the group is **Sumburgh Head,** bearing a lighthouse, and its loftier neighbour Fitful Head. This district figures largely in *The Pirate*. The Shetland airport is at Sumburgh, which has an hotel. At **Jarlshof,** near Sumburgh, are the remains of an ancient Pictish village recently excavated. At Scousburgh on the west side of this narrow neck of land there is an hotel (*Spiggie*).

The inhabitants of these islands are engaged chiefly in fishing, farming, knitting and the rearing of sheep and ponies, for which the islands are renowned.

Index

Where more than one reference is given, the first is the principal.

INDEX

YOUR HELP IS REQUESTED

A great part of the success of this series is due, as we gratefully acknowledge, to the enthusiastic co-operation of readers. Changes take place, both in town and country, with such rapidity that it is difficult, even for the most alert and painstaking staff, to keep pace with them all, and the correspondents who so kindly take the trouble to inform us of alterations that come under their notice in using the books, render a real service not only to us but to their fellow-readers. We confidently appeal for further help of this kind.

THE EDITOR

WARD LOCK LIMITED
116 BAKER STREET, LONDON, W.1